The bands of the 60s, 70s, and 80s played on the record player of my mind throughout the writing of this book. The social upheaval of the time, expressed through music and lyrics, gave me courage to become a rebel, to see the lies hidden within my home life, and to leave. Every effort was made to obtain permission for excerpts of songs used in this book, and those I wanted to use. My deepest gratitude to these brilliant writers, composers, and performers of my early years for the soundtrack of my escape, and for accompanying me while I wrote about it:

Leon Russell – Rickie Lee Jones – Led Zeppelin – Yes – Pink Floyd – Joni Mitchell – The Beatles – Jackson Browne – David Bowie – Janis Joplin – Bee Gees – Traffic – Jethro Tull – The Moody Blues – Stevie Wonder – Dave Mason – Gordon Lightfoot – Emerson, Lake & Palmer – Jimi Hendrix – Chicago – Roberta Flack – Renaissance – Peter Frampton – Shawn Phillips – Earth, Wind & Fire – Paul Simon – Sly & The Family Stone – Jefferson Airplane – Carole King – Bob Dylan – Steely Dan – King Crimson – Marshall Tucker Band – Marvin Gaye – Carly Simon – Stevie Ray Vaughan – Aretha Franklin – The Band – James Taylor – It's A Beautiful Day – Allman Brothers – Blondie – Simon & Garfunkel – BB King – The Pretenders – Electric Light Orchestra – Santana – Genesis – The Doors – Black Sabbath – The Rolling Stones – Aerosmith – Roberta Flack – Indigo Girls – Tracy Chapman – Bruce Hornsby & The Range – Grand Funk Railroad – Peter Gabriel – Supertramp – Cream – Crosby, Stills, Nash & Young – Stevie Nicks – and many others

"A playwright recounts past abuse in this debut memoir. . . Willow's prose remains eloquent throughout even when describing raw, harrowing episodes . . . the author reveals herself as a strong woman unwilling to succumb to her past."
–**Kirkus Review "Get It"**

"Startling and deeply engaging, this moving memoir explores the dark world of the author's childhood from her perspective as a grateful survivor. The tightly written story transports readers to a world where nightmares live as suppressed memories. It took tremendous courage to tell this story of trauma and the bad decision that grew from it. Ann Willow writes with easy grace and an open-hearted spirit of forgiveness for her younger, struggling self. What she learned and shares here has broad applications, a timely guidepost for today. *Remembering Changes Everything* is a memoir to remember."
–**Anne Hillerman**
NYT bestselling author of *Leaphorn, Chee & Manuelito Mysteries*
Executive Producer of *Dark Winds*

"I didn't want the words on the page to stop. In a strange way, I looked forward to the twists and turns in *Remembering Changes Everything*. However, I never gave up hope that Hanna finds that inner peace which she seemed to be chasing from the opening of the book. Ann's way of writing is quite riveting and illustrative. Her story stays with you!"
–**Tracey Anarella**, A-Roll Pictures, Director/Producer of *Not Black Enough*

"Willow's vivid descriptions and strikingly straightforward recounting of her life's extraordinary events captivates the mind in a way that makes it both unimaginable and understandable. The bare, open style of narration creates a compassionate glimpse into a life of pain, danger, and difficult choices that few others have ever had to face."
–**DelSheree Gladden**, USA Today bestselling author of *The Aerling Series*

"Trauma teaches the art of silence, but in the pages of this book, silence is shattered, and secrets find their voice. It's a profound privilege to accompany a survivor on their path to healing, and witnessing their transformation into a beacon of support for others is incredibly rewarding!"
–**Kandyce Walker, RN**, Trauma Recovery Institute

Remembering Changes Everything

Ann Willow

Published by Ann Willow 2024

Book I: Aboveground Memoir Series

For Elsa

Dear Reader,

If you have survived abuse, tell your story. Discover who you truly are and were always meant to be. It's okay, and right, to move beyond whatever trauma you've endured, to know it was *never* about you, it was something wrong with *them*.

My name is Ann. Not the name given to me at birth, but legally became my own name, chosen carefully in 1993, when I drew up legal papers stating honestly the reason for my name change. The judge signed the document with sad eyes and the banging of his gavel, and I skipped out of the courtroom. My daughter's name is Elsa, the name I gave her at birth, naming her after my Grandma Elsa, the person in my life who was always there for me, which I realized while writing this book. I hope when you reach the end of our strange tale you will view us not as victims, but as warriors.

This memoir is based on my true story, meaning dates and details may not be exact, and I have combined certain events and dialogue for readability. I've written this book from memory and the numerous journals I kept during this time. This story is from my perspective, as I lived it. Certain memories are sketched on the canvas of my mind in vivid detail, while others are obscured by time, drugs and alcohol, or the intentional processes of brainwashing conducted by my abusers.

I think of all the missing children and know my life will have meaning only when I do my part to expose the kidnappers, rapists, and traffickers exploiting their innocence. Thus, I write my story for the ultimate love of a child, for all of you with abused and missing children, and for those of you who were abused and may be missing.

In descriptions of Satanic or Occult Abuse, I want to make it perfectly clear that I do not stand in judgment of anyone's spiritual or religious beliefs, nor ethnicity or political affiliation. My concern is in exposing those people who use their authority and belief system to use and abuse vulnerable populations of society, regardless of what those beliefs are, or where or how they came to be. I hope that by doing so, I may help empower their victims. Depictions of abuse may be triggering for some. If you are reading this book in the early stages of trauma recovery, you may need a strong support system.

Certain terminology in this book represents the era in which this book takes place, used only for historical purposes: Multiple Personality Disorder, MPD, now called Dissociative Identity Disorder DID; Manic-Depressive Disorder, now called Bipolar Disorder. References to Black People will sometimes be referred to as Negro or negro; policemen vs. police officers; housewife vs, stay-at-home mom/dad; and others. No offense at all is intended.

Everyone involved in my story has their own memory of events, which may differ from mine. They are welcome to write and publish their account of what happened.

Some names and locations have been changed.

Ann Willow

CONTENT NOTE: This book may contain content objectionable to some readers; discretion is advised. For those in early stages of trauma recovery, depictions of abuse may be triggering, so please lean on your support system. I hope my book will be a source of validation and healing, and that sharing my story will inspire you to share yours.

East was Lake Michigan. That's how I learned my directions.
West was everything on the other side of Eden's Expressway,
over the bridge to Adrienne and Alex's house.
South was downtown Chicago.
North was Wisconsin.

Remembering Changes Everything

a true story

1984 to 1989

Down there by the river is a man
Whose horn is twisted into shapes
Unknown to the wicked and the wise
And he bears the look of an animal
Who has seen things
No animal should ever see
He has been driven beyond all towns
And all systems, until now
Though it is long past too far
He keeps going

--Rickie Lee Jones, "Flying Cowboys"

In 1984, a series of events opened a vault of secrets buried deep within my unconscious mind. The door ajar, memories of my past slipped out one at a time, sometimes in great numbers. As the door swung wider, I looked deeper into my history. Terrified of the truth, I ran for thirty years.

I am a grandmother now. And as would a grandmother, I take the hand of the little girl, teenager, and new mother I once was, and walk with her back in time. I stand by her, love her, protect her. I give her the voice to tell the secrets she has longed to reveal . . .

The Changing Time. Somewhere in the wooded environs of the wealthy North Shore suburbs of Chicago. I don't remember how I got to this clearing in the woods, a grove surrounded by a dense stand of tall trees, the circular area worn to dirt. Around the perimeter are posts upon which blazing torches offer golden light. In the center of the circle, a huge bonfire points flaming fingers to the sky.

I am three years old, naked, squatting before a large animal slit from tail to jaw. A man stands to my left, slightly behind me.

I stare straight ahead, bewildered, feeling as though I've just woken from a dream.

I look downward in shame at my nakedness—dirty, ugly, and bad. I pee on the soft, dark dirt, adding a deeper pool of shame to my tiny person. The man swings a silver ball of puffing smoke. He wears all black, like a priest I saw in a Catholic church. I feel awkward and insignificant in his presence. Even in my tender toddlerhood, I am aware of his black costume in contrast with my white, naked skin, and the importance of being white.

I'm not afraid, really, having already shut off fear as much as possible to survive. What I endure most keenly is the pain of abandonment, the self-consciousness of shame, and the anxiety of guilt, always wondering what I've done wrong. Nobody at this ritual sees me or thinks of me as a baby. To them, I am merely a vulnerable object to be shaped and molded into the role they've planned for me.

One moment I squat beside the beast, the next, I'm lying on a rough stone altar before the dancing, taunting firelight, gazing up at a pitch-black sky, the stars obliterated by the light of the fire.

Watching, waiting, hoping this will be over soon, I observe the scene as a visitor from another place who does not belong here.

Girls, twelve or thirteen years old, dance around the fire in white dresses. They twirl, flowing hair swirling about their pale faces. Flat, unblinking, crystal-blue eyes reflect the wagging, accusing fingers of fire. As the young girls on the verge of womanhood spin past the altar, they dip over me with vacant faces, their ice-blue eyes looking upward. They chant a monotonous song, twirling in a half-circle before me, or so it seems from my view—unknown hands turned my head to the right, facing the fire, and a voice told me not to look to my left. I sense people who don't want to be recognized are standing there, watching. With my face positioned this way, the girls spin on a slant, twirling faster and faster until I'm dizzy, feeling I will vomit.

The dancing halts.

The priest-man lifts me off the altar and takes my hand.

He leads me to another man sitting on the red velvet cushion of a black wooden chair with

ornately carved woodwork surrounding the high back, like a throne. He must be a prince of some sort, in his early twenties, and like the priest-man, wears black: black turtleneck shirt, black pants, shiny black shoes, and even shoulder-length black hair swept up and away from his pale white face, exposing a high, furrowed forehead. The only colors in what seems a black-and-white snapshot of him are his icy blue eyes—like the girls'—and the blood-red cushion upon which he is throned. A round silver medallion on a silver chain hangs around his neck.

The prince half smiles as I reach him, the left side of his mouth slightly curved, so I think maybe I've been a good girl?

He pinches the chain holding the round medallion and swings it from side to side below his chest, a lazy pendulum hypnotizing me into submission. Drawing nearer the pendulous medallion, it comes into focus, depicting three black, triangular mountains behind a lake, their peaks pointing into a silver sky with a black moon. The moon reflects silver upon the ebony lake, with tiny silver waves rippling its surface. I cannot see, nor will I for many years, that the ripples are words of an ancient language passed down from generation to generation of this coven of black witches.

I have no idea I am being raised to take my place in the circle of this coven. I am unaware that this ceremony is only one of many in my indoctrination.

Lulled into compliance by the swinging mountains and lake, I toddle toward the shiny disk. As I reach out my hand to touch it, the chair begins moving backward.

The priest-man releases my hand and pushes me forward. I run toward the throned man, but backwards into the forest he zooms on his throne, swinging the medallion, sinisterly grinning, holding my eyes with a mesmerizing stare. I race after him, fast and furious, with chanting and whirring sounds all around me.

3

The scene's periphery is unfocused, like a wildlife film focused on the cheetah chasing its prey, the surrounding scenery a blurry haze.

Tick tock, tick tock. Time has no meaning.

Tick tock, tick tock. Sudden silence.

No more chanting. No more backward racing motion of the man on his throne. He is gone, has disappeared. I stop.

Tick tock, tick tock. The stillness is so complete, I can hear it, a ringing in my ears. It slows, then stops.

Tick tock, tick tock. Time resumes amid the quiet of the forest, beginning anew. The crossing of a threshold, a fusion of space and time.

Now I stand in a smaller grove encircled by giant, fully leafed summer trees. The air is chilly here in the darkness of the grove. The full moon eerily illuminates the scene with pale, silvery light. Wondering what will happen, I am afraid now, a cold fear shivering through my body. I frantically look around, waiting for a rescue I know won't come.

I think I hear my name whispered behind me, so faint I'm not sure.

"Haaanna . . ." I turn to face the voice.

I hear my name whispered to my left. "Haaanna . . ." I turn.

Then in front of me, to my right, behind me, to my left.

"Haaanna . . ."

I spin around and around, searching for the women's faces who call to me in whispers, "Haaanna . . ."

They stop.

The leaves rustle in the sudden gust of a light breeze. I hear them approaching, the women, feet shuffling softly as if wearing moccasins. One holds a staff in her right hand, using it like a walking stick, tap, tap, tap on the ground; it comes up to her shoulder, with a crystal ball sitting on top. In another's right hand is a bell raised to her shoulder, in her left a stick. A third woman swings a globe of golden light, barely giving off enough light to illuminate the scene. As

4

they come closer, a buzzing sound rises to a murmur of whispers which circle me in a crescendo of monotonous chanting. I know it is not in English, nor Swedish, which are the languages I hear at home. It is different, yet familiar. I cannot see the women's faces, hidden by hoods pointed forward to hide them, creating black holes where their faces should be.

They slowly surround me. I am immobilized, frozen like a statue of myself. I push away my fear like shoving open a heavy iron gate leading to freedom. I am a glowing white light. I grow taller and taller, brighter and brighter, rising above them, strong and brave. They will never have me. As I rise higher and higher, I see a speck of a child on the forest floor, surrounded by six hooded women chanting the incantation intended to transform her, me, into a witch.

With the tinkling of the bell in a witch's right hand, the Changing Time begins, and my toddler self, unable to resist the weight of their ominous chorus, succumbs to the adults ruling my existence, charting its course. They rob me of a chance to travel down the myriad paths open to all babies, directing me instead down a secret path, a path upon which I will walk in shadows of loneliness that will shade my life.

High overhead, angels lift my spirit to fly far, far away. Though my human form falls under the witches' black spell today, I will someday choose another destiny. One which my predecessors, people of lies, have not planned for me. They will be violently displeased when they discover I have found my way . . . Out.

One

August 1984

"I gotta get out of here."

"What are you talking about, Hanna?" Mark was in the driver's seat of my cute, burgundy-red Volkswagen Scirocco. He'd driven from the bar because I was too drunk. He turned to me, the leather seat making that creaky-crunching sound.

"Come on. You wanna go home? Want me to take you home?" Mark asked for the fourth time.

I was living in the North Side Chicago neighborhood of West Rogers Park. Mark and I were at his apartment in Skokie, a suburb north of the city where we'd grown up. Mark still lived with his mother in the same apartment they'd lived in when we were in junior high school.

"No, no, no, no! I have to get out of here. I'll die if I stay!"

I curled into a circle on the passenger seat of my cute little car, my long blonde hair draped over my face like the last curtain call.

"I can't wait another day, Mark. Help me. Please help me."

"*Ugh!* I can't figure out what you want. You're acting crazy." He opened the car door.

I grabbed his wrist. "Please, Mark, don't go. Please don't go. Help me."

"What the hell do you want me to do?"

"I don't know. I don't know. I gotta get out of here. Gotta go, gotta go . . ." My voice trailed off. I could hear it flying away as if it had taken the last flight out, leaving me behind.

"Don't leave me," I begged in a husky whisper, to Mark and my vanishing voice.

"Hanna, stop! I'm home, so I'm going in now. You'll be okay. Goodbye!"

He pried my fingers off his wrist with a sigh of disgust, slammed the car door shut, and I gave up. I imagined him taking a seat beside my tired and weary words, flying away to parts unknown, leaving me to sit in my misery.

I'd bumped into Mark a few weeks before at a bar in downtown Chicago. He was an old friend from junior high school, a year older than me, a guy with a crush on me back then. When we were kids, my mother gushed over Mark when he'd come to the house with the rest of the gang my twin sister and I hung out with. I thought she was crazy, having thought of Mark as an overweight goon, though funny and kind in his way.

Mark and I hadn't seen each other since high school, seven or eight years earlier. When I saw him at the bar, I didn't even recognize him. He'd changed so much—lost about a hundred pounds, grew his hair long. Wow, he was handsome. I liked the way he looked, and knew how to look good myself. Upon first meeting me, nobody would suspect I was a wreck. The thing is, I didn't know why I felt like such a wreck, smashed and broken.

Marked still liked me, although this night may have changed his mind about that. I opened the passenger door to beg him once more not to leave me, but my voice was gone, had already boarded the plane. I gently closed the door, head bent, my curtain of hair blessedly blinding me from the sight of him walking away.

Maneuvering over the gearshift, I climbed into the driver's seat and drove a few blocks to my parents' house—the house I'd grown up in—to ask my mother for money. She gave me twenty dollars, apparently not noticing, or not caring, that I was drunker than drunk. I staggered back to my car, slid into the driver's seat, and drove to O'Hare airport to catch up with my sad voice, tired of searching for words.

* * * *

It's Wintertime. I am a child. I've been asleep and am awakened by voices. It's dark outside. I'm in a car? Snow. Cold. I've been dreaming about a place that gives me comfort. A happy dream of warmth and safety. Car doors. Joyful voices. They're leaving. Don't go! Take me with you! A longing deep within my soul. But I must be quiet. Very quiet. My whole childhood spent in silence. Not a word to anyone.

I still dream about the place I belong, but can't remember where it is when I wake up.

Two

I parked in the long-term lot at O'Hare airport. I wore a royal blue dress of thick, soft cotton, just above my knees, sans underwear. (I don't know why I remember not wearing underwear.) Other than the dress, my purse with depleted checkbook and the twenty dollars my mother had given me were all I had. And a smile. Damn, it was muggy; the humidity so thick it was like trying to breathe underwater. What a relief when the terminal doors whooshed open to frigid air conditioning.

I dashed to the airline counter and wrote a check for a ticket to Dallas, which wasn't going to clear my bank. I hadn't been working much, and when I did, I sold ads for my cocaine dealer's coupon flier—you know, those coupons in the mail for two-for-one steak dinners, discount eye exams, and such—both of us struggling to pretend we lived ordinary lives with an ordinary job. Everything I earned went directly up my nose with the cocaine I bought from him as soon as he paid me, typically only a fraction of what he owed. It was fine with me when he offered cocaine as payment.

On the airplane, far above the city of Chicago, I held a vodka and tonic in my left hand while writing a suicide note to my parents with my right, exonerating them of any blame. Wanting to enjoy my last few hours, or days, on planet Earth, I chatted with other passengers and the flight attendant, feeling happy and free.

I was on my way to find Jerome, a boyfriend who, a few years before, didn't try to stop me when I left him for Michael, the guy I'd been in love with since the age of fourteen. Jerome wasn't the jealous type, so whenever my inevitable fights with Michael erupted and I wanted Jerome's attention, he always let me back in when I drove to the little house we'd once shared at the Wisconsin border. Even if he wasn't home, I was welcome to let myself in with the key I hadn't returned. Sometimes he'd find me asleep in his bed, which had once been mine, too. We'd lie there together for hours, me talking, him listening.

On that muggy night in August 1984, flying to a new life or to Heaven, I hadn't spoken to Jerome in almost five years. His brother told me Jerome lived in Abilene, Texas, wherever that was, and I'd have to fly to Dallas to get there.

I watched Dallas come into view, forming pinpoints of light like stars thrown across a black sky, growing into shapes of street lights, and then the various colored lights of the runway as the plane touched down just before midnight. One day laid to rest as a new day began.

Tipsy, I sloped into a seat in the terminal, shocked I'd done it. I left Chicago.

I dropped my forehead into my hands, adjusting to the possibility that maybe my departure marked the start of a new life, rather than the suicide I had envisioned. The world I left behind already seemed long gone, flashing before me like a life remembered at death. I'd spent my last few months in Chicago living a double life.

My parents were the children of immigrants, raising us kids in an ethnic Swedish home. In the mid-1980s, they'd been married forty years, and had lived in the same house for over thirty of those years. My paternal grandfather built their home in the early 1950s, one of the first to go up in the post-WWII housing boom of the Chicago suburb of Skokie. My grandfather built other homes in the new neighborhood, bought primarily by Jewish families, many of them refugees from the war and some concentration camp survivors.

My parents appeared to be typical suburbanites of the era—father the breadwinner, mother a housewife who didn't even drive a car. Yet, I sensed something different about them, a not-quite-spoken ethnocentric attitude of superior descendancy from a white, Nordic, non-Jewish bloodline. I was aware of the irony of them raising their children in a Jewish neighborhood, and in the back of my mind, wondered why. Most of our friends were Jewish kids from school. Didn't they know this would hugely influence our ideals?

A large man, over six feet tall and well over two hundred pounds, my father dominated me, my sisters, and our petite mother with an abrasive, critical, and distant demeanor. His persona was righteous ultra-conservative, proud as hell he'd been an army intelligence officer in London during World War II—his glory days. By the 1980s, he had switched careers from insurance agent to a partner in his friend's lucrative import business specializing in gourmet Scandinavian food, which provided us with ample financial stability.

In sharp contrast to my father, my mother possessed a certain graciousness about her that inspired strangers to confide their life stories, to which she'd listen with sparkling aquamarine eyes and a warm smile. Unlike my father, she never talked politics, just voted as he instructed her . . . well, she said she did.

Emma, my twin sister, and I were the youngest in the family. Lorain was two years older, Ellyn eight years older, and Donald eleven years older than us.

My siblings had all been married and had kids by 1983. But not me. Traditional marriage and family were way too bourgeois. I flatly refused Michael's marriage proposal that year when I missed a period. We'd been living together, and even though he was the love of my life, I was way too hip to consent to a *wedding*. Relieved I wasn't pregnant, I left our tumultuous, on-again-off-again relationship in the fall, when I could no longer tolerate our drunken fights, occurring almost every day. I rented an apartment with Emma, who'd been living at our parents' house with her three-year-old daughter, Lily. Though I hadn't told Michael where I'd moved, he found out. He'd wait for me outside, persistent in his cocksure "Come on, Han, talk to me" confidence, certain I'd take him back, which I always had. Though I caved in and let him in once, and then left with him for a weekend in Ft. Lauderdale, we never did get back together.

My new apartment with Emma and Lily was on the third floor of a lovely old building in West Rogers Park, a culturally rich Chicago neighborhood.

Mr. and Mrs. Rosen, a liberal, middle-aged Jewish couple, lived on the second floor. They kept kosher—their kitchen cluttered with dishes, pots, and pans separated for meat and dairy foods. Bookshelves filled the rest of their apartment, jammed with hundreds of books. I read all of Mrs. Rosen's Agatha Christie mysteries, which we'd discuss for hours at her dining room table, a portrait of a rabbi overlooking us from the wall like a kind and benevolent teacher. The Rosens must have known something was wrong, but they never questioned me. They provided a haven to pretend I lived the joyous, intellectual life I really wanted.

Hasidic Jews walked past our building on Sabbath days. The men wore tightly curled strands of hair beside their faces, like bouncing springs sewn into their ever-present black top hats. The women covered their heads with lace and wore black ankle-length dresses, stockings, and shoes. If I happened to be on the sidewalk, they would look down, never acknowledging me in any way. I'd look down, too, feeling inferior and ashamed, thinking they viewed my worldly lifestyle as dirty and wrong.

A few streets down Devon Avenue, the main artery through West Rogers Park, a Croatian Roman Catholic cultural center filled an entire square city block. It was as if they'd dragged a hunk of Croatia across the ocean and plunked down

12

their own island in the middle of a city thousands of miles from their homeland. Like our Hasidic neighbors, the Croatian Christians also kept to themselves—a paradoxical pair of insular enclaves within a city of hundreds of people. Their ability to isolate themselves fascinated me.

A smattering of Italian, Russian, Puerto Rican, Greek, and Asian immigrants also lived and worked in our new neighborhood. Mr. Wang sat behind the cash register of our favorite Chinese restaurant while Mrs. Wang whipped up delicious dishes from her Beijing grandmother's recipe book. And the Greek restaurant down the street welcomed us with music. When I say *our* and *us*, I mean Michael and me, as these had been his favorite restaurants too, before I left him.

The immigrants who'd found their way to Chicago captivated me. I never understood the prejudice I'd witnessed way too often in the suburbs—hatred and fear of anyone's skin color or religion different from themselves.

People were people: the funny ones, serious ones, kind ones, cruel ones, happy ones, melancholy ones, the thieves and the benefactors. The only thing separating us was ethnicity, based solely upon our ancestral modes of survival. To me, the rich diversity of humans on Earth brought texture and beauty to life. I liked my new city dwelling, exemplifying the diversity I loved.

My bedroom in our new apartment was spectacular. It was horseshoe shaped, like an immense bay window created by seven walls. I often woke up on Saturday mornings to three-year-old Lily prying open one of my eyes, greeted by her adorable face so close she was out of focus. Her soft breath ruffled my eyelashes, her white-blonde hair tickled my nose, and her Earth-from-space-blue eyes were blurry globes, as if I'd woken on the moon with a hangover. I'd groan, opening my other eye, which she took as an invitation to lay her head on my pillow and shove a stack of books at me. I'd read, no matter how tired, or actually hungover I may have been, hoping she wouldn't notice me skipping pages. But she always did, and then I'd have to tickle her. We'd lie like that for hours, it seemed, snuggled together in my fabulous bedroom.

My last winter in Chicago, 1983-84, was one of the coldest on record, the kind that defines "blistering cold." On one such skin-blistering morning, Lily came out of her bedroom dressed in shorts, a T-shirt, and sandals.

"Why are you dressed that way?" Emma asked.

Lily casually walked to the door. "I'm ready to go."

"You can't go to daycare like that. It's the middle of winter."

"No, it's not."

"Uh, yes, it is," said Emma.

It was so cold that just opening the door to the outside, any exposed skin felt as if it would peel off. And the snow seemed never to quit. If we got a parking space near our apartment, most of us left our cars parked and took the bus or caught a ride. It might sound ridiculous to non-city dwellers, but parking spaces were a precious commodity that winter. Driving down Chicago streets, we'd see chairs, and even sawhorses, staking claims to parking spaces. Encroachers were shot at. Really.

"I'm tired of winter," Lily whined. "I want summer. I want the beach!"

"It's *not* summer. It's snowing outside." Emma, exacerbated, bustled about, running late for work.

"No, it's not winter anymore," Lily said with authority. "It's summer."

"Come look." I led her to the living room windows and scraped away a thin patina of ice. "See? It's snowing. You'll have to wear warm clothes. And a coat."

Lily's expression turned to horror. "I want the beach! I want the beach!" she chanted. "I want summer! It's summer now!" She stamped her foot.

It took both Emma and me to wrestle Lily into warm clothes. She sulked with an angry face, stomping her boots down each stair.

Chuckling, I turned to Emma and said, "Wouldn't it be nice if we could get what we want by simply dressing for the occasion?"

Emma rolled her eyes and followed Lily down. At the bottom of the stairs, Lily opened the door.

I felt the icy air rush up to the third floor like the ghost of an iceman seeking redemption and a warm place to stay.

That was my daytime life, when I pretended to be normal . . . until summer finally came and I left them.

My other life was the one I lived at night.

I sold those ads for my cocaine dealer's coupon clipper after I'd been fired for too many Monday and Friday absences from a marketing job downtown. An employment requirement for my new job with my dealer was to provide my checking account information so he could deposit money to cover his checks that always bounced. I didn't mind, as long as he supplied the cocaine I wanted. Sometimes I'd lay awake all night, waiting for him to score. It was perfectly okay to keep calling him because he'd be awake too, waiting.

My father paid my rent and utility bills, as any money I earned went directly up my nose or into the bowl of a water pipe. Though he was a suit-and-tie-horn-rimmed-glasses type, I think my father liked to fancy himself a cool John Wayne, straight out of a 1940s war movie, playing the hero when he threw money at me and my sisters. I didn't mind. I was an addict, eagerly accepting his funding. At the time, I didn't know and wouldn't have cared that my father knew how I spent my money, that he needed me fucked up on drugs to control me.

I preferred smoking free-based cocaine over snorting it. In the mid-1980s, free-basing was a huge undertaking, a science lab project. The end product—pure crystals of cocaine—we cocaine addicts tenderly scraped from a Petri dish with a razor blade's sharp-edged caress. We'd carefully tap every delectable morsel into the bowl of a water pipe, obsessively checking and re-checking to make sure we hadn't spilled any, sifting through the carpet and licking off anything white from our fingertips. So lovingly did we regard our cocaine high that we fueled our Zippo lighters with rubbing alcohol instead of butane, to prevent black burn marks on the glass pipe. After all that trouble, plus paranoia of cops—peeking around curtains and window shades—we didn't transport free-based cocaine; we savored our crystal high at someone's apartment after the bar, or on Sunday afternoons with people deliberately chosen for trustworthiness. For me, that would be Michael, before we broke up, and my brother-in-law Rick. One time, Michael and I were so desperate for cocaine that we drove around the seediest Chicago neighborhood hunting for it.

Drug and alcohol consumption was only a symptom of my baneful life, an attempt to escape a malady buried deep within me.

I didn't know why fits of grief haunted me, driving me to drink and drug. I didn't know why I drove off alone to scream and pound the steering wheel in agony and remorse. I had no idea why I wanted to die, terrified that my soul did not belong to me. I couldn't grasp the source of my torment, imprisoning me on a charge I was never told—except for the guilty sentence imposed by my mother each time she proclaimed, "My, Hanna, you sure have a wild imagination." One day, I would know the motive for her accusing words that muffled my reality. But not yet.

I was miserable.

So, I sought escape in water pipes and bars with loud music.

Getting ready to go out partying, I would sit in front of my dresser mirror applying mascara and eyeliner with a glass of champagne, swaying to music. In the mirror, I'd practice the slow dance moves of my preferred blues bars. As my cocaine addiction took over and money became scarcer, I resorted to cheap vodka and wine, arriving at the bar half-wasted. My favorite was Biddy Mulligan's on Sheridan Road to see Koko Taylor and dance with the Black guys, better dancers than the white guys. I loved the anonymity of a packed dance floor, a nameless member of the crowd crushed in the middle of pulsating bodies. The music and movement were elixirs, soothing my yearning for comfort.

Then there were the nights I wore all black. Those nights were different. Instead of my happy-go-lucky romp to the bar to dance with people of all races, I went to well-lit establishments frequented by white businessmen. My arrival would be a grand entrance, sashaying through the door with my long, wavy blonde hair draped across my shoulders like Veronica Lake, 1940s sex symbol and star of the movie, *I Married a Witch*.

The tight black jeans and three-inch-heeled black boots I wore accentuated and lengthened my spidery legs, stretching my height to just under six feet. I was aware of men watching me, a beautiful young woman, but I didn't see myself that way and I didn't care about them, other than their eagerness to buy me drinks. Standing tall, I might nonchalantly swing my hair, and perhaps prop a foot on their bar stool, flaunting what those men wanted. I didn't want them to touch me, and never allowed them to, as my occult teachers had instructed me in lessons begun in childhood. Lessons I'd locked up in the amnesia drawer of my mind's filing cabinet of lost memories.

What happened in the Chicago bars on those mysterious nights I dressed in black? Where did I go when the tap on my shoulder portended the whisper behind my left ear that made me smile? When I walked out the door, was there *really* a man in a black woolen overcoat, facial features obscured by his bent head? Did he brush against my right shoulder as he entered the bar, slipping me a piece of paper? Was it a piece of paper? Or did he shove a small packet of cocaine into my hand, payment for a job well done? Was it a *job*? Did I hear a man screaming in agony as I stepped out onto the icy sidewalk? Was I used as a lure to even a score? Does any of this even matter anymore?

Maybe it matters to others who don't understand the reality of their lives. Perhaps you. So, I keep writing.

17

I drifted through the darkness of my life, only feeling comfortable leaving my apartment at night. Even when I made myself go out to sell ads, I'd only solicit companies open after sunset. I had a one-night stand with a nice man I met at a Lincoln Park optometrist's office that stayed open until 10 p.m. He asked me on a date to horse races and dinner. I got drunk and embarrassed him in front of his friends. When he drove me home, I persuaded him to come upstairs, seduced him, and then kicked him out.

My affair with a handsome married man, an old neighbor, lasted until I left Chicago. Another affair was with a married man I despised. And another was a brief fling with a handsome man who worked for my father—he never asked me on a date, only to his house, which he kept cold and dark. Then there was Mark, who I was with on the night I left.

I was tired of shallow relationships with shallow men. Tired of my own shallowness. Seduction didn't do it for me anymore, and the drugs and alcohol were failing me as well. But I knew nothing else.

In the spring, I got a call from a young man who said he was my brother, that we had the same father.

"*What?* You're full of shit. Who the hell is this?"

"I am so sorry I bothered you," he said. "I hoped you'd be ready to hear it."

I hung up on him and called my mother to ask if it were true. All she said was, "Oh! don't tell your sisters!"

Not wanting to deal with the possibility that my father had another son somewhere, I quickly forgot his name. His phone call unnerved me, dragged me deeper into the confusion and misery taking over my life. I began thinking about him whenever I watched shows about people finding long-lost relatives, wishing I could remember his name.

I free-based more cocaine and drank more cheap wine, numbing my mind into oblivion. The days wore on until I couldn't take my life any longer.

I was at my sister Lorain's apartment when I decided to leave, dog sitting while she and her husband, Rick, were on vacation. They left me a book, *No One Here Gets Out Alive*, a depressing biography of Jim Morrison's turbulent life and death. Disturbed beyond measure, I stopped listening to The Doors that day, Morrison's voice a haunting reminder of his tragic life and death. His biography of hopelessness spoke to me, forced me to face my unhappiness, for which I hadn't a clue of its source. All I knew was that my life would be over soon, if I stayed in Chicago.

So, I ran. All the way to Texas.

* * * *

Fall. Halloweentime. We walk in a single line to the witches' fire burning in the cool forest. I stand, as usual, locked within the fortress of my child body, staring out, watching. Pushed forward from behind, I am a captive forced to witness.

Demons fly about. They dart and zing with menacing grimaces, making a frightening noise of shrieks and demonic laughter. But they're not as strong as God's loving arms spread before me, hovering above the altar.

The trees weep.

The angels weep.

God and Jesus weep.

For the tiny victim's soul carried home.

But they weep most grievously for the witches who have committed the awful crime.

Jealous of the child on the altar, I wish I were the special one leaving life. I want to be the one embraced in Jesus's loving arms.

My spirit is trying to sneak away from the scene, wishing to disappear. But I can't, so I hide inside my body, forced to witness the secret ritual.

19

I am silent and immobile like the trees surrounding me, rooted to one spot, hating myself for not running, hating myself for being born.

It is difficult to leave the other children when the ritual ends, knowing what I know.

I don't want to look at them. I don't want to know how they got here, because I know how they got here, and I don't want to know.

I feel removed. I am merely a spirit observing the charade.

Fallen autumn leaves crunch beneath my feet in pre-dawn mist, walking single file out of the forest with the others. Mystical auras of love protect the trees from the anguish of dark secrets they must witness. Like soldiers on duty, above it all, these superior beings are my friends. They watch over me with sheltering limbs, shedding tears of sympathy colored ochre, orange, and wine-red.

Three

I strode over to the ticket counter to book a flight for Abilene in my search to find Jerome. The ticketing agent said the next flight would depart Dallas in the morning, with two seats left on the six-seat commuter plane. As we discussed my options for the night, a man walked up behind me and said, "Hey, I know you."

Turning around, I didn't recognize him. "You do?"

"We went to high school together. You have a twin sister. Right?"

"Yes, I do."

"Everyone knows the twins in school. Plus, you two had that long blonde hair. And tall." He motioned with his hand that I was still a bit taller than he.

I smiled and extended my hand. "Nice to see you, uh . . ."

"Gabe." He splayed his fingers out on his chest in exaggerated self-importance, as if the gesture would be enough for me to remember him.

"I didn't go to high school much." My excuse for not remembering him.

He chuckled. "Yeah, I know. You were one of the 'Mulford Freaks.'"

I chuckled, too. "Uh huh, I sure was."

Gabe was referring to Mulford Street, behind the high school, where school administrators allowed students to smoke cigarettes. We smokers were called "freaks," a shortened version of the hippie-freak movement, of which we were the tail end. In fact, during the years I attended high school, my only picture in a yearbook was a single photograph of me lighting a cigarette on Mulford Street, placed among the scattered photos of high school life.

"What are you doing here? In Dallas? At midnight?" I asked.

"I live in Denver now. I just arrived for a business meeting in the morning. What are you doing here?"

I said I was on my way to visit a friend or something. He dipped his head, and I knew the sadness in his eyes was for me. Maybe he noticed I had no luggage or smelled alcohol on my breath.

"Would you like something to eat?" he asked.

"Oh, I don't know. I need to find a place to stay. My flight doesn't leave until tomorrow."

"You can come to my hotel with me. No strings. Honest." He crossed his heart. "We can just talk, and you can leave in the morning, or whatever. I have to get up early for my meeting, so I'll be leaving around 7:30."

"Well . . ." I felt embarrassed, suspecting he'd figured out I was flat broke.

"I'd like to talk with you," Gabe said. "Honestly, I'm not trying to . . ."

I scrutinized him, my head tilted to the side, hand on my hip. Something about him reeked of sincerity, and I needed a place to stay.

"Okay then. Thanks, Gabe."

We walked to his hotel, adjacent to the airport, to check in.

Gabe wanted a quiet restaurant. My eyes, however, fixated on the opaque glass doors of a bar in the hotel lobby, so I suggested we go there. With a look of disappointment, or maybe disapproval, he shrugged his shoulders and sighed, "All right, come on." He opened the door for me like a gentleman.

Music and loud voices blasted us from inside the packed bar. It was shocking to see so many people crammed in there after midnight on a weekday.

I ordered a drink. Gabe ordered pizza.

I have no recollection of what we talked about, though whatever it was, I felt his compassion for me and wondered about it. I thought I'd been doing a fine job of keeping up appearances. Gabe's kindness toward me was extraordinary. I was accustomed to men paying me attention, but his was different. He listened with rapt attention, patting my hand as would a brother. I sensed he cared, wasn't looking for a weakness in me to exploit.

While Gabe finished his pizza, I swallowed one last drink and nonchalantly pulled out my checkbook. He placed his hand over mine to stop me and said, "Now listen here. I'll be insulted if you don't let me pay." He smiled, eyes glowing with the wisdom of an older man.

Gabe insisted I sleep in his comfortable hotel bed while he took the floor, making a bed from a couple of extra blankets. My protestations would not move him from this arrangement.

He turned out the light. "I'm glad I ran into you tonight," he said with such tenderness my eyes stung with tears I was glad he couldn't see. "I'll probably be gone in the morning when you wake up. Order anything you want from room service and I'll be back around noon."

I pretended to be sleeping when Gabe left in the morning. I ordered toast and left him a check for the cost, wanting to pay my own way, though I knew my empty checking account wouldn't cover even that meager amount. I wrote him a note to thank him and left, hoping he'd forgive me.

How was it this kind man happened to be at the Dallas airport? Perhaps he was the first angel sent to help me on my journey.

A perky travel agent in the hotel lobby booked my flight to Abilene and a rental car to pick up when I got there. I ripped out two more hot checks from my checkbook and handed them to her.

"Have a pleasant trip," she good-naturedly proclaimed, and I walked over to the airport, showed my ticket at the gate, and strolled across the tarmac to the tiny commuter plane preparing for the forty-five-minute flight to Abilene.

I had flown on a small plane only once before; in fact, with Jerome, whom I was taking this flight to find.

When Jerome and I were a couple in the late 1970s, we took a trip to visit his brother Perry, a pilot for Port Clinton, Ohio, an island community on Lake Erie. I didn't know there were islands in the Great Lakes. Perry flew us to the largest island in a tiny red-white-and-blue plane called The Ford. (I still have the T-shirt Jerome bought me, crinkled with age.) The islanders didn't allow cars on their island, only golf carts and bicycles. We rented a tandem bicycle for the day, meeting up with Jerome's family for lunch at a cafe in the lovely business district of antique and trinket shops sprinkled along the lakeshore.

I tagged along on most of their family adventures to visit wacky relatives, all of us piling into Jerome's mother's colossal motorhome. Josephine, Jerome's mom, personally invited me, most likely to ensure time with Jerome, who wouldn't have likely gone without me. Josephine embraced me into her family during the few years I was involved with her son. Secretly, I loved the feeling of belonging, of being a treasured member of his family.

The rickety plane ride to Abilene left me breathless and trembling. I wanted to at least *see* Jerome before making my decision to live or die, wanting it to be *my* choice and *my* way, which was *not* death by plane crash. I felt a desperate need to talk to Jerome before I made that decision, counting on his love as my salvation, although I would never have admitted it, not even to myself. I didn't understand the need for love, like the need for air, water, and sunshine. But I knew Jerome would accept me, welcome me, and, yes, love me.

I found Jerome by sheer obsession and bizarre luck. By asking every person in a diner I stopped in for lunch, I met an older woman who knew Jerome. She invited me to sit at her table and wrote out directions to a new subdivision where

24

she thought he might be working as a roofer. Determined to find him, I drove my rented car up and down every street. Turning the corner on the last block under construction, there he was, standing on the roof of the two-story house he was shingling. I pulled up to the job site, got out, and leaned against the car, shocked that I'd found him. I smiled, waiting for him to notice me.

The guys turned to see who'd driven up, and from his vantage point on the roof, Jerome shielded his eyes to get a better look. He froze with a jolt of surprise, teetered, and almost fell off. Then, slowly, he climbed down.

As he approached in his familiar sensual swagger, I smelled his life working outdoors: the sawdust of freshly hewn wood, scents of flowers on a warm breeze. He looked great, still fabulously well built, with a nice tan and hair streaked with wisps of white-blonde strands of sunshine, all of which presented him as the picture of excellent health.

He sauntered over, not smiling, and stood before me, staring.

"Hi Jerome."

He stared at me, mute, and then found his voice. "What are you doing here?"

"I've come to find you."

Our eyes locked.

"Wh . . . *what*?" he stammered.

"I need a friend, Jerome. You," I said, pressing my finger in his chest. "Are you still my friend?" I leaned back on the car, one ankle crossed over the other, arms extended down the front of my body, fingers laced. I felt a bit vulnerable, yet confident.

"Um . . . sure. Yes, of course." He hugged me, never diverting his eyes from mine. He didn't even blink, his eyes stuck open in surprise. "What's wrong?"

"I don't know."

He released me from his embrace and took a step back to take me all in. I must have appeared to him as a ghost, materializing from the mists of the past.

Coming to his senses, the spell that had moved him in shocked slow-motion broke, and he became livelier, his old charming self I had known. Mr. Cool. Suave, I used to call him.

"Come on," he said. "I'll introduce you to the guys before we go."

"Are you done for the day?"

"Close enough." He hugged me. "I can't believe you're here!"

I giggled, overjoyed to see him. He took my hand and introduced me to the crew.

I wish I could bring you to Jerome's house to continue with a heartwarming story. But I can't.

Jerome lived with his girlfriend and a roommate, Neil, one of the guys he worked with—a tall, well built, funny guy who told silly jokes.

Jerome had recently turned thirty, his girlfriend was eighteen, maybe twenty—a strike against him, though I didn't tell him that. The girlfriend moved out of Jerome's bed to sleep on the filthy couch when I arrived. She was upset, of course, but didn't make a scene or anything. She liked me, and I liked her. I felt terrible for her and thought Jerome was such an asshole for dumping her—another strike against him, yet it didn't deter me from sleeping in his bed.

I wasn't in my right mind, obviously. Utter desperation had driven me into a self-absorbed state of mind wherein I thought little of other people's needs and wants in relation to my own. In other words, I didn't think *I* was an asshole for replacing that girl in Jerome's bed. And the strangest thing is, she stayed.

Now four of us lived in a tiny house with a tiny living room, tiny bathroom, a kitchen only one person could stand in comfortably, and a single bedroom divided by a wall partition into two narrow sleeping spaces. My first experiences in the vast state of Texas were tiny: the tiny airline that flew me to Abilene in the tiny plane, and now Jerome's tiny house with the tiny rooms and our tiny attitude toward that young girl's feelings.

And now that I'd found Jerome, settled in, and our sleeping arrangements were set, I relaxed and turned myself over to him, the weight of my life falling from me onto him. Miraculously, I stopped thinking about the next drug or bottle of booze for the first time since the age of twelve, my desire for them having vanished. I had a beer here and there after I'd first arrived, out of habit. When that stopped, I fell into a foggy withdrawal, a sort of mind-numbing stupor for the few days it took to come down off the cocaine and alcohol. And when I did, I heard Jerome's concern for me.

We were in the dusty front yard, so unlike what I'd known. Instead of soft, northern Illinois green grass, Jerome's Texas yard was finely grained, rusty-colored sand, coating my feet like an unfired patina. It was dusk. I was leaning against Jerome on a lawn chair, the kind that folds out for sunbathing. Detoxing had been like a bewitched slumber. As I came out of it, I looked down and noticed I was wearing a pastel pink, one-piece outfit—the top part sleeveless and form-fitting, the bottom part shorts with flared legs, like culottes, only much shorter, resting way up my thighs, right below my butt. It was a comfortable, thick cotton. Stroking the soft fabric, I vaguely remembered walking through a department store and Jerome picking out that outfit. *Figures.*

Those tactile things are what I noticed first—the scratchy feel of sand on bare feet, the softness of clothes on skin.

Then I heard Jerome's voice as if coming from a distance, speaking in mid-sentence, ". . . worried sick. Don't you think you should at least call them?"

"What?" I turned my face to his, disconcerted by the closeness, as I was on his lap.

"You need to call your family. They must be worried sick."

"What are you talking about, Jerome?"

"Your folks, silly. Don't you think they're wondering where you are?"

I sat up and turned to face him.

"Wondering where I am? Why would they?"

"You disappeared, Hanna. Vanished!" He made a "poof" sign with his fingers. "Of course, they're wondering what happened to you."

Jerome's eyelids and eyebrows were triangles framing his eyes like oddly shaped picture frames. Deep trenches of vertical lines buckled the space between the triangles, and his mouth turned downward in a pout. His alarm, his concern for me, was most prominently illuminated in his eyes—pupils constricted to pinpricks in the center of hazel-brown irises, brighter than I'd remembered, even in the darkening evening light.

"Wondering what happened to me?"

He shook me gently. I moved like a rag doll. "You have to call home. What about your sister? Don't you think she's worried sick? You left one day and never returned. And what about your little niece? She must be missing you."

"Jerome . . . uh . . . call home? I don't want to go back to Chicago."

"I'm not telling you to go back. Just call." He peered into my eyes. "They probably think you're dead."

"I, uh, hadn't thought of that."

I wondered how much I'd told him while in my withdrawal delirium. Enough for him to know I'd been living with Emma and Lily. Had I also told him my plan to find him before deciding if I would live or die? Maybe I had, and that's why he moved his girlfriend out to the couch. Perhaps that's why she wasn't angry, was friendly to me, and used a gentle voice when we spoke.

"I don't know, Jerome. You think they're *worried*?"

"We have to let them know you're okay." He looked into my eyes. "Right?"

"Um . . . I don't know . . . um, maybe."

The triangular shape of his eyes distracted me, and I realized it was a look of concern. Extreme concern, grief almost. Concerned for *him* now, I placed my hands on his cheeks. "Okay, if you think so," I said. And just like that, his face softened and he exhaled.

He smiled, alarm lingering deep within his eyes. Or maybe it was a pause of uncertainty. He must have been wondering if I'd gone mad, not understanding my desperation to leave Chicago and what it was like to get off cocaine and alcohol.

In that moment, fully detoxed, killing myself went on hold. I was so worried about the bad checks I'd written for the airfare and car rental that I hardly slept. With Jerome's continued urging, I finally called my father, my first words a request to cover the checks. He hesitated before answering, "Okay, I'll deposit the money and send you your stuff. What's the address?" His voice cracked, making me wonder if he felt more than anger.

Next, I called my sister Lorain. Her husband, Rick, answered the phone. "Oh Hanna, I'm so relieved to hear your voice," he shouted. Oddly, or perhaps not, he added, "We were worried some sort of cult had abducted you. I'm glad you're all right."

My father put money in my bank account and shipped a box of clothes Emma packed from my closet in our apartment. I didn't call to thank her, nor did I apologize for leaving. It never occurred to me she would be afraid, only that she'd be angry and yell at me.

Choosing to live, in Texas, I wanted to start my life over. I wanted a job, a regular job.

Jerome drove me to a temporary employment agency the day after I called my father.

I received my first work assignment as a receptionist in the office of an oil speculator in historic downtown Abilene, which in the mid-1980s was crumbling. Wrapped up in cocaine and alcohol, I hadn't even known the U.S. was in a recession.

Everything about Abilene differed from everything I'd known in my life back in Chicago. I learned about the oil-based Texas economy from the man I worked for, a geologist who used his education to search for deep pockets of oil for giant gas and oil companies. Things had slowed down because of the recession, but he hung in there, waiting for the tide to change. I knew nothing about oil, the wealth of it, thus had never considered the driving force behind it— our U.S. romance with the automobile. Dotting the landscape were pump jacks, which I had never seen. They looked like hungry mosquitos ravaging the land. Jerome agreed, laughing at the way I wrinkled my nose from the noxious fumes of crude oil pumped raw from the earth. I couldn't help but think of them as sucking up Earth's life force, opening veins for rapacious vampires.

Like my former rush from cocaine, the excitement of an alien environment quieted the screaming in my head, for a time. My new high would be Texas. I found great fun exploring my new digs. Which included, I am ashamed to admit, Jerome's roommate, Neil.

Neil was taller than Jerome, with a fantastic body. He made me laugh, his green eyes sparkling when he laughed at his own jokes, more of a chortle than a laugh, with a warm and beautiful smile. Neil's father owned a ranch in a small town outside Abilene, another side of life heretofore unknown to me. Neil took us all out there one afternoon, late in the day, the sun slanting golden on the fields, where long shadows of sparse trees made slivers of shade for cows trying to escape the hottest part of the day. It was my first time on a ranch. I loved it, enthralled with the novelty.

Neil's father sauntered over as we parked in the dirt drive by a barn. He touched the brim of his sweat-stained cowboy hat, tipping it slightly in greeting.

The ranch was quiet. Quiet enough to hear an occasional cow mooing in the field, two horses nickering in a corral, a light breeze blowing through the upper branches of apricot trees in the orchard and the pecan trees surrounding the house, and the hinge of a rusted gate that squeaked with each gentle gust. The loudest sound I heard that day was the shrill call of a peacock. Neil's father, who'd been talking to Neil, pointing at the horses with one foot propped on a wooden slat of the corral fence, turned at my shriek. His bluebonnet eyes lit up, and he took his time curling his lips into a grin. He shook his head from side to side at a snail's pace and proceeded to calm me down in a slow drawl with long, drawn-out vowels. "Looky here, now," he said. "That there's 'jus the mating call of a peacock looking for a hen." He pointed to a strutting male coming around a corner of the house, tail feathers spread in a beautiful fan of iridescent eyes.

Mouth agape, I stared wide-eyed, having never seen a peacock outside of a book. Neil's father broadened his smile. Amused, he turned to Neil, a lazy thumb thrown my way, and asked, "She a Yankee?"

The two-storied ranch house was old, constructed of a light-gray, almost white brick, with wooden pillars out front. It reminded me of plantation homes I'd seen in history books, albeit in slight disrepair, giving it a down-home-countrified quality to my enchanted eyes. I was hooked. I loved it. All of it.

Jerome didn't freak out too badly when I told him I was leaving. Not at first.

He assumed I was going back to Michael, which I'd done when I left him the first time, in Illinois. He sighed, eyes drooping. "Okay, Hanna, I get it. I know Michael is the one you love."

When I mustered the courage to admit it was his roommate this time, he went berserk. "Have you gone completely out of your mind?" he yelled. "Neil is a total loser! Don't you see that? He drinks all the time, smokes joints like they're cigarettes, and misses a lot of work because he's too hungover to make it. I don't know why the boss hasn't fired him." He placed his hands on my shoulders and looked deep into my eyes, his eyes those triangles of grief. "Please don't do this. You can leave, of course, but don't go with *him*."

For a reason I could not explain, I laughed while Jerome and Neil fought in the dusty front yard on that sunny October morning when I left Jerome standing in anguish and drove off with Neil.

I still feel ashamed.

Neil and I rented an apartment in Round Rock, Texas, about twenty miles north of Austin. For the first few weeks, we fought like crazy each time I hunted him down at the local bar. So, I decided it was time to get married. That would fix him. "We get married, or I'm out," is how I put it.

Thus, on the night of December 31, 1984, we drove an hour south to Lockhart, Texas, for our wedding ceremony. Lockhart was my idea, thinking it a charming place to "lock hearts." At midnight, standing before the justice of the peace who agreed to bring in the new year with us, my mouth said "I will" while my mind screamed *No!* I ignored my mind. I figured, *well, I've never been married before, maybe that will help*, though I hadn't a clue what help I needed or wanted. . . . To ease the tormenting thoughts ceaselessly fluttering in my mind, I suppose, though those thoughts were elusive butterflies I could never quite catch.

We had our choice of December 31, 1984, or January 1, 1985. We chose the new year and spent the rest of our honeymoon night in a cheap motel—Neil's idea—so we'd have money for his beer and grass. Such was the starting point of our life as a married couple.

Over the next three years, the process of remembering unfolded. Clouds of illusions began to dissolve, freeing up fragments of my history to sneakily slide open my mind's amnesia drawer of lost memories. They came in a haphazard jumble, pulled randomly from the files . . .

I'm sick of everything! Boyfriends. My parents. Every person and every thing!

I get in the car and drive, drive, drive, getting nowhere. I don't know my destination or where I want it to be.

32

I'm driving down the street that Steve, my friend from sophomore year Earth Science, lives on. I don't know why I'm on his street. But that's a lie. I want to "accidentally" run into him. He'll be walking out of his house, see me, and wave me down with a big smile. He'll look at me the way he did in our class, when he liked me and wanted to know me. Me. He'll say, "It's okay, Hanna, I'm here. Everything will be all right." He'll hug me and hold me close. And never let me say goodbye.

Searching. Running. I don't know what I'm searching for or what I'm running from. I feel like a child, even though I'm eighteen. Please help me! I beg, to no one, to everyone. My plea bounces off rooftops and ricochets off trees as I speed past, my foot smashing the accelerator to the floor. I grasp the steering wheel with a thread of hope from John Lennon singing "Imagine" on the radio. Imagining what it would be like if everyone lived in peace, I join John Lennon, entering the realm of dreamers.

Four

The famous Texas bluebonnets bloomed mid-March, blanketing roadways in solid blue, extending outward into every farmer's unsown field. It looked as if someone dumped gravel-loads of unpolished sapphires along my route to work, driving from our rented townhouse in Round Rock to my new job at KLRU-TV, Austin's public television station. I'd always wanted to work for public television, so I took the job offered—Accounts Receivable Clerk and secretary to the Chief Financial Officer. Not the most glamorous position, but got my foot in the door. Neil was working on a construction crew, building homes in a new subdivision carved out of a rancher's recently sold field. I'd been his helper until I started my new job, arriving at job sites in his 1962 Chevy pickup, which I loved to drive.

Grandma Elsa was turning ninety on March 28, and my parents were having a party for her. My new boss gave me time off to go to Chicago for her birthday party, and for a wedding reception for Neil and I, even though my parents sorely disapproved of my elopement with a man I barely knew. They were cordial to Neil during our stay, not quite warm. We stayed at Emma's with her and Lily to avoid the disapproving sidelong looks from my mother and father.

Summer came to Austin with a scorching heat I was unused to, chasing me across Mansfield Dam to spend my weekends stretched out on a plastic float, drifting on the cool water of Lake Travis. Neil, working outdoors all week, usually opted to stay home. We'd fight about it, and by the time I'd get home, he was usually be drunk or gone, resulting in fierce resentments. Fueling my anger was the possibility that he would never stop drinking. I'd had such high hopes for our marriage, thinking it would change him. Instead, a rift grew between us as wide as the highway separating those springtime bluebonnets.

In the Fall, my parents came.

They arrived late in the afternoon, impatient from their two-day drive. They complained about everything, unimpressed with their first trip to Texas, even the winding roads, which my father sarcastically claimed, "The city designed them that way to give a false impression." Whatever that meant. His criticisms tugged at my heart. I wanted to share my new life with him and my mother. I wanted their approval.

As they talked, and I listened, I noted the intensity of their negativity, and a disrespectful attitude toward me, particularly from my father. Something was out of place. I saw them as peculiar for the first time, as if I'd never really known them. Completely discarding the fact that I'd fled Chicago to save my life, I assumed my revelation was due to my eleven hundred mile move away from them, which was about a million miles, culturally.

Growing up in the rushed Chicago Metropolitan area, people were in a hurry, briskly walking down city and suburban streets, avoiding eye contact for fear of having to stop for a chit-chat.

At home, my sisters and I received tacit rules about life—how to look good, mostly. Until the day I left Chicago, I couldn't shop for clothes without at least one of my sisters' advice and approval. And looking good wasn't solely about our physical appearance. Looking good encompassed a whole range of unspoken laws about how we were to present ourselves to the world, what we were and were not to say, even to each other.

My new Texan friends were quite different—their Texas drawl and slow-paced lifestyle, for starters. They thought differently about family and friendship, too, providing support and encouragement to one another—values in sharp contrast to where I'd come from. Far away from the world of my youth, my family's influence no longer stifled me. Hence, when my parents came to visit, I had a fresh perspective on life, if not clearly defined.

My parents slept in our bedroom, their first time sleeping on a waterbed. That part was funny. Neil and I slept on a twin bed in our spare bedroom across the hall, giggling when my parents plopped down on our waterbed, sloshing about, my mother huffing and puffing, "Oh my!"

I woke up one morning to find her alone in our bedroom, quivering from head to foot, trying not to cry, with a terror-stricken expression bulging her eyes, staring blankly out the window. She was smoking a cigarette, sitting on my rickety cane-back chair I'd found in one of the abandoned houses Neil and I rummaged around in for fun. Ashes fell everywhere except into the ashtray she unsteadily held on her knee.

I went to her, arms open. "Mom, what's wrong?"

"Nothing. What could be wrong?" she said defensively, pushing me away.

I walked downstairs. My father was sitting on the sofa with a smirk on his face, reading the newspaper, which he pulled up over his face when I came down. I asked him what was wrong with mom. He dismissed me, and her, with a sarcastic "*pshew*," peering at me over the edge of his newspaper. At that exact moment, like an alarm clock jolting me awake, I knew beyond any doubt that *he* was responsible for her faraway eyes, and always had been.

I'd see my mother upset and shaky numerous times, my father dismissing and diminishing her pain with sarcastic smugness. Now, looking into his cold, calculating, cobalt eyes, unbelievably devoid of feelings for his wife, I realized something was terribly wrong. In that stunning moment I suspected, for the first time, that maybe it wasn't me who was all wrong; maybe it was *them*.

I never found out what happened that morning. After my parents left on their long drive home, I sat in shocked quietude on a living room chair facing the door, feeling a tornado had just ripped through my life.

My moment of truth.

My parents were fucked up. Especially my father.

I wondered about something else I'd never forgotten . . .

It's Summertime. Emma and I are taking turns pushing each other on the swings in the backyard. It's getting on toward the end of the day, close to suppertime. The sun is sliding low behind the three-story apartment buildings across the alley, casting long shadows over the play area behind the garage where my father anchored a swing set in the dirt.

We feel alone, Emma and I, like it's just us against the world. Something has happened, and there is no peace in that house. Maybe it's because our father came home early and disrupted our mother's routine with his belittling demands and insults—"Marjorie, can't you do anything right?" "Marjorie, I thought I told you . . .," blah, blah, blah, treating her like a child. Or, with disgust, he'll say, "Marjorie, pshew . . .," not even finishing the sentence, so stupid is his wife that she's not even worthy of an insult.

When I think of my mother, it seems strange to call her mother because I sense she's not. I don't know why I think this, I just do. Sometimes I look at her with suspicion and search the mirror for something that looks like her, like how Ellyn has her same dark brown hair underneath her bleached, platinum blonde. But I have found nothing I share with my mother.

This I know for sure. The lady who calls herself my mother is a mystery. She's someone I want to be like sometimes (she has a certain grace and elegance about her); someone I never want to be like at other times (she allows my father and everyone else to treat her like dirt); and someone I am never afraid of because I can see her scared and lonely parts. Like a couple of months ago, when Emma and I found her sitting at the kitchen table with a black eye and I saw the telltale, greasy signs of Vaseline she'd already patted on her eye, just like she puts Vaseline on everything. *Emma and I sat next to her like bookends, worried, sad for her. "What happened?" we asked.*

"Nothing," she declared, trying not to cry, smoking a cigarette, her chin trembling.

We said no more and sat beside her, pretending we didn't see the black eye. Who hit her? Why?

It must have been our brother, Donald. We're scared of him. Or else it was our father.

It was one of them.

The holidays arrived. And passed. Bringing Neil and me into a new year, 1986, and our first anniversary.

Migraine headaches started when the bluebonnets came up. The doctor said it was from stress. I thought only wealthy business executives were stressed out, not an ordinary person such as me. I was so out of touch with myself that I wasn't aware I needed to relax. The doctor prescribed biofeedback sessions, which taught me to stay calm by breathing correctly—deeply from the abdomen, rather than shallowly from the chest.

I also attended 12-Step meetings for alcoholic families, realizing Neil had a drinking problem after the honeymoon phase of our marriage wore off—which was on our actual honeymoon, spending more money on Neil's beer and reefer than that one night in a rundown motel. In the meetings I attended twice a week, I learned that people raised in alcoholic homes often get involved with alcoholics, attracted to a familiar lifestyle. I realized all my previous boyfriends had likely been alcoholics, but I didn't understand why, as I'd only seen my father drink when he and my mother hosted dinner parties, and I'd never seen my mother drink. Then I learned about the many other faces of addiction, which explained a lot, such as my father's obsession with work and money, and my mother's prescription drugs, which I'd never thought of as addictive, having been prescribed by doctors. My new friends from the meetings said, "Your husband suffers from a disease. You should stick it out. Maybe he'll get sober one day."

I tried.

By the end of August heat, the migraine headaches abated. The man who'd conducted the biofeedback sessions recommended I see a counselor. I shrugged off that notion. I knew how to quiet my mind now. Everything would be fine.

However, towards the end of 1986, my new relationship with my new man in my new marriage lost the exciting feeling of new beginnings that I craved. I got a promotion at work, but that too had become rote. Chicken fried steak lost its appeal once I got the hang of making it, as did fajitas, both new foods I'd dug into with gusto, though I never mastered the art of frying up chicken and catfish. I still had fun on trips to my father-in-law's ranch, but it was the same old fun: riding out to the field in the back of his pickup truck to dump day-old bread for the cows; sifting through the beautiful antiques scattered about the house, hidden under layers of dust; and waiting for dinner, ravenously eating everything put before me. It was the thrill of the unknown I craved, using my new life as a drug to keep me too busy to think. Thus, my father-in-law's ranch routine no longer did it for me, either. And I had stretched my explorations of the Austin area to its very edges, as far as I could go without an overnight bag.

Stuck in limbo, I was back in the same uneasy discord I'd suffered in Chicago when the cocaine, alcohol, and men had stopped working. I had even taken a month leave of absence from my job in downtown Chicago to backpack across southern Europe with two friends.

Once again, I wondered what was wrong with me. All the time. As if worrying were a twenty-four-hour-a-day job. All my efforts to not think ceased to work, and all I did was think. I'd lost the ability to live life as a carnival, playing games I could never win, trying out all the rides in search of a tilt-a-whirl to spin away my thoughts, seeking the spine-tingling anticipation of where the ride might take me. But it never took me anywhere. I always ended up right back where I started. Spinning.

I didn't know I was stuck on a roller coaster ride of diversions, trying to prevent a painful memory from popping open that amnesia drawer in my mind like a giant, scary jack-in-the-box. Instead, I took it out on Neil. All the time. I blamed him for not fixing me, whatever I needed fixing, which I hadn't a clue. All I knew, what I believed, was that it was Neil's responsibility to quit drinking and make me happy, neither of which occurred. I grew tired of worrying and looking for him during his drunken sprees, and his refusal to hold down a job.

Thanks to the 12-Step meetings, I came to accept that Neil was not going to change, but that I could, with help.

At the bottom of a purse, I found the therapist's phone number the biofeedback practitioner had given me. I stuck it on the refrigerator with a magnet and looked at it for a few days, getting the courage to call Claudia in the autumn of 1986.

"I'd like to hear about *you*," said Claudia in our second session. "Not other people and what they're doing or not doing."

I didn't know what she meant. I'd never talked about myself other than what I wanted, and how I perceived others.

"What about you, Hanna? How are you behaving towards your husband?"

"I'm, well, I'm pissed that I have to hunt him down all the time. I mean, what else is there?"

"Yes, you believe you must look for Neil when he doesn't come home. I get that, sure. But what I mean is, what are *you* doing? Do you have to chase after him? Is this marriage what you want?"

"I have to look for him when he disappears, don't I?"

"No."

"What am I supposed to do, then?"

"Nothing. What can you do?"

This reasoning echoed what I'd heard in the 12-Step meetings. I still didn't get it, though.

In our fourth session, Claudia asked me to tell her about my family. "Family of origin" is what she said.

"What's 'family of origin?'"

"The family you grew up with. Your parents, siblings, perhaps aunts, uncles, cousins. Grandparents."

"I don't know," I said. "What's there to say?"

"Well, Hanna, you told me you got on a plane and took off without telling your family. And that you'd planned to commit suicide, right?"

"Well, yeah, if I couldn't find Jerome. But I found him, and he took me in, as I knew he would. What does that have to do with my family?"

"Is it possible that things weren't that great in your family? Things that may have driven you to want to commit suicide?"

"I don't think so. I was just unhappy."

"Why?"

"I don't know."

"You've been blaming your husband for your unhappiness. Is *he* the root of your troubles?"

"What do you mean?"

"Let's move on," she said. "Tell me about your weekend."

I continued therapy sessions with Claudia, once a week, trying to grasp the idea that my husband was not to blame for all my troubles. She introduced other concepts as well, such as dysfunctional family dynamics, which frightened me. I did not want to believe that *my* family might be dysfunctional, meaning "not performing normally," according to the dictionary. If I were to concede my family was dysfunctional, then I'd have to give up the notion I had control over my life. I had always found comfort in the faulty belief that if people only did as I wished, then I could change things and control the outcome, which, honestly, never ended the way I wanted, or thought I wanted. Not wanting to accept that truth, I hoped Claudia would teach me how to get everyone to do my bidding. She assured me that would never be a therapy goal, and reassured me that many people come from dysfunctional homes. In her sly therapist way, she even suggested that perhaps I could create my own family.

I began drinking a glass of wine now and then to cope with my burgeoning awareness of my broken marriage, my broken self, and my totally messed up family of origin. Inevitably, the occasional glass of wine turned into a drinking binge. At our KLRU Christmas party on the set of *Austin City Limits*, I couldn't stop drinking once I started. I went home with a co-worker, his wife and kids out of town to visit her family. He and I partied into the wee hours of the following day, beginning an affair, of course.

Neil was sitting on the stairs by the front door when I got home. I expected him to yell, but he didn't. His voice was frantic. "Where have you been? I've been worried sick. Why didn't you call?"

"*Humph*. Now you know how it feels," I said, walking past him up the stairs.

He followed me. I was nervous, thinking there'd be a huge fight, but there wasn't. Neil wasn't even angry. He was worried and hurt. I glanced his way before I slammed the bathroom door to take a shower, his eyes dark, wrinkled from lack of sleep. I knew how he felt, relishing the pain I saw in his eyes, revenge for the times he'd let me suffer.

I continued my affair with the man from work, though the clandestine excitement of illicit love still was not enough to keep my confusing thoughts at bay. Nothing eased my messed-up life I was now forced to face. Deep inside my mind's filing cabinet the amnesia drawer slid open, coaxing me to peer inside. There was more to my family history. Much more. But to accept it was not something I was ready to do. After the Christmas party, I blamed Claudia for my uncomfortable thoughts, flew out of her office, terrified, and never returned.

Alas, the door had been pried open and left ajar.

Across the sea from my childhood, memories flowed in with the tide of what I'd never forgotten, but hadn't thought of in years . . .

Seventh grade. Yesterday, my sister Emma and I got into a fight in the hallway outside Miss Jacobson's room. Emma yanked out one of my earrings, making my ear bleed. It was one of the big silver hoops that rest on my shoulders. I had to walk into Miss Jacobson's English class like that, and it really pissed me off. I guess Emma and I pretty much hate each other right now.

Vanessa was already in class and didn't see the fight, so I rushed over to my seat next to her to complain.

This class is where I met Vanessa. She taught me how to do needlepoint and we spend our classroom time stitching matching floral pictures instead of doing schoolwork, which Miss Jacobson doesn't even seem to notice. Half the time, she's not even in the room.

Vanessa and I have grown to be close friends. Brian, too, another kid I met in this class. The three of us huddle in the back of the room together, listening to the radio and talking about everything. I get to be myself with them. Brian listens when I try to explain how I feel when I hear Led Zeppelin's song, "Stairway to Heaven," which is constantly playing on the radio. He didn't think I was weird when I told him I feel far away and spacey when I hear that song.

At the bus stop in the morning, I eat the sack lunch my mother puts together. I spend my lunch hour at school mooching money from kids to spend on cigarettes for Vanessa and me. And after school, we walk a few blocks to downtown Skokie, which we call Uptown—"Are you girls going Uptown today?" my mother asks on Saturdays—where Vanessa and I steal gum from the Ben Franklin dime store to make gum wrapper chains, yards and yards of it. We also swipe Great Lash mascara in the hot pink tube with a hot green cap.

This year, psychedelic colors are popular for miniskirts, too—hot pink, hot green, and even hot orange. I, however, wear tight, tapered bell bottoms with men's work shirts. I don't want to be noticed, like in a miniskirt. I'm uneasy when people look at me. At school, I can fade into the back of a classroom—incognito.

On weekends, I walk across the bridge to Vanessa's house.

We listen to songs that make me sad, like Carly Simon's song, "That's the Way I've Always Heard it Should Be." The melancholy music, the lyrics about her father's cigarette glowing in the dark, her mother reading a magazine in another room . . . I feel sad, like what's family all about if everyone is unhappy, pretending they're not? When I hang out with Vanessa, I'm with her, but I'm not. We don't know it yet, but in the future, we're going to discover we have something in common we'd imagined was only nightmares we'd never told anyone.

I don't say much with my other new junior high friends. I am an observer, gazing upon their lives as an outsider. Maybe that's a good thing, the way it's supposed to be? My body is a fortress. My spirit, locked within, gazes outward, inhaling the unlimited life around me.

And I survive.

. . . Summertime warmth is over now. On to eighth grade.

Brian lost weight over the summer and grew his hair long. He's cute! I never noticed last year in Miss Jacobson's class when Brian and I became friends. I was so surprised when he asked me to go steady a week after school started. All the girls wanted him, but he chose me to be his girlfriend! He gave me his ID bracelet, so it's official.

I'm kinda self-conscious around him now. He's so nice!

Brian invites me to his house almost every day. We hang out in the basement with his older brother and his friends. We laugh a whole bunch, especially when they put Cheech and Chong's Up in Smoke *album on the turntable, the one with the giant joint on the cover. My favorite cuts are "Sister Mary Elephant" and "Dave's Not Here." It's hilarious! Brian and I sit close together on the couch, holding hands and laughing our butts off. I have so much fun with Brian that I forget he's my boyfriend. Then, I'll notice his ID bracelet jingling on my wrist and feel shy.*

I wonder what he wants from me, really *wants. He's too nice. He makes me feel self-conscious, looking at me as if he can see straight through me. Smiling, he holds my hands and kisses me gently, never even trying to put his hand up my shirt. It scares me. I think he truly likes me and I don't know how to deal with it.*

Five

Michael slumps on a gray chair in a gray room. Staring up at me, his thick brown hair covers one of his beautiful hazel-green eyes, filled with such pitiful anguish that I go to him and touch his pale cheek. His brow creases in bewilderment, his ghostly face frozen in grief. His eyes search mine for an answer, though I do not know the question. It seems we discovered something we weren't supposed to, and someone (who?) warned us to forget it or something terrible would happen. So, we forget.

It's 1973, the year we met. Michael is eighteen. I am fourteen.

I awoke from the dream with a start. A morning in early January 1987, right after our second wedding anniversary. Neil, who actually had a job that day, had already left for work.

Groggy and disoriented as if rising with a hangover, though I was stone-cold sober, I sat up on the edge of our waterbed and watched shafts of sunlight slanting through the window of our upstairs bedroom. I noticed the tops of trees outside, bare of leaves, but my focus was concentrated on those shafts of sunlight, the dust floating in them, thinking we only see all that dust in beams of sunlight. Not even the brightest light bulb illuminates it. Only the sun. I wondered what

46

happens to our lungs, inhaling those particles of dust we don't see, imagining them accumulating into lung-shaped pillows.

I didn't know why those were my first thoughts upon waking. I didn't know it was my way of trying to shove that dream into a drawer of my unconscious mind's filing cabinet, though it refused to fit. Encircled by a foreboding aura of truth, the dream felt real, as if Michael and I *had* been in that gray room, with forbidden knowledge we were told to forget. If indeed the dream hinted of an actual event, perhaps what we'd forgotten had contributed to the turbulence of our ten-year relationship. And a strange sense of knowing other things I wasn't supposed to know, and didn't want to know, slithered out of a drawer deep inside that filing cabinet—an uncomfortable, familiar foreboding of my life in Chicago.

Gazing upon those sunlit-revealed specks of dust, I didn't know my life was about to launch into an upheaval that would catapult me into a new dimension. Those dust particles, invisible unless exposed to sunlight, were like tiny bits of my life; invisible fragments that had remained unseen until the strange dream, as if the dream itself were a shaft of sunlight.

When I awoke that morning, I didn't know I was pregnant. It makes sense, though, that the child growing within me would send up memories on light beams—illuminating relics of long-buried events whispering from the depths of our ancestral consciousness. Connecting us. And portending our trials to come. Thus, the survivor deep within me awoke from a primordial sleep, bonding with the baby, determined to save her from my fate.

Unaware of what would soon transpire, a lingering aftertaste of the dream stalked me for weeks. I felt like a zombie. Stunned, unable to concentrate, I only half-heard, half-sensed the world around me. My world. I couldn't understand why that dream shook me so.

Neil came home drunk, again, this time with blood pouring out of his head and flowing down his ashen face as he passed out in a kitchen chair.

"Neil, what happened?" I begged, shaking his shoulders, trying to wake him.

My body trembled, feeling for his pulse, which I couldn't find. I called 911 and kept yelling and shaking Neil, as instructed by dispatch. He came to when the shrieking siren pulled into our driveway, narrowly missing his motorcycle he'd dropped there. Neil slurred, "It's no big deal. I just skidded on my bike in the driveway and hit my head when I fell." He refused to get in the ambulance or receive medical attention, flailing his arms when the paramedic tried to bandage him.

That was it for me. The end of the marriage.

My greatest heartbreak was not the marriage breakup, but the possibility of never having a baby. I didn't think I'd meet a man with whom I'd want to have a child before I reached thirty, as if that were the magic age beyond which society forbade a woman to birth babies. Hence, when the doctor announced I was pregnant soon after my decision to leave, I wept with joy. I knew I was carrying a little girl the moment the doctor confirmed her existence.

The haunting dream of Michael lingered, his perplexed, grief-stricken, beautiful face etched in my mind as a tapestry, tightly woven, unwilling to unravel. His image tugged at my heart, nibbled on my brain.

On March 1, 1987, determined to be a good mommy, I left.

Neil wanted me to stay, but I refused to raise my child in the insanity of an alcoholic home. For the baby's sake, I hoped we'd be friends, and begged him to get sober one last time.

On the far north side of Round Rock, I moved into a mauve-carpeted apartment with a sliding glass door that opened onto a large balcony facing a wooded creek bed. Neil made a wooden platform for wild bird seed I scattered, and I occupied my time watching a family of cardinals. Did you know the father feeds the round, fluffy babies? That fascinated me. I read everything I could get my hands on about human babies. Did you know amniotic fluid has the same salt content as oceans? I felt earthy, connected to Mother Nature. Eve.

I cried after spending time with Neil, whose goal was to bully me into letting him move in. He tore my heart into ribbons with words I didn't want to hear. Sometimes he came over drunk, and I'd have to kick him out. My entire existence was the upcoming arrival of our baby, which I wanted to share with him, angry he wouldn't be my friend. I shoved his bullying tactics aside and kept letting him in, hoping he'd stop.

Judith, from work, was also pregnant. Together, we ate our way through our pregnancies, meeting for lunch or dinner at least twice a week. Judith and her husband, Denny, invited me over on weekends. We ate, of course, and watched movies. I think they felt sorry for me, going through my pregnancy alone. But I didn't feel sorry for me. I smiled all day long, thinking about my baby.

In early July, Augustus was born—Gus for short.

I cuddled him on weekends, looking forward to my baby, due in October. Judith gave me her maternity clothes and waited with me.

On a swelteringly hot, humid, central Texas evening, my baby decided to come. I'd just trudged home from my pre-natal exercise class after work, where I'd sat out, fatigued beyond belief. I changed into a bright turquoise dress with huge embroidered flowers that Judith had given me, grabbed a peach from the fridge, and went to lie down on my bed. Plopping on the edge of my waterbed, I felt warm liquid and knew it was amniotic fluid. I freaked out—the baby wasn't due for another six weeks.

Neil didn't answer his phone, so I pulled a towel off the rack in the bathroom, shoved it between my legs, and drove myself twenty miles to the hospital, parking at the emergency room entrance.

I jumped out of my car and waddled in, yelling, "Help me! Please. My water broke and my baby isn't due until October."

The ER admissions clerk looked me up and down and said, "You probably just peed on yourself, but wait over there," pointing to the waiting room.

When a nurse finally called me back to an examining room, he balked in horror at the blood-soaked towel between my legs. "Don't worry, honey, your doctor will be here in a jiffy," he said, patting my hand.

Dr. Sundara rushed in, ultrasound equipment ready and waiting. "It looks like the placenta has pulled away from your uterus," she explained, "which has caused the blood and premature labor. The baby is in position for birth, though, so that's good. Do you want to know the gender?"

"Yes!"

Dr. Sundara smiled, exclaiming, "It's a girl!"

I wasn't surprised.

Neil still didn't answer his phone, so I called my friend from work, Pamela. She sat beside me and held my hand until Neil arrived later that night.

Dr. Sundara ordered a drug administered via an IV drip to stop the contractions, but it didn't work. Like it or not, the baby was ready to be born.

Two days later, my contractions weren't strong enough to dilate my cervix, so Dr. Sundara administered a different drug to intensify them into bone-crushing earthquakes. My cervix still refused to dilate, and my baby girl was in distress. Dr. Sundara ordered a caudal block, hoping that would work. The giant needle inserted into my spine sent Neil swooning from the room, held up by two nurses. But it worked. The lower part of my body relaxed and my cervix opened like a flower.

One hour and three pushes later, right after midnight, out swam my precious baby, riding the waters of life-giving love. All 4.28 pounds of her. Blinking open her enormous globe eyes like twin blue planets, I swear I saw the universe in them, stars shining from deep space. My baby gasped a startled brand-new-baby spasm of surprise, and her lungs filled with oxygen for the first time, inhaling life. My darling Elsa—an angel come to Earth from far across the Milky Way, her wings clipped when she took hold of her human form.

The world stopped turning.

"She looks just like me!" My surprised first words. Then, more softly, "Welcome to this world, my darling, beautiful little Elsa."

A nurse held my daughter in front of me to let me touch her tiny fingers and toes. What a miracle is the birth of a baby. Weeping with joy, I stared into Elsa's starlit eyes. In dazzling glory, Elsa's lovely spirit displayed itself to everyone present, until her pediatrician, Dr. Braun, whisked her away to the neonatal intensive care unit. I craned my neck after their hasty retreat, my arms outstretched in a longing gesture to cradle my angel in my arms.

On a new axis, the world began turning again. And my life changed forever.

Neil slept for brief minutes, jumping up to run to the ICU nursery, bringing back encouraging news. Relieved, I allowed myself a few hours of sleep before I woke up with a start, hunting for my baby.

I found her hooked to an IV with tiny round sensors stuck all over her teeny body. Frantic, I turned to a kind nurse who explained, "Your baby is doing great. Those sensors are monitoring her heart and blood pressure, that's all. Everything is normal." Her smile reassured me and I relaxed. When she shooed me out of the neonatal ICU an hour later, I called my family.

"*Elsa?*" My sister Lorain's first indignant word. "Why did you name her *Elsa?*" No congratulations or any other sentiment. "Everyone made fun of me growing up when they found out my middle name was Elsa, calling me Elsie the Cow. Do you want her to be made fun of?"

"I named her for Grandma Elsa. Her name is not Els*ie*, it's Els*a*. And by the time she gets to school, chances are nobody will even know Elsie the Cow."

I hung up, hurt to the core.

Grandma Elsa, on the other hand, clapped and cried, "Oh, that's wonderful!" I wept, elated that she approved. I decided to call the baby Little Elsa.

Easygoing from the start, Little Elsa didn't cry, not even when she was born. Her calls for attention were mere kitten mews. She was home for a month before she cried a real baby cry. I freaked out and called the doctor's office to tell them my baby was crying, to which they were not sympathetic.

Already her own person in the ICU, Elsa's personality was delightful. Tiny as she was, she managed to flip herself over and stick her cute little butt in the air, knees folded under her—a preview of her future independence.

My heartbeat during and after Elsa's birth was irregular, and my legs so swollen they looked like helium balloons, but felt like cement blocks. Dr. Sundara kept me in the hospital with Elsa for a few days, under observation. In a faintly lit, curtained-off area next to the ICU nursery intended for mothers to learn how to breastfeed, I spent hours in a useless struggle with my baby, too little to latch on to my breast. Disappointed, I fed her from a bottle, all the breast milk I could squeeze out of me with a hospital breast pump.

When the swelling in my legs receded, Dr. Sundara sent me home. I bought an electric breast pump and set an alarm clock every three hours, pumping and pouring breast milk into cellophane envelopes. I drove twenty miles to the hospital each morning, stashed them in the ICU refrigerator, and spent the time allowed cuddling and feeding Elsa. By day's end, I nearly collapsed from exhaustion.

Neil, an excellent coach during labor, now rushed to the neonatal ICU every day after work, his only consistency since I'd known him. He scooped up Elsa the moment he arrived, grinning so true his eyes sparkled. And he had a regular, full-time construction job, getting a paycheck instead of cash at the end of the week. I felt hopeful. Not for our marriage, but for him. Maybe for a genuine friendship, as parents. Hence, I dismissed the concerns of the nurses and my obstetrician when they cornered me in the neonatal unit one evening before Neil arrived.

"So, when are you getting the divorce?" Dr. Sundara asked.

Two nurses stood by the door, their arms crossed over their chests as if guarding the exit.

"We suggest you divorce him right away, if that's what you have in mind," said the lead nurse. She was gentle, yet firm.

It wasn't the first time they'd gathered to discuss my divorce.

"I am planning to divorce Neil," I said, "but I'm wrapped up in my baby right now. We don't live together, so I don't see a problem."

They looked at me without replying.

What was going on? Was there something they weren't telling me? Did they see something I did not? Did they know Neil drank?

I did not pose those questions to the concerned medical team. I found their unyielding interest a bit extreme, albeit difficult to ignore their force in numbers. As a euphoric new mommy, refusing to face unpleasantries, I did my best to ignore them and sealed their comments in my mind's filing cabinet.

Dr. Braun moved Elsa to an incubator in an adjacent ICU room after gaining a few ounces and jaundice was eradicated with light therapy. Her condition was less critical now, so visiting hours were longer and I was allowed to stay all day.

A baby boy, six months old, inhabited the incubator across the nursery from Elsa. He barely moved. A nurse confided that the baby was suffering from a syndrome called Failure to Thrive because his family hadn't come for him yet. Volunteer grandmothers came in to hold him, but it wasn't enough. I convinced a nurse to let me have him one afternoon. The little guy looked up at me with lifeless black eyes while I rocked and hummed, whispering, "Don't give up."

I wondered what it would be like to take him home. Little Elsa would have a brother, and this little guy would have a sister. Paul McCartney's pop song,

"Ebony and Ivory," played in my mind, the one he recorded with Stevie Wonder. Elsa and the baby boy would grow up the same age, only a few months apart, like piano key twins, living "together in perfect harmony."

It seemed silly, but there it was; the idealism that comes with motherhood, longing to believe in a world that would change to fit my ideal of a utopian life for my baby. I imagined them both as my babies, ambassadors for peace and love between the races. The piano key twins on a mission to free the world of hate.

I was certain the little boy, at least in part, was left at the hospital because of the effects of racism inflicted upon his family. I had been watching him for days, caged in that incubator. I couldn't stand it if no one came to get him. I wondered what was going on in his mother's life, picturing his family in a chaotic dance of futile problems, feeling that I understood his family's inability to take him home. But they weren't putting him up for adoption, either. I considered offering to take him until they were ready for him, even though I was a single mom of a preemie who would require a lot of care. That little guy wasn't a preemie, but he was going to require a lot of care, too. I tried to penetrate his soul with laser beams of love, rocking him to the beat of Paul and Stevie's song.

And then.

A vague memory rocked loose from my mind's vault. I was lying in a crib, listless, like this baby boy, wishing for someone to comfort me, rescue me. In the baby's eyes, I saw his crushing acceptance of rejection and remembered my acceptance of loveless abandonment, lying in a crib like a stone, wishing I would fade away. I was back in my baby body, in the grayness of early dawn light. Alone. Separated from my twin sister. No longer crying, having given up.

I shook my head, my eyes flickering back to the present. *Whoa! What was that?*

Looking at the baby boy in my arms, an uncomfortable, confusing panic fluttered in my solar plexus. I tried to push aside the horrible feeling of neglect I'd just remembered, handing the boy back to the nurse on duty.

Failure to Thrive Syndrome, the nurses had said. In my case, a better term would have been Failure to Believe. For, once again, I returned to denial, neatly filing all notions of neglect by dysfunctional parents into the file marked "My Parents are A-Okay."

Then they arrived.

* * * *

1964. I'm standing on a cold stone floor in a room made of rock, like a cave. There is a long, narrow window high above. Sunlight streams into the room's darkness, a golden shaft of light upon which angels alight. I can see them, but I can't see them. I just know they are there.

Words flow into my mind on waves of sunlight, whispering, "Do not be afraid. You are not alone." I touch my chest, my soul filled with gladness. Peace flows through me as if they've poured warm water onto my heart. I kneel in the shaft of light and pray. Surrendering to the Light, I make a vow to be a voice for children when I grow up.

A door opens. I turn to look. The black robe I'm wearing swishes with the movement. Someone, a man I think, also in a black robe, hood covering his face, pushes me aside. His white hand snakes out of its sleeve. It pulls a tasseled gold rope and a black velvet curtain falls over the light.

But it doesn't matter. I made my vow. I am the Light.

Six

My mother arrived at the hospital in her usual fashion, bright and bubbly. People typically loved her, so the neonatal nurses' obvious disapproval of her and my father—who arrived in his customary sullenness—surprised me. They were polite to my parents, but wary.

Dr. Braun, examining Elsa on her rounds, greeted my parents with great cheer in her thick German accent. The nurses observed their introduction . . . suspiciously?

I didn't understand, and I didn't want to understand. I wanted everyone to rejoice with me in the miracle of my baby, for the universe to applaud her birth. Was that too much to ask? I was a new mommy. All I thought about was everything Elsa.

My parents had come on the sixteenth day of Elsa's hospital stay. On day seventeen, I took my precious angel home.

I gingerly dressed Elsa in an adorable outfit I'd bought for her first time wearing clothes. Looking outside the hospital's glass front doors, I scanned the parking lot, hesitating to walk out and strap Elsa into a car seat. It felt as though Neil and I were tossing her out into a harsh world of hectic humanity with noisy traffic. I wanted to un-birth her back into my womb, where she'd be safe and warm.

Neil drove while I fretted and patted Elsa in the back seat, instructing him to slow down and, "Hey, be careful over those bumps."

How was I to know how miraculously, yet tragically, my daughter's tumultuous birth would change my life? How was I to know how deep into my family's secrets I would dig? It's a good thing I didn't know our future, my baby and me. I would have barricaded us in a closet in that hospital and refused to leave.

My parents were waiting for us at my apartment. But my father did not know it was only my apartment, not Neil's. When I'd called my mother a few days before their arrival, figuring I'd better tell them I left Neil the previous March, she said, "Oh no! Don't tell your father! It'll kill him." That was my mother's comeback whenever she didn't want to deal with my father, who always found a way to blame her for everything. So, I didn't tell him. After all, it would be selfish of me to give my father a heart attack because I had left my alcoholic husband. I succumbed to the pressure to conform and allowed Neil to move in. Temporarily. To please my mother.

My father bought me a new dining set because I didn't have one, and a new bedroom set because he disapproved of a mother sleeping on a waterbed. Whatever. And then they left.

Two weeks later, Neil's mother, Violet, came. She stayed long enough to help me get Neil to move out, which wasn't easy. He slammed things around and refused for an entire week. Violet left soon thereafter, and I settled into my new life with precious Elsa.

KLRU-TV gave me extra maternity leave to care for preemie Elsa.

I agreed to return to work after Christmas. Until then, I would go into the office a few hours each week to do the payroll, carrying Elsa with me in a baby basket that Judith bought in Mexico.

That fall, Alexandra, Alex, called to beg me to bring Elsa to Chicago. Alex and her twin sister, Adrienne, were my and Emma's best friends from junior high and high school.

"I don't know, Alex. My parents asked me for Thanksgiving, but I'm not too keen on traveling with a preemie."

"Oh, but it'll be so much fun! Please come."

Secretly wanting to show off my new baby, I let Alex sway me. I called my parents and let them buy me a plane ticket.

Little did I know how significantly our lives would change at midnight on Thanksgiving, when Elsa would turn three months old.

We landed at O'Hare airport on a frigid, sunny afternoon. I bundled up Elsa in the baby basket, which Judith had padded with a pink-and-white checked cushion and matching blanket she'd made. Alex and Emma were at the gate, waving. I tucked Elsa into the backseat of Emma's car and she dropped us off at Alex's house.

Alex's precocious toddler, Abby, adored Elsa. Whenever Alex called out, "Abby, where are you?" in a sing-song mom voice, we'd find her squeezed into Elsa's basket with her. Alex's nine-year-old giggled on the sofa. He was five the last time I'd seen him. And was still the sweetest, most beautiful little boy—a perfect combination of his equally gorgeous parents.

Alex made a baked mostaccioli casserole for dinner, the pasta swimming in a sausage tomato sauce, smothered with browned, gooey mozzarella cheese. Alex's second husband, father of Abby, couldn't get enough of it, making yummy sounds throughout his four servings. After our lively dinner, he took the kids upstairs to bed.

Alex grabbed the bottle of Merlot from the table, I got wine glasses, and we went to the living room to lounge on their comfy, overstuffed couch. We placed Elsa, asleep in her basket, between us.

"Can you believe it's been over, what, four years since we've seen each other?" Alex said.

"I know! That's crazy. It feels like yesterday," I said.

"It's great having you here, Hanna."

"I'm glad you talked me into coming. Good to see the kids, too."

Alex changed the subject. "You know what I've been thinking about since you said you were coming for Thanksgiving?"

"No, what?"

"The crazy shit we did when we were kids."

"Yeah," I said. "Especially when we did LSD." We laughed.

"Our escapades were hilarious, in a sad sort of way," said Alex. "We were so young to be dropping acid." She and Adrienne were only thirteen, Emma and I only twelve . . .

We're at the bowling alley, our hangout. Emma's boyfriend, Clark, has finally shown up with the acid.

Even though it's almost curfew, we're taking it anyway, and by the time Adrienne and Alex's dad picks us up, we're "peaking"—the climax of an LSD trip, before leveling off for the next twelve-hour high. We've been waiting for him at the door, finding something funny with every person who walks in, especially our friend Mark, who we call Goon. We're laughing uncontrollably when their dad pulls up. He demands to smell Alex and Adrienne's breath for alcohol, which makes us laugh harder. Then all of us twins cram into the backseat of the car, stifling giggles, the sides of our faces throbbing from acid-induced, cheek-splitting grins we can't suppress. Their father keeps shifting his eyes from the roadway to the rearview mirror on the way back to their house.

We spend the night holed up in the twins' bedroom, giggling.

Alex's giggles turn into sobs as she points at a skeleton she sees in the wood grain of their bedroom door. We see the skeleton too, but watching Alex crying about it, we laugh until we can't breathe.

Then Alex starts leaving the room, walking ghostlike to the landing at the stairs. We follow her.

Every time she goes out there, she says, "It looks like a picture, it looks like a picture," in a dreamy voice, meaning the living room down below. Adrienne and I run back to the bedroom, stomachs aching from laughing. Their dad comes out of his bedroom to smell Alex's breath again, tells us to hush up, and marches back to his room, slamming the door. Adrienne and I just about suffocate from laughter. "Be quiet!" he yells. Adrienne and I stuff rolls of toilet paper in our mouths to silence our shrill laughter.

Emma is trying to shush us, but she can't. So, she calls Mindy, a friend in the neighborhood we consider a goody-two-shoes because she doesn't get high.

Mindy sneaks out of her house around midnight to come help Emma get things under control. We sneak downstairs to let her in and then tiptoe back up the stairs, Adrienne and I in hysterics.

"Why did you take acid?" Mindy reprimands us after we close the twins' bedroom door. "Don't you know how dangerous it is?" Her braces flash in the light of the candles we've placed around the room.

Adrienne and I are dying of laughter. She throws herself stick-straight sideways onto her bed like a log, shaking in fits of hilarity, which makes me lose it completely.

Mindy and Emma are trying to gain control, but Emma is tripping, too, alternating between giggling with Adrienne and me and weeping with Alex.

As we even out for our sleepless night—compliments of LSD—we eventually quit laughing and crying. We drift into restless sleep as daylight grays the room. Mindy scurries home before colors take form and her parents wake up.

Around noon, Emma and I go home, walking downstairs in a hurry to avoid the twins' parents sitting at the kitchen table. Their dad watches us with suspicious eyes.

Alex and I laughed till our sides ached.

"I did so much acid, Alex, until I was sixteen, after we'd drifted apart a little bit during high school."

"Yeah, going to different high schools after junior high will do that."

"I did a lot of acid with Dianna, remember her?"

"How could I forget? She was crazy."

Alex and Adrienne went to the same high school as Dianna, who was two grades above me, one grade above them. Dianna had a reputation as a "slut," which was partly true; however, there were boys involved and nobody had a derogatory word for them.

"Crazy fun!" I laughed. "Dianna and I did a lot of acid together. Sometimes I'd turn philosophical and sit cross-legged to give a lecture on my favorite topic when I was high on acid: Carlos Castaneda and his experiences with don Juan Matus, the Yaqui Indian who taught him how to 'stop the world.' It's all in Castaneda's book, *Journey to Ixtlan*."

"I vaguely remember you talking about that. But you spent more time with Dianna than me and Adrienne."

We laughed, envisioning me sitting cross-legged, espousing the mind-expanding benefits of psychedelic drugs.

"I was such an *expert*," I said, giggling.

"I can see that," giggled Alex.

"I still have *Journey to Ixtlan*," I said. "Checked it out from the Skokie library years ago and 'forgot' to return it."

"I never read it, but I remember our acid trips together. Altered reality. I should see if our library has *Journey to Ixtlan*."

Elsa woke up for a feeding at 2 a.m. Alex lazily walked up the stairs to bed, turning back to say, "I love you."

"I love you, too, Alex."

A few hours later, I awoke to the delicious aroma of bacon. Opening my eyes, it startled me to see Abby standing over me, staring at baby Elsa. I slid over, patting the pull-out bed for Abby to get in next to Elsa, who was just waking up, her kitten mews barely overlapping the sizzling bacon.

The doorbell rang, waking up everyone else, and Emma walked in, Lily in tow. Lily was seven now, with a bright, open face shining like a movable sun. She sat next to Elsa and gently stroked her little face, which Abby did not like. Abby had been sitting in my lap with the baby in hers, my arms around them both to help Abby hold Elsa's bottle.

From the kitchen, Alex saw Abby push Lily's hand away. She slammed her spatula on the counter and headed for the living room. I shooed her away. "Don't worry about it, Alex, it's okay. We're fine."

Nevertheless, she came in and said, "Abby, the next time I see anything like that, you'll be in the kitchen all by yourself."

I tried to imagine Elsa at Abby's age, acting naughty, finding it hard to believe I'd ever have to put her in a time-out.

After eating way too much bacon, I packed our stuff to go home with Emma and Lily. The plan was to spend the next two days with them.

At the door, Alex and I draped our arms around each other. "I'll miss you, Alex," I whispered. "You, too!" she said, not whispering.

Abby cried at the door, watching us precariously step over winter ice to Emma's car parked in the driveway.

It was a short drive to Emma and Lily's apartment. I dropped our stuff on the floor by the front door and we plopped on the couch.

"Being with you and Lily reminds me of our apartment in Chicago," I said, forgetting that I'd left them there without saying goodbye. "It was fantastic! Wasn't it?"

"I guess so," Emma said.

Alex's twin sister, Adrienne, came over for lunch to meet Elsa and introduce us to *her* new baby, Bobby, born a month before Elsa. Her daughter, Langley, now five, climbed on my lap. "Well, hello, Langley," I said, hugging her.

She pushed me away, not my hug, but the closeness of it, to look in my eyes. Her flawless face, a pearly disk, glowed like the moon, just like her beautiful mother. Her butterscotch eyes were bottomless wells of wisdom.

Adrienne said, "Every day after you left Chicago, she stood at the window saying, 'Hanna? Hanna?'"

"Really? She was only like what, a year old? I'm shocked she remembers."

"You were at our house a lot. She loved you."

I was messed up on cocaine and alcohol before leaving Chicago. Love hadn't been on my mind. I was at Adrienne's house all the time because I sold those coupon ads for her husband. And bought cocaine from him, my primary reason for going there. I cared for Langley, was always happy to see her shuffling around the house, but surprised to hear she loved me.

"She liked me that much?"

"She adored you. Asked about you every day." I hugged her tighter.

Langley stayed on my lap, fiddling with a paper doll. Adrienne laid a blanket on the floor for sleeping Bobby and picked up Elsa, cradling her. How cool to have friends I'd known since my pre-teens, still bonded in that particular way kids bond for life. Now we were sharing the mom thing—more aunts for our kids.

Emma and Adrienne made sandwiches, and while we ate, Emma reminded us of our crazy hitchhiking antics . . .

Summer, between 7th and 8th grade. Emma and I have been having a blast hitchhiking with Adrienne and Alex.

Emma and Adrienne wait a few blocks down while Alex and I stick our thumbs out for a ride. Our distinct looks make us noticeable—Emma and I are 5' 7", blonde and blue-eyed, and our twin friends are 4'8", with brown hair and eyes.

Two guys pick up me and Alex in a two-door Mustang. Three blocks away, the driver almost veers off the road when he sees our duplicates, Adrienne and Emma. Alex and I laugh our asses off. Both guys look at us, smile, and the driver slams on the brakes. "Out of sight, man!" Laughing, he bends into a comma as he leans forward to let Adrienne and Emma cram into the back seat with us.

His friend says we're way too cute, and they decide they're not letting us out of the car. Since it's a two-door, we're trapped. We all start talking at once, and they get pissed! They tell us to shut up, but we won't. Finally, they get tired of listening to us and dump us off on a side street.

We still hitchhike. We figure there's strength in numbers, so we're not scared.

"We had to do some fancy talking to get out of that car," Adrienne said. "Does anyone remember what we said?"

"No," I said.

"Verbal castration," Emma said drily.

Adrienne laughed. "Yeah. And we still hitchhiked!"

"Uh-huh." I snickered. "Strength in numbers."

We promised to stay in touch when we hugged and kissed goodbyes.

Emma went to her room to lie down, Lily went to her room to read, and I laid on the couch to nap with Elsa, spooning her in her basket. I fell asleep with a tender heart, thoughts of Alex and Adrienne lingering, when I first met them in junior high school . . .

Autumn. 1971. I just started seventh grade—a new world. Rather than walking along house-lined streets to elementary school, I wait on the corner for a bus to take me to the junior high school on the other side of town. It looks more urban over there than suburban—all apartment buildings, not even one house. I'm meeting kids with moms who have jobs. This is my first encounter with single moms working their asses off to pay the rent.

Sometimes I walk home with Sandy to her dark and lonesome apartment after school, staying until her sad mom comes home in the shortening autumn daylight. Walking home in the dark, I ponder their bleak life together.

Other days I go home with Grace. Although she lives in a single-mom home, their apartment is always bright and sunny, with lots of noisy activity. Her mother is a singer. In contrast to the reserved Swedish household I live in, Grace's Jewish home is fun. She has two sisters, and they love each other, with hugs even. I like their boisterous conversations; nobody is criticized for their thoughts and opinions.

Like me, Adrienne and Alex live with both of their parents in a house way over the bridge in Morton Grove. Their mother lays in bed all day with the curtains drawn. She's pretty and sweet, yet far away, like lost in another world. Still, I like going to their house. They have makeup mirrors in their bedroom with bright, artificial lights. I love watching them put on makeup, dabbing on sky-blue eye shadow and using safety pins to separate each lash after applying mascara. I don't use eye shadow, but the safety pin trick works well. My twin sister, Emma, comes with me. We compare twin stories, laughing like crazy. It's nice to know other twins. Alex and I are the twins with rounder faces, so we're called Pumpkin Heads. They have narrow faces, so we call them Skeleton Heads. At our house, we have slumber parties in the backroom, as we call it, which is a room addition on the back of the house where Emma and I sleep. We Pumpkin Heads share the narrow couch I sleep on, and the Skeleton Heads share Emma's. The four of us have a blast staying up until daylight. I think they're going to be my best friends.

At school, we smoke cigarettes outside a back door, propping it open with a purse. Sometimes we get up the nerve to light a joint, which we get from Emma's new boyfriend, Clark. When school lets out, we walk across the sports field to his apartment, hanging out in his dark bedroom lit by black lights illuminating Peter Maxx posters taped to his walls. We listen to Pink Floyd, Yes, and Led Zeppelin, smoking pounds of reefer with Clark, Mark (aka Goon), Ed, and a guy with glasses we call Bob Me.

Clark turned us on to acid, too, and downers like Quaalude and Seconal. We got drunk for the first time on a Friday night when his mom was out. Clark pulled out every bottle from her liquor cabinet and we mixed them together in orange juice, drinking until we puked. I can't say I liked the puking part, but I loved getting drunk.

Junior high school. Where the "bad kids" are. Finally, I feel like I belong!

Alex and Adrienne, who I hang out with all the time now, complain about their dad constantly. They're pretty sure he bugs their telephone, and he grills them about what they do, where they go, and who they're with. I don't get along with my father, either, though in a different way. It's hard to explain our relationship; we don't really have one. All he does is criticize me, make demands, or ignore me. We're all sick of our fathers, so we agree we're running away.

The plan takes shape after my dad's criticism turns violent. He says I have a smart mouth because I told him I don't appreciate how he treats my mother, my sisters, and me as if we're complete idiots. He points his finger in my face and says, "Shut your mouth!"

66

"Fuck off!" I scream.

He pushes me into Donald's old bedroom (now Lorain's) and shoves me on the floor. I see my mother standing in the kitchen, hands on hips, watching. My father's hateful grimace hovers over me, his jowls trembling. He puts his fist in front of my face, the fist with his bulky ring he calls a fraternity ring.

"Go ahead, motherfucker, hit me. Then you can tie me up and lock me in the closet. And I still won't do anything you say!" I stare right into his eyes, refusing to be intimidated. "You can't make me do ANYTHING! Fuck you!"

He gets off me and storms out of the room.

My mother's putting dishes away now. "How dare you speak to your father that way," she says, not even looking at me.

I call Alex and Adrienne. They say they're ready to go.

As soon as it's dark outside, I open a window in the backroom and Emma helps me slip out.

I'm not wearing any shoes, because I rarely wear shoes, and I only have five dollars. But it'll be okay.

I meet Alex and Adrienne just past downtown Skokie at Mark and Bob's house. They're always nice to us, and funny. Their mother said we can sleep in a tent in their yard, and I can't believe it. Mark and Bob set up the tent and toss some sleeping bags in there.

We climb inside the tent and Mark brings us peanut butter cookies and peanut butter sandwiches.

When he goes back inside, Alex whines, "I hate peanut butter. Oh my God, the smell is making me sick," and she curls into a circle inside her sleeping bag, covering her head. Alex and Adrienne start crying, but not me. They want to go to their oldest sister's house tomorrow, even though I don't want to. That's not exactly running away, in my book. I want to go far away, like maybe out west somewhere.

Around midnight, we huddle together like a litter of puppies and fall asleep. The tent is soggy with dew when we wake up. Mark and Bob come out to see how we're doing and help us climb out into fresh air. Since the twins have more money than I do, they're paying for the cab Mark and Bob's mom calls for us. The boys stick around until it arrives, telling jokes.

Susan, a housewife, wrings her hands with worry when we get to her house. She serves us canned Spaghetti-Os at the kitchen table with her two kids. The twins spend the entire afternoon on the phone, fighting with their dad. I'm sure he knows where we are.

At dinnertime, I convince Adrienne and Alex that it's time to move on, before their brother-in-law gets home from work. I suggest we hitchhike westward, toward Colorado. When we step out the door, a car pulls up, and we figure it's an unmarked police car. Two men get out and approach us. They tell us that, yep, they're police detectives. They're friendly, but say we must go with them to the Skokie police station, where our fathers are waiting.

At the station, a detective takes the twins and their father to one room, and another detective takes my father and me into a different room.

My father refuses the chair our detective offers. He stands in the interview room with his arms crossed over his chest, polite, but obviously anxious to get out of there. The detective suggests family counseling, which the police department offers, and hands my father a piece of paper with the information. As soon as we walk out of the police station, my father rips it in half and throws it in the gutter. I knew he'd never go for it. Deep inside, I wish he had.

Alex and Adrienne's dad agreed to family counseling, once a week for two months. I'm glad for them.

Seven

Thanksgiving Day. When everything changed.

Late in the morning, Emma and I trudged out to the car to drive to our parents' house with seven-year-old Lily and baby Elsa. I borrowed a coat from Emma, which she yanked off a hanger as if it were the most difficult thing she'd ever done. When I packed for my trip, I didn't think about a winter coat, not that I had one. I didn't need one in Texas.

"Wow, it's freezing out," I said, teeth clicking. "And look at all this snow. More than that last winter I lived in Chicago with you guys, I think."

"Maybe. And it was freezing that year, too. Colder than this year."

I shivered. "Well, it's still damn cold. Can we turn up the heat?"

Emma slid the heat lever to the hottest hot, and warm air rushed into my face. I looked at Elsa to make sure her blanket was over her.

"Uh, Emma?"

"Yeah." She kept looking straight ahead.

"I don't want to go to mom and dad's house. I really don't want to see them and I don't know why."

Panic tightened a fist around my throat.

"I called the airline this morning to change my flight, but there's a fee, and I can't very well ask our father to pay it. He paid for the plane ticket. They're expecting to see the baby."

I withheld from Emma that I was *afraid* to see our parents. Deathly afraid.

She drove on, silent, staring forward.

"Can I have a cigarette?" I asked. I hadn't smoked since I'd found out I was pregnant.

Emma diverted her bewitched, forward-facing stare to glance at me sideways, knowing I had quit smoking. She handed me her pack of Marlboros and said, "Our family is so fucked up." Nevertheless, we both stared straight ahead, mesmerized, continuing forward on a magnetic track yanking us toward our childhood home. No detours.

Emma had been in counseling on and off for many years. She'd distanced herself from our parents somewhat, though not entirely. She explained that she'd learned that our family was dysfunctional, due to our fucked-up parents not raising us right. "That's why you feel anxious about bringing Elsa to see them," Emma said. I didn't tell her that I'd run out of my therapist's office because I wanted nothing to do with dysfunctional families. The survivor in me knew she was right, but I shoved her words into my mind's filing cabinet, into the drawer marked "Things That Cannot Be True."

By the time we got to our parents' house, I was smoking again, and my breast milk completely dried up.

At the door, our mother informed us we were going to a restaurant for Thanksgiving dinner. That was a first. Holidays were celebrated at our house or at Uncle Vern's and Aunt Eva's. One of us would go pick up Grandma Elsa at the retirement home in Rockford (eighty miles northwest of Skokie) to join us. When I asked where Grandma Elsa was—whom I did want to see—my mother said, with her tight, thin-lipped expression reserved for disgust, "Vern and Eva want her this year." I dropped it, sensing her chagrin.

Thanksgiving dinner at a restaurant felt strange, albeit great to escape washing dishes. I sat next to my mother, looking around the table at just us. No Grandma Elsa. There must have been an argument or something—ultra unusual for our family. The norm was making believe everything was simply wonderful all the time. When I got up the nerve to ask why we weren't wanted at Vern and Eva's house for Thanksgiving this year, my mother looked away, pretending I hadn't asked. She switched subjects, saying, "Why don't you and the baby spend the night at the house?"

My stomach lurched and tightened around all that Thanksgiving food. Laying my fork beside my plate, I excused myself to the restroom, thinking I might vomit.

Something wasn't right. Surreal. Mysterious. But I couldn't put my finger on it. When I finished my restaurant pumpkin pie, I bundled up Elsa for the drive back to my parents' house, eager for the day to end.

Buckling up in Emma's car, she said, "What's up? You seem really spacey."

I told her I didn't want to stay at our parents' house, and started crying big, heaving sobs.

Emma said, "What? You're staying at *their* house tonight?"

"Yeah, I guess so."

"Why? When did you decide this?"

"Mom asked me to stay with the baby, and I said okay."

Emma insisted we go home with her, but I didn't want to go there either. I wanted to run to the airport and catch a plane to Austin.

We drove in silence all the way to our parents' house.

"I'm using Dad's car to go to Vern and Eva's to see Grandma Elsa," I said when we got there.

Emma stared at me as we walked to the front door.

"Lily and I will wait for you."

"Whatever," I said.

Inside the house, I tried to grab my father's car keys, which he dangled before me like a carrot. "It's too snowy," he said for the third time, jingling the keys in my face with a sarcastic grin. I got the feeling he was making fun of me for wanting to see my grandmother. His mother.

"Too bad. I've come all this way to introduce Grandma Elsa to her namesake, so I'm going." I snatched the keys and stormed out.

The snow glittered in the headlights. It was beautiful. I hadn't driven in a snowstorm for several years and never thought I'd miss it. I got right back into the adventure of winter driving.

Little Elsa and I arrived at Vern and Eva's to a festive mood, with every light in the house turned up bright. Eva's parents, Danish immigrants, were also there, everyone relaxed in front of the fireplace in the den. To join them, I walked through the formal dining room where the remains of their feast lay scattered across the table. It felt weird, as if I were intruding on their holiday.

I knew better than to ask why we'd spent Thanksgiving apart.

Grandma Elsa grumbled in her sing-song Swedish accent, "How could you even *tink* about traveling alone with a new baby, such a long way from Texas?"

"I wanted Little Elsa and her great-grandmother to meet each other," I said, kissing her cheek.

While Grandma rocked her new great-grandbaby, murmuring in Swedish, I chatted with Eva's mother, who was equally aghast that I, a woman, had travelled alone with a baby from Texas.

As snow accumulated outside, Uncle Vern took a few pictures of Elsa and me beside the fire. Aunt Eva offered pumpkin pie with freshly whipped cream. The snow turning blizzard-like, I said my goodbyes, not knowing when I'd see Grandma again, and drove back to my folks' house in the sparkling snowscape.

The house was dark when I walked in the back door. My mother had been waiting for us, and grabbed the basket with my baby in it.

Emma and Lily came in behind me, the storm door slamming behind them, jolting my nerves like an electric shock. I moved into the kitchen, where the only light in the house was from the tiny light over the sink and a faint golden glow from the living room. I say "moved" into the kitchen because I felt I was levitating, as if my feet weren't walking on the floor, step by step, but that my body was flowing slightly above ground level. I took a glass from the cups and glasses cabinet and turned on the faucet for water. Emma stayed put with Lily at the back door.

I glided through the kitchen to the dining room door and glanced across the dining table into the living room. On the couch on the far wall sat my mother, leaning over sleeping Elsa in her baby basket, which my mother had placed on a dining room chair in front of her. Three slender white candles glimmered, one on the coffee table and one on each end table bookending the couch, making a triangle of flickering candlelight. The house was dark except for those candles and little light over the kitchen sink.

My mother's hands moved in a sweeping motion over my baby. She looked up when she noticed me watching, a strange smile wavering in the candlelight. I'd seen that expression on her face before, but couldn't recall when. With that tiny smile, my mother stared at me. Dizzy and confused, I turned around to retreat to the kitchen, feeling I was floating like an ethereal being, an angel or a ghost.

Emma and Lily stood near the back door. I could see them through the cutout above the kitchen sink, which had been a window in the original house. Through it, Emma whispered, "Come over here."

I leaned over the sink, Emma framed in the opening. "You and Elsa can't stay here," she whispered with a stern face. "Come home with us."

"Why?"

"You can't stay here. Please. Come with us, you—"

"What's wrong with you, Emma? You're acting bizarre."

73

"Hanna, you didn't want to come here today. After dinner, you cried because you didn't want to spend the night. What the hell?"

"Yeah, but now that I'm here, it's okay. I don't know why I didn't want to come."

"Yes, you do. Get Elsa and come on!" Emma slapped her hand on her thigh as if scolding a stubborn dog.

"No." I said, not bothering to lower my voice. "We're staying."

She pleaded with her eyes, then opened the door and stepped out into the cold without looking back. Lily looked backward at me as she gently closed the back door. I heard the outer storm door creak before it slammed shut behind them.

I turned and walked into the living room.

"What was *that* all about?" my mother asked.

"Nothing," I said, glancing around the room.

Why is the house so dark? Where is my father?

Emma didn't know why she pleaded with me to leave with her that night.

It had always been that way with her: moments of clarity when she spoke the truth, not fully conscious of what she was saying, disconnected from the survivor deep within her—a strong, wise child, alive and well in that place where the flame of her true being had never been extinguished. There were times she would deny any recollection of what she'd said or why, claiming to not even remember an incident. If you were to ask her, she would have gazed off with a faraway stare, looking off into the past somewhere above your head and said, "No. That never happened."

Emma learned well how to forget, as had I. And in her need to block ugly parts of her life, she'd also buried her genuine, authentic self in forgetfulness.

* * * *

Summertime. 1960s. I'm in the back seat of my father's blue Oldsmobile with my twin sister, cruising toward downtown Chicago. "Downtown" is playing on the radio. We sing along with Petula Clark, quietly, so our father can't hear:

Just listen to the music of the traffic in the city
Linger on the sidewalk where the neon signs are pretty
The lights are much brighter there
You can forget all your troubles
Forget all your cares and go
Downtown
Everything's waiting for you

On Saturday afternoons, we go downtown to our father's office in the Prudential Building. Our father says the Prudential Building is the tallest building in the world so far. We ride the elevator to the top floor and look across the smoky city and Lake Michigan far below.

Then we go to Clark Street for his haircut. There are so many people to watch in the city. All the colors of the world.

I hold on tight to the good parts of our Saturday afternoons with our father— watching people, listening to Petula Clark, and stopping by Grandma and Grandpa's apartment for ginger ale and Grandma Elsa's homemade cookies.

But he takes us other places, too, parking in gloomy, rundown city alleys.

Can I be free knowing my father leaves me and my twin sister alone in the car for strange men to peer in the window at us? They have deranged smirks, and they shake and grunt, their eyes rolling up into their heads. It's terrifying.

Twins. What a novelty for pedophiles. Adorable, blonde-headed, blue-eyed little girls who never make a peep.

What fucking perverts there are in this world.

Sometimes our father takes Lorain, Emma, and me to Kiddy Land for our Saturday outings with him. He just stands there, smoking cigarettes and staring at us on the rides. I feel uneasy under his gaze. When we get back in the Olds, he flicks on the radio. He doesn't talk. It's like his mind is somewhere else, so far away he's not really there. It's gloomy on those days. Maybe it's just him.

The next day, on a warm summer Sunday, our family will take a voyage up the Lake Michigan shoreline in my father's big boat of a car, the blue Oldsmobile. Emma and I sit in the back seat with our sister Lorain. Our mother, relaxed on these drives, smiles as she gazes out the front passenger window.

On these trips, our father drives us through neighborhoods of the wealthy North Shore, to Baha'i Temple in Wilmette. We gape in astonishment at the beautiful, round shrine made of stone—marble, I think—encircled with ornately carved designs. Inside the temple are words carved in every language of the world in the same stone as outside, circling the dome above. I love it here.

There's a beach across the street. When we go there, my sisters and I run in the sand to the waterline, crossing a barrier of hundreds of dead fish washed up on the shore. We assume every beach is littered with dead fish you must step over to get to the water. You can smell them for miles.

After Baha'i Temple and the beach, we go to No Man's Land for fresh peach ice cream. Or we'll stop at Cock Robin Ice Cream Parlor near our house for square ice cream cones filled with square blocks of grape, lime, and orange sherbert.

Sometimes Grandma and Grandpa come with us on Sunday drives, all of us piling into the Olds. My father grills hamburgers on our patio in the evening when we get home.

After supper, Grandpa tells us stories from Sweden in his sing-song accent, a poetic Swedish melody.

When I close my eyes, I can see the dark, thick forests of Sweden when he was a boy, filled with the ghosts and trickster fairies who are the stars of his stories. He told us his parents sent him to work on a farm when he was only twelve years old! He lived there, sleeping on hay in a barn with another boy. They must have been so scared.

My mother washes and sets Grandma Elsa's hair before supper, chattering away in her lyrical voice, telling Grandma stories about us kids and the gossip in the neighborhood. I love my mother when she's this way. Her eyes sparkle.

Grandma Elsa doesn't have much of a sense of humor. She's very serious. But she must love my mother's carefree flip of a hand and lighthearted chit chat as she rolls up her snow-white hair in curlers. My mother's lightheartedness is so contagious.

I like to sit with them, watching these roll-up moments, always taking place in the kitchen; the brightest room in the house.

I often dream about my mother's kitchen. I bring my current life to sit at the round table, in the happiest room of her house.

Eight

1988. A cool January morning at KLRU-TV. Gazing out my office window at university students walking along the sidewalk below, I couldn't understand my panic, why I felt I would die if I didn't get help. I turned from the window to stare down at the yellow pages on my desk, open to the page offering treatment for alcoholism and codependency.

From Thanksgiving night in my parents' strangely lit house to this moment in my office, everything was a blur. I had been maneuvering my life like an automaton, a hypnotized zombie from a voodoo ritual, only half-alive. The only thing that felt normal was my baby.

Now, as if awakened from the voodoo spell, hysteria took over, which I downplayed, writing myself off as a drama queen. I assumed my troubles lay rooted simply in my choice of men: alcoholics. No big deal. So, for lack of better insight into my malady, I chose codependency treatment from those pale-yellow pages, an out-patient program to begin mid-January, three nights a week for six weeks. Neil disapproved, of course, but agreed to watch Elsa.

By the end of our second week learning about "enablers," another name for codependents, our counselors took us on a trek beyond the effects of alcoholism on the family, to delve deeper into the creation of dysfunctional family systems: abandonment; neglect; and physical, emotional, and spiritual abuse.

A nice woman with five kids hinted she had a terrible family secret, which I wrote off as a dramatic quest for attention—as I'd done to myself that day in my office when I sought help from the phone book. At the end of week three, she tearfully told the group she'd been the child victim of incest by her father.

I'd never heard anyone admit such a repulsive thing. It freaked me out. Treating her as if she were toxic goods, a revolting, low-class piece of shit, I stopped talking to her and wanted to quit the program. My counselor talked me into staying.

Soon thereafter, a picture began flashing on and off in my mind. A single image of a young man standing before me with a gun. It wasn't a dream. It was a strange photograph blinking on and off in my mind. He was Jake, the boyfriend of Maria, a friend I'd met when I was fourteen.

When I told my counselor, he brushed me off with, "Oh *please*, you're just trying to get attention. Right?" he added, his voice seething with condescension.

That sounded familiar. My mother always told me I was "just trying to get attention" whenever I'd try to tell her disturbing things. Though I wasn't yet aware of it, "trying to get attention" was set as a trigger by my parents' coven via systematic brainwashing techniques to erase my mind of anything except what *they* wanted me to think.

Hurt beyond words, I didn't mention it to my counselor again.

Though the vision of Jake was not my imagination, of that I was certain, I didn't understand why the picture flashed on and off like a strobe light in my mind. Again and again, returning as a specter from the grave of my youth, Jake threatened me with his gun. One day, more of the vision came with him: Jake driving a yellow-beige car down Sheridan Road, Maria and me in the backseat, and someone I couldn't see in the front passenger seat. Heart pounding, I tried shoving the vision into my mind's filing cabinet of things I wished not to see. But the drawer was already unlocked, sliding open. An uneasy feeling crawled into my consciousness that these visions connected directly to that dream about Michael slumped on a chair, he and I knowing something we weren't supposed to know.

Not wanting to be accused of "only seeking attention," which meant accused of lying, I didn't dare tell my codependency counselor.

Codependency treatment ended when Elsa began projectile vomiting every time I fed her. Still small at six months, she wasn't big enough to afford losing weight, not even an ounce.

Dr. Braun admitted Elsa for five days to Austin's children's hospital at St. David's, hooking her up to intravenous feedings, which stopped the vomiting. I changed my work schedule to four hours in the morning and moved into Elsa's hospital room, sleeping on a bed thoughtfully built into the wall for parents. My boss wasn't pleased, but my baby came first. Period.

Neil never mentioned a word about the hospital. He never visited Elsa. Not even once. His silence baffled me.

Within twenty-four hours of her release from the hospital, Elsa started vomiting again. She laid like a rock, her skin ashy-gray. I called my mother, worried sick.

"Don't worry about it. There is nothing wrong with that baby," said my mother in her carefree way, precisely as she'd said every other time I'd gone to her with worries. I pictured her folding towels at her kitchen table, a small grin curling the edges of her mouth. Flipping her hand in an off-hand way, she'd flick away my concern like she would an annoying housefly.

As if to reassure me, she added, "Listen, I'll have Donald call you."

"*Donald?*"

"Yes. He's in the medical field, Hanna," she said, her tone rather sarcastic.

"Donald lives in Michigan, you know. It's not like he can stop by to look at her. What would he know, anyway? He's not a doctor." He wasn't even a nurse. He was an Inhalation Specialist, trained to resuscitate hearts.

"Oh, he'll know," said my mother.

To my utter surprise, Donald called the following morning, a Saturday. I hadn't seen him for six or seven years, maybe more, and I doubt we'd even spoken.

The moment I picked up the phone, Donald barked, "What's wrong with the baby?" not offering a hello or any other greeting.

Shocked to hear my *brother's* voice, I stammered out the lowdown on Elsa's condition.

"That's normal," he said rather truculently, as if I were merely an overly fretful new mother to be treated with disdain. I imagined him on the other end of the phone scrunching up his nose to keep his glasses up, a habit he did so often it was almost like a tic.

"Really, Donald? How would *you* know what normal is?"

"Nothing's wrong with the baby. Sometimes they turn grayish, or blue."

"Yeah, like when they're starving to death or can't breathe. Again, Donald, what makes you an expert on babies? You're not a doctor, and you haven't even seen her. Why would you think it's normal for a baby to vomit and turn gray? And she just lies there, barely moving."

"You're overreacting. I do work in a hospital, ya know."

I looked at the phone in disbelief. "That makes you an expert? *Working* in a hospital? And besides, you can't even see her."

He chuckled. "I'm telling you, the baby is okay. You're acting too worried. Let it be." Was that a threat? "This is all in your imagination, and your worry is bad for the baby."

I pulled the phone away from my ear and looked at it as if *it* were insane.

What was I supposed to do, agree to stop seeking medical help for my baby?

And my "imagination?" How many times did I hear that growing up? And never heard in Texas. Not once.

"Hello?" Donald's voice oozed with condescension. "You there?"

"Yeah, I'm here."

"Don't worry about the baby. She's fine. Let it go."

That definitely sounded like a threat.

I feared my brother, for good reason. Donald was a lot older than me and my twin sister, eleven years older. When Emma and I were little, he stalked us through the house whenever our parents went out, usually finding us in the basement, hiding. Or we'd be trying to sneak down the basement stairs and he'd jump out from under them. You'd think we would have learned to stay away from the basement, but no. Our older sisters, Ellyn and Lorain, escaped on those days, racing for the door the moment our parents left, slamming it on Emma and me. Too young to follow, they left us at the mercy of our horrible brother.

One time, when he was studying biology in high school, he brought home a dead cat, which he skinned and left on a board on the ping-pong table downstairs. He locked Emma and me down there several times with that skinned cat.

Twenty-five years later, my brother's evil voice entered my ear via cross-country phone lines. Now, all I had to do to escape him was to hang up the phone.

"Well," I said. "Thanks for your input, I guess. I gotta go."

I hung up in a daze, wishing I had also said, "Drop dead, Donald, and go fuck yourself."

Yet, for a heartbeat, I wondered if Elsa's illness *was* my imagination.

I stood in my quiet living room and stared at the closed curtains for a long while, thinking, remembering . . .

Our parents left. Ellyn and Lorain run for the door.

"Please don't leave, Ellyn!" I scream, terrified, grabbing her shirt, which she yanks from my hand.

"Take us with you! PLEASE!" begs Emma. "Please don't leave us!"

Twelve-year-old Ellyn gets out first, followed by Lorain, six, who shuts the door in our faces. Emma and I, four, can't get the door open to run after them.

Our brother, Donald, is somewhere in the house, waiting.

He's in the hallway, I think. Laughing.

We run to the basement to hide. I don't know why we do this, because he always finds us there. The stairs creak as we creep down, one at a time. Halfway down, where the gray-painted plywood railing begins, Donald jumps out from under the stairs and grabs my ankle. Emma shrieks, tears streaming onto her pink shirt. She's holding my arm, but Donald is fifteen and we're only four. He squeezes my ankle, and I start tumbling down the stairs. I grab the railing.

"Get down here. Now!" shouts Donald, his face twisted into something so awful I can't look. He's turned into an evil animal.

"Okay! Okay!" Emma and I shriek as one. And we creep down, clutching each other, sobbing.

"Shut. Up!" Donald barks like a wolf. He holds my ankle all the way to the bottom in a vise-grip clasp I'm sure will leave a bruise.

At the bottom of the stairs, Donald shoves us to the picture of a bloody dagger he painted on the side of the chute—a wooden box hanging from the ceiling with a hatch to release dirty clothes from the floor of a hallway closet upstairs. Donald stands behind us and smashes our heads together in front of that horrible painting. I scream and holler, clamping my eyes shut. Donald tears Emma away and she screams so loud it's not possible for Mr. and Mrs. Verva next door not to hear her.

Everything goes black after that. I think I pass out from fear. Except . . . I swear, at one point, I'm almost positive I see Donald with a grotesque, twisted, animal face with horns on his head, blood all over his teeth and chin like he's been eating a kill. It can't be true, it just can't!

When I got to work Monday morning, Pamela and Sofia handed me several names of pediatricians. "For a second opinion," said Pamela.

Were it not for them, chances are I would have waited or not sought further help at all. Without the seeds they planted—along with the 12-Step meetings for families of alcoholics, the codependency treatment program, and my old counselor Claudia—it would have been difficult to withstand the false reality my family tried to create; their gaslighting techniques making me think I was crazy.

Pamela and Sofia were beacons of light on the stormy seas of my life. As was Judith, who no longer worked with us, but remained in our lives.

My friends gently forced me to question why my parents and my brother—over a thousand miles away—wouldn't take me seriously and were trying to bully me into submission. Pamela, Sofia, and Judith didn't have to see Elsa to believe something was wrong with her, based solely on my word.

When I gathered my strength to tell Neil I'd made an appointment with another pediatrician, he forbade me to take our baby for a second opinion.

"What the hell, Neil? Look at her gray face! And she lies there like a rock."

Unable to shake my resolve, Neil demanded to go to the appointment with me. I want to say I made a mistake allowing him to come, but in hindsight, I'm glad I did. Glad because it exposed Neil's insanity—he yelled all the way to the doctor's office.

"Neil!" I hollered. "Why the hell don't you want your baby to get medical care? She's almost six months old and weighs less than ten pounds."

"There's nothing wrong!" he yelled. "Listen to your mother!"

"And she's *losing* weight. She can't eat!" I yelled.

Neil's demeanor abruptly shifted. Calmly, coolly, he said, "You know, your parents and I could put a stop to your insane preoccupation with that baby."

"Are you fucking out of your mind?" I yelled.

"You need to stop being so obsessed with her," he said with that calm.

Incredulous, it reminded me of a saying of his, said as a joke if anyone accused him of being untrustworthy: *Well, I told ya I was a snake before I bit ya.*

I pulled over, shaking with fear and rage. "Get out!"

"No," Neil said with calm venom, boring his eyes into me like a hypnotizing cobra. "Turn the car around and go home."

"Are you crazy? We are taking Elsa to that pediatrician, and that's that. Either sit there and shut the hell up, or get out!"

"There's nothing wrong with her, Hanna." Neil's voice was way too calm.

We were late, so I sped away from the curb with a, "Fuck off, Neil."

The pediatrician's hands shook as he examined Elsa. He asked the name of her current pediatrician. Neil stood over the examining table with a smug, angry demeanor—arms crossed over his chest, feet separated in a stance of defiance. The doctor glanced back and forth between us as if at a tennis match, watching to see if anyone had the ball.

"Here's one problem," he said. "Your baby's ears are clogged with wax, which I'll have to remove to get a good look." He grabbed a silver instrument with a minuscule round wire at the end of it and scraped her ears. "They're infected. I'll prescribe antibiotics for that." Then he demanded, "Who's her pediatrician?"

He jotted Dr. Braun's name on a pad of paper, stuffed it in the pocket of his lab coat, and wrapped up Elsa in her blanket and returned her to me. Trembling with fury, he locked eyes with mine as he spoke.

"Dr. Braun needs to be reported to the medical board," he said. "I don't know what else is wrong with this baby, but she appears malnourished, which she *is* if she can't hold down formula.

"I strongly suggest you allow me to make arrangements for the Texas Children's Hospital in Houston, the best hospital for kids in the United States."

Silent tears flowed down my cheeks. I said I'd think about it after Neil nudged me, having moved to plant himself behind me.

Neil resumed haranguing me as soon as we walked out the door, proclaiming the doctor was overreacting, too.

I shelved my incredulity to drive safely. Staring straight ahead, with no emotion, I dropped off Neil at his dilapidated house. "Fuck you," I said under my breath.

I called my mother when we got home to tell her the second opinion. Still, she remained unconvinced there was anything *really* wrong with Elsa.

The next day, I took Elsa to her babysitter's house on my way to work. Mrs. Melder, a grandmotherly woman who adored Elsa, asked how the appointment went. I provided the highlights, excluding Neil's oppositional behavior. She asked when we were leaving for Houston, and looked puzzled when I said, "I'm considering it." Without comment, she scooped up Elsa with a bright smile and wished me a good day.

My office mates crowded around my desk. I repeated everything I'd said to Mrs. Melder, plus Neil's behavior.

Later that afternoon, Pamela knocked softly on my office door, then opened it. "Hi Hanna, you busy?" I motioned her to come in and to sit in the chair beside my desk. Pamela cleared her throat. She seemed nervous. "Hanna," she said. "We're concerned for *you*, as well as the baby." She waved her hand to the outside office, where Sofia and Judith's desks were stationed.

"Me?"

"Yes, you. Your family . . . um . . . They're so far away."

"Yeah, I know."

"They can't possibly know what's wrong, or *not* wrong, with Elsa." Pamela cleared her throat again. "And Neil, not wanting you to take Elsa to Houston . . .

well, uh . . . we love you and Elsa, and want her well. Why don't you take her to just *one* more doctor?" she said, poking her index finger upward for the number one.

"You mean for a *third* opinion?" I asked.

"Yes." Pamela handed me a slip of paper with the name of a pediatrician she'd gotten from several friends she'd enlisted in the search. "They informed me that Dr. Faget has a very gentle disposition," she said. "Maybe you'll feel better getting *another* opinion. To convince Neil," she added.

"All right, Pamela."

We stood. Pamela hugged me so tight I couldn't breathe. She opened my office door and Sofia, her desk right outside my office, swiveled in her chair toward us. Judith, across the room, also looked our way. It was odd to me that they were not smiling. Butterflies flew around my stomach, my friends' worried faces forcing me to look more closely at the bizarre reactions of my mother and brother to my ill baby, as well as Neil's refusal to support me getting medical care.

I nodded my head at them and closed my office door. I sat down, exhausted from the adrenaline rush of reality I did not want. Finally exhaling, I stared out the window at the students walking along the street below.

I didn't tell Neil I made an appointment with Dr. Faget.

The following Friday, I arrived early for Elsa's appointment.

Dr. Faget walked into the examining room, looked at Elsa in my arms, and asked if she could arrange for Elsa to be admitted to the Texas Children's Hospital in Houston. I answered, "Yes, please do."

She proceeded to examine Elsa, concurring with the second doctor's diagnosis. In contrast to him, Dr. Faget was serene and mild-mannered, with warmth and sincerity reflected in doe-brown eyes. She told me about rare cases she'd seen of babies allergic to both dairy and soy products, the key ingredients in baby formula. She gave me samples of a unique non-dairy, non-soy baby formula they had in the office. "Try this," she said. "And in the meantime, I'll make the plans for the kids' hospital." She hugged us as she placed Elsa in my arms.

"Do you really think it's that serious?" I felt I had to ask, even though her validation and confirmation of my concerns were a relief.

"Oh yes, this is a serious case, and rather unusual. You are doing the right thing."

She smiled and walked us to the outer office with her hand on my back.

Elsa had her first bottle as soon as we got home. Later, Neil sat on my couch with a blank stare while I relayed the news. He glared when I told him Dr. Faget was sending Elsa to Houston, and then left my apartment without a word.

I fed Elsa her new formula twice more that night.

Saturday morning, I noticed her gray pallor was gone. I rushed her outside into the daylight. Sure enough, a bit of pink dusted her cheeks. Thinking I only saw what I wanted to see, I put her down for her nap and anxiously counted the minutes until her next feeding.

I heard her stirring two hours later. Before she was fully awake, I snatched her up, bottle ready. Her eyes were still sunken, but her color was better. When I laid her down to change her diaper, her arms started moving. By the time she'd finished her bottle, her eyes were brighter, and when I put her up against my shoulder to burp her, I could feel she had more strength. I spread a blanket on the floor and laid her on her back, examining her. Her arms and legs were moving. Overjoyed, I called Dr. Faget first.

"Terrific," she said. "Call me tomorrow morning with an update. Until then, the plan is still the kid's hospital in Houston."

In my joy, I wanted everyone to know, even my mother.

Choosing to overlook her consistent denial, I called her. She listened on the other end of the phone line, then said she was too busy to talk.

Neil sure took his time coming over, now that Elsa was improving. He moseyed over Sunday afternoon, sullen and quiet. His behavior made no sense. He'd come over to argue every day during Elsa's illness, except while she was hospitalized. I tried stashing his new apathy in my amnesia drawer, but it never quite made it; my friends and Dr. Faget wouldn't let me forget.

Home from the hospital, I went back to my routine with Elsa, more deeply appreciating our simple, structured life: regular work hours for me, daycare for Elsa, and her nightly splash-time in the bath, followed by a bedtime song and story. Elsa was still behind for her age, yet progressing. Her attempted developmental milestone at six months was struggling to sit up on her own. Pamela, Sofia, and Judith asked about her every day. It was with them I shared my joy.

Still needing psychological help, I began individual counseling with the psychologist from the codependency treatment program, Ray Gunn, PhD.

Nine

With prominent forehead and ardent hazel eyes, Ray emanated intelligence. He was handsome, with well-designed confidence, always looking dapper in a crisp white shirt and tie, often clipping suspenders to his expensive trousers.

Ready to confront my life in our first session, I blurted, "This image keeps snapping on and off in my mind, a flashing picture of this guy holding a gun, like a photograph in the dark with a strobe light pulsating the image into my brain."

Thinking he'd never believe me, I hesitated before telling more.

"I see," he said, nodding his head encouragingly. "That's quite descriptive."

"It's creepy, because it seems like maybe it really happened. He was my friend's boyfriend, when I was fourteen. It seems so real."

Ray nodded his head.

Developing trust in Ray over the next few weeks, I took another chance and told him my dream about Michael in the gray room.

Unlike my counselor in the codependency program, Ray took me seriously. When I told him I'd been pregnant with Elsa but hadn't known it, he said, "That makes sense. Hormonal changes during pregnancy can trigger memories of abuse. So, your dream *could* be a memory."

"I'm sure I was fourteen in that dream," I said. "Like in the flashes of that guy holding the gun. Could they be related somehow?"

"It's possible," Ray said, assuring me we'd sort it out, together.

Finally, someone to talk to who didn't think I was crazy or just trying to get attention. Free to fully concede a link between the dream and the guy with the gun, I now named him. "His name was Jake."

I reflected more critically on my family life, as well. I remembered school pretty well, but only bits and pieces of my home life.

Emma, also in counseling, started calling me every day. Or I'd call her. Sifting through the questions of our lives, she reminded me of the time I became terrified of Jesus Christ, petrified He would appear before me. We were eleven. Neither of us had forgotten those few strange weeks, but this was the first time we'd discussed it, seeing how truly fucked up it was . . .

It's Wintertime. I'm scared all the time. Jesus wants to kill me.

A black shadow hovers above the doorway of the backroom, where Emma and I sleep now—an addition to the house. We've been sleeping in here since we turned eleven a few months ago. The black shadow creeps across the ceiling towards me. I'm too scared to run out, afraid it will fall on me like a net. It has something to do with Jesus, and I'm terrified of Him. I fear this whole back part of the house. I cry every night.

Lorain and my parents act like they hate me, and are deaf to my shrieking torment, as are our neighbors next door, apparently. Nobody does anything to help me. My mother won't listen to me, and I'm too afraid to talk to my father. I wish Ellyn still lived at home; maybe, just maybe, she'd listen to me.

Emma's scared, too, even though she doesn't see the shadow. She's worried for me. I heard her in the living room last night asking our parents, "Can't you hear her screaming?"

I heard our father say, "For crying out loud, make her shut up."

Emma came back wringing her hands with worry. I didn't want to scare her with my screaming, but I was petrified.

Last night, after Emma's fruitless quest for help from our parents, I was positive Satan was going to take me away. Jesus scares me, but not Satan. I had to tell Emma, so she'd know why I'd be gone in the morning. I wrote her a goodbye note, telling her Satan was coming for me in a spaceship, and not to be afraid because I wasn't.

When I woke up this morning, my arms were still crossed over my chest, the way I'd look lying in a casket.

I'm surprised I'm still here, and a little . . . disappointed? Emma is so happy I didn't get taken away by Satan that she won't stop hugging me. She's smiling and laughing and planning our day.

I curled into a corner of Ray's office couch. He wheeled his chair over and looked into my eyes with intelligence and compassion I felt I didn't deserve, his hazel-green eyes seas of sympathy.

"I'm sad, because after that, Emma and I hated each other."

"Yeah?" Ray encouraged.

"She attacked me one time at school, ripping out one of my earrings and making my ear bleed." I looked over his head, gazing into the past. "I mean, we *really* hated each other. I wonder if she blamed me for that dark time. When I woke up alive that morning, I started pulling away from her. I didn't want to be around her anymore. Maybe she was still afraid, and I'd hurt her feelings by pushing her away. Maybe she was angry and didn't know how to express it, so she took it out on me."

Ray nodded his head. "Perhaps," he said.

I grimaced at the memory, ashamed to have to admit it. "I took it out on her, too. She got really clingy, always trying to tell me what to do. I don't remember what happened, but one day I pushed her on the floor in the backroom and stomped on her head."

Ray nodded his head, eyes sparkling with wisdom

In early April, my childhood friend from the neighborhood, Linda, called. She wanted to come to Austin to see me, said she had something she wanted to discuss with me. I, of course, said, "Sure, come on down." As children, Linda had been Lorain's playmate, mostly, as they were the same age, older than Emma and I. Linda and I became close later, in early adulthood—we went out dancing and drinking together, and visited her parents in Florida when they moved down there, where we went canoeing on a river with alligators.

Linda grabbed Elsa from my arms at the airport, to which Elsa wasn't pleased.

"Here, let me have her," I said.

Linda reluctantly handed back panic-stricken Elsa, who had never before seen her.

"Give her a little time to get to know you." I smiled and hugged Linda. "Hello! Glad you came!"

Elsa fell asleep as I pulled into the parking lot at our apartment. I gently lifted her and tiptoed inside, placing her belly down in her crib, covering her with a cotton blanket.

In the living room, Linda was sitting on the couch looking out the window with a serious look, almost like worry.

"It's so good to see you, Linda. What's up?"

"I really want a baby, Hanna."

"I know." I sat beside her and took her hand. "I'm so sorry, Linda."

Linda attended college for many years. She finally finished in 1985, at the age of thirty, with a graduate degree in nursing. She married Edward before she was out of school—I was a bridesmaid at their wedding—and after graduation, they decided they wanted a baby. They tried for three years, but Linda couldn't get pregnant because of acute endometriosis. In her early twenties, several doctors had told her that having a baby would cure the endometriosis, and that because of the severity of it, she would have to have at least one baby by the time she reached twenty-five. After that, her chances of conceiving would diminish with each year. Linda, in school throughout her twenties, said she was way too busy to become a mother then.

"I wish I could help you, Linda."

"Well, actually, you can."

"How?"

"Will you be a surrogate mother for us? We will use Edward's sperm to artificially inseminate you, pay for everything, and give you an additional $10,000," Linda spewed in one breath as if she'd been rehearsing and needed to say it before losing her nerve.

I was not expecting that.

"Oh, I don't know Linda. I'd have to think about it. I've got so much going on right now. Little Elsa has been in the hospital, and it's just crazy right now. I'm in counseling every day."

Linda knew this, as we had spoken here and there in recent months.

"Hanna, *please*! The baby would be so beautiful, and I'd let you see him or her once in a while, if you wanted to."

"I'm not sure, Linda. This is a huge thing to consider. I'll have to give it some thought."

Linda was thirty-three years old in 1988, when she arrived in Austin to beg me to carry a baby for her. She and Edward had spent thousands of dollars on fertility treatments. They were desperate, and I mean *desperate* for a child. I felt terrible for my lifelong friend.

"Please do this for me, Hanna."

I hugged her and asked if I could think about it overnight. Her shoulders slumped as she shuffled into the bathroom to get ready for bed.

I insisted she sleep in my room and made up a bed for myself on the couch.

Lying awake most of the night, I thought about it. Agonized over it. But in the end, I knew I wouldn't be able to go through a pregnancy and give up the baby. I couldn't do it. And it would have been my egg with Edward's sperm, which, honestly, felt kind of creepy.

I explained my feelings in the morning. Not the creepy part about Edward's sperm and my egg, but my reasons for not being a surrogate birth mother.

She pleaded with me. "You're my last hope," she begged, tears streaming down her face like rain on a window. I cried too. She got in my car for the ride to the airport, so sad I could hardly bear it and almost changed my mind.

"I guess Edward and I will look into adoption," she said, grabbing her suitcase from the back seat at the departure doors, refusing my offer to park and wait with her to board the plane. I imagined her shuffling down the jetway, sagging into a window seat for her flight back to Chicago, and staring out at the changing landscapes below, hoping I would change my mind.

A few weeks later, Linda called, "Just to talk," she said, "about nothing much, you know, what you've been doing." We chatted about Elsa and Linda's new nursing job before she went off on a tangent, proclaiming with sound assurance that, "single mothers shouldn't be allowed to have children." *What?* "They are a burden on the state and society because they don't have enough money to raise a child and have to ask for assistance." She insisted that only married couples with careers should be permitted to have children. *Whoa Linda!* She was my friend, so I listened, feeling awful that she wanted a baby so badly she would grasp at straws like that. However, I didn't think she was referring to *me* in her rant against single mothers. I wasn't receiving state aid. I had a job.

Months later, I would discover Linda's agenda.

My little darling and I continued adjusting to our routine: daycare while I worked the job I loved at KLRU-TV, picking up Elsa in the evening for dinner, bathtime, and bedtime songs. I was so happy she was doing better now with the Nutramigen formula.

But by the end of April 1988, despite my joy over Elsa's recovery, I felt uneasy and self-conscious around people. I jumped at the slightest noise and woke up from dreams I couldn't recall.

Emma, too. We talked on the phone every day, trying to figure out what else went wrong in our lives. On a Saturday afternoon while Elsa was napping, Emma called to ask me, "Do you remember something about pillows?"

"Hmmm . . . *Yeah!* Now that you mention it, I remember dad putting pillows over our faces. Right?"

"Uh huh. Do you remember a game we played, putting pillows over each other's face?"

"Oh my God," I admitted with a sigh. "I do."

The game came racing to the surface of my consciousness. "It's weird, because I've never forgotten it, but put it aside, didn't know what to think."

Emma having said it made it real. I allowed myself to remember . . .

Lying on my childhood bed, my father holds a pillow over my face, one knee propped on the side of the bed to give himself leverage, pushing and pushing down on my face. I'm four, five, six. Emma and I have been playing a game with pillows, practicing how to turn our faces under them so our father won't realize we can breathe. So, I do that.

My eyes fix on the light from the window, not wanting to hear Emma crying. Our father tells her to shut up through clenched teeth, clamped shut from the exertion he's putting into smothering me. I am both Victim and Observer, having left my body, watching from a distance. Perhaps it's Emma I'm witnessing him smother, knowing how it feels.

"Did our *father* really do that?"

Emma sighed, "Yeah."

"Why?"

"I don't know, Hanna. I don't think he wanted us to *die*; he just wanted us to pass out or something."

"Torture us. Make me watch him smother you, and vice versa. Why? To silence us?"

"Undoubtedly," Emma said.

We hung up without saying goodbye.

After a sleepless night, I thought more about my father. And my mother. Things I hadn't forgotten but never thought about because it was too bizarre.

One incident was my father forcing Emma and me to play a game with him in the bathtub, a game we hated. We were young, three or four, in the bathtub with our father. I saw our mother's reflection in the mirror over the bathroom sink. She'd stand out of sight of the doorway, watching us through the mirror. Our father soaped up a washcloth and puffed it up in the water like a balloon. He instructed us to grab it, laughing, gliding it around the surface of the water, keeping it out of reach until he placed it over his penis. In the mirror, my mother's mouth would be straight-lipped, her arms crossed over her chest. It was her disapproval stance. I thought she directed it at Emma and me, that we'd done something wrong.

Sometimes our father pushed our heads under the water. I'd never forgotten his hateful, grimacing face, wavering above me through the water as I struggled to understand why he hated me. To survive, Emma and I devised a game to practice holding our breath, timing each other.

We didn't have a game to prepare for the times our father put our heads in the bench vise attached to the worktable in the basement . . .

I'm craning my neck to look up at my father.

A mop of hair flops over his forehead and his teeth clench from the exertion he puts into forcing my eyes away from his, tightening the vise on the sides of my head. I struggle and turn just enough to see his face. I plead with my eyes and murmur, barely able to speak, "Daddy, why do you hate me?" He stops and lets me go.

Emma never forgot the bench vise, either. One more piece of the million-piece jigsaw puzzle we'd taken apart as kids and were methodically piecing back together as adults.

In Ray's office Monday morning, I recounted the latest in my mysterious upbringing—pillow, bathtime, bench vise.

"Those were the experiences Emma and I had never forgotten. And never talked about." I looked out the window at leaves rustling in a light breeze. "Ray, I suspect there's more we *have* forgotten."

"Perhaps," he said, his eyes lit with mirth. "Why don't you try journaling? Will you do that?"

"I guess so."

"Great! Get some paper and a pen and start writing. Don't think about it, just write words, any words that come to mind," he said cheerily.

All week after putting Elsa to bed, I sat with a spiral notebook and pen. On Memorial Day weekend, 1988, I began writing an incest story: *My father comes into our bedroom and picks a twin to . . .*

I threw the pen across the living room.

My eyes, shocked open, were dry and unblinking, my breath a shallow panting. *What the hell was that?*

I walked over to retrieve the pen, but couldn't finish the sentence.

Ray was home when I called. "I was a victim of incest! By my *father*! Shit!"

"Oh Hanna, I'm so sorry. So, so sorry." I heard the sadness in Ray's sigh. "But I'm glad you remember."

"Well, I'm not. I hate this. It's a horror I can't describe. There are no words to define the torment, the reality of my father's assault on his little daughters' innocence. I don't understand how I could have forgotten. It happened all the time! And to Emma, too."

"Your mind blocked out the abuse to protect you from it."

"Protect me?"

"Yes. In psychology, we call it Traumatic Amnesia, or Repressed Memory Syndrome, a symptom of Post Traumatic Stress Disorder, PTSD."

"You mean like war veterans get?" I asked.

"Yes. Exactly like veterans of war."

I had a name for my confusion. PTSD.

We scheduled an appointment for the following afternoon, after Ray rustled around his home office desk for his appointment book.

When I arrived at Ray's office, I plopped on the couch and covered my face to hide my shame.

"It wasn't your fault. You were a little girl. Do you understand now why you would want to forget? Your father smothered you with pillows, shoved your underwater, and squeezed your head in a bench vise. They were tactics used to keep you quiet about the incest."

Sexual. Abuse.

Two simple words when strung together described my childhood. And would not, could not, be unstrung.

"It makes sense, I suppose." My soul ached in despair. "I get why people develop Traumatic Amnesia. To bury memories that feel like they'll kill you."

Ray patted my hand, his eyes intense with wisdom.

"I think there's more, Ray."

"Probably, Hanna." He leaned back in his chair, nodding his head.

"What am I going to do? I can't live like this, knowing something is terribly wrong, but not knowing what."

"When you're ready, we'll try light hypnosis to help you remember more clearly. We'll walk back into your past, together."

I fell in love with Ray that day.

Lorain gasped when I told her. "Oh my God! Emma told me the same thing yesterday. I swear! She wasn't ready to tell you, and I didn't know how."

"I can't believe it, Lorain. It happened all the time."

"So that's what was wrong with you two. It explains a lot."

Over the next few days, Lorain had a few unsavory memories of her own. Now the truth embroiled the three of us in shameful misery.

Emma and I didn't speak for a week. We couldn't. But when we spoke again, the true story of our sordid childhood came out.

"Dad came into our room," Emma said with a strangled sound as if struggling for air. "Lorain told me you remembered too."

"Yeah. He came at night."

A furious rush of adrenalin surged through my body. The old panic returned, gripping my throat, and I wanted to run.

"Our *father* got in our beds in the dark," she whispered.

"Yep. He picked a twin. And we were *not* dreaming."

"No, we weren't." She started to cry.

"It happened all the fucking time!" I shouted.

"How could we ever have forgotten?" she cried.

"Well, *duh*, because he put pillows over our faces."

"And threatened to drown us," Emma added.

"Our history is coming back," I said. "It's true. Our *father* smothered us, tried to drown us, and came into our room at night."

"My God, what a disgusting, fucking pervert!"

"And he was so damn angry! So mean and uncaring about rubbing his clammy little dick on me from behind, rubbing me raw," I reluctantly admitted.

It made me sick to my stomach to say those words.

"When I tried to get away, or cried, he'd shake my shoulders and whisper a harsh 'Quiet!' like a hiss."

"Fucking perverted pedophile snake," Emma correctly ascertained.

In silence we sat together on the phone, gagging on the truth as if once again submerged under our father's bathwater. A raging flood washed over us, battering us with the debris of our shocking reality.

With a sigh of mourning, Emma said, "I went to our mother in the mornings, after she changed our wet sheets—"

"Yeah. I remember . . ."

My father came into our room again. This time, he stomped to the bed farthest from the door—Emma's bed. I covered my face with my sheet and blanket and tucked them around my head, tight. I didn't want to listen to the sound of snapping rubber. I flew far, far away inside my mind.

This morning, my bed is soaking wet. So is Emma's. I was too afraid to run to the bathroom last night, and my mother isn't happy she has to change our sheets. "Again?" she angrily asks us.

I feel shame deep in my bones.

Another morning, after he'd chosen my bed, I wait a while before I go to my mother, as I've done so many times. "Mommy, my body hurts." That means I hurt between my legs, bad.

She turns her eyes away while she slides a glob of Vaseline between my legs.

Every time Emma and I try to tell our mother about our father, her response is always the same. "Oh," she harrumphs, "That didn't happen. You two were only dreaming."

"We can have the same dream?"

"Of course you can. Twins have the same dreams all the time."

"Why would we dream about Daddy doing that to us?" I ask, my voice low, almost a whisper.

"Oh, go out and play. Can't you see I'm busy here? I've got to finish folding towels and go downstairs to get sheets out of the dryer. I don't want to hear another word."

Emma concluded in a whisper, "She always shushed and shooed us away with her thin-lipped look of disgust."

"I love you, Emma."

"I love you, too, Hanna."

Our shared years of bewilderment and fear, not wanting to know the truth, yet knowing it now—beyond any shadow of a doubt we wished we could hold on to—heaved in sorrowful intensity. Our fanciful illusions of childhood were sucked down the drain with our father's bathwater. We became painful reminders to each other of the horror of sexual assault perpetrated by a father in a shared childhood bedroom. Our shame was too great. We said goodbye that day, seldom speaking for the next few months.

With the turn of the key opening the door to my past, the confusion and worry that had ruled my life transformed into a strength I didn't know I possessed. I'd always punished myself, wondering what was wrong with *me*. Finally, I could place my anger where it belonged, an elating vindication of my innocence. I felt powerful. "Taking your power back," is how Ray put it.

Marjorie—I ceased calling her my mother—had to have known about Evert's nighttime roaming. Stupefied as to why she hadn't protected me and why she had spent her life with Evert, whom I quit calling my father, I decided to confront her. I doubt I will ever forget our conversation.

Anger fueled my courage to make the call when Evert, retired, would most likely be out playing golf.

* * * *

Wintertime. I'm in junior high school. I savor the winter night as I walk down Oakton Street, watching my smoky breath puff in unison with my footsteps, boots crunching along the snow-packed sidewalk. The lights of store windows fade as I leave the outskirts of downtown Skokie. I love nighttime winter streets. A fresh, snowy scent cleanses my breathing, soothes my fears. I wander alone, reveling in the beauty of the soft, moonlit snowscape. This is where my spirit lives, in the light of the moon on snow.

I head for the library. My sanctuary.

Bob and Mark live across the street. I'd like to go say hello, but . . . I don't know. I'm embarrassed, I guess, from when I ran away with Alex and Adrienne, and Bob and Mark's mom let us spend our first night in a tent in their yard. They were so nice to us. I don't know how to be friends with them or if I should even try. So, I turn away.

As I approach the door, the bright, artificial light from inside creates a golden spotlight circling the building like a halo, the darkness beyond a black shroud obliterating the light of stars, robbing the moon of her glow. It's okay though, because this place is a beacon in the dark, an island oasis for castaways.

The door opens, a rush of warmth greets me. I finally feel safe.

I love this library, basking in the warm safety of nobody knowing where I am. I enter as a sad girl of thirteen, alone at the house I live in. A house full of people I seek comfort and understanding from, which never comes. There is so much chaos, I can't think straight.

Searching the library shelves for comfort in stories, I leave that world for another, simply by turning pages. I can choose whatever I want, and any book that scares me may be closed.

Tonight, I sit at a table along a far wall. I open a book and feel cleansed of self-doubt and confusion. Like rainwater seeping through limestone, my sense of unworthiness dissipates as my tears reach an underground river, my wounded heart purified on its journey, flowing to rest in a pool of redemptive goodness.

I enter tonight's chosen book about sailboats and sailing, and become an expert boat woman. Drawing up anchor, I quietly sail away.

> Wheel gull
> Spin and glide
> You've got no place to hide
> Because you don't need one
>
> "The Lee shore"

Ten

Marjorie answered the phone.

I lit into her. "Why have you stayed with him all these years?"

"Hanna? Is that you? Emma?"

"It's me, Hanna."

"Oh, you two sound so much alike, I can't tell the difference," she said light-heartedly, as if it hadn't been *weeks* since we'd spoken.

I ranted about the incest, insisting she'd always known, and demanded she explain her reason for not protecting me.

"Your father is all I've got!" she snapped, as if that were a sane answer.

"What do you mean, he's all you've got? You had five children. Five! We would have taken care of you. How could you stay with a man like that? I mean, really, I don't understand."

"Oh right, Hanna."

In my mind's eye I saw Marjorie's intense, stern face—straight-lined lips, a creased brow—focused on whatever activity she was busily performing. Undoubtedly, she was sitting at the kitchen table folding towels, or standing at the counter mixing cake batter, or ironing sheets and Evert's boxer shorts.

I was offering her a way out, assuming she'd be relieved for an excuse to get away from Evert. I couldn't imagine she *loved* him. He treated her as a doormat to wipe his feet.

After more bantering—listening to her self-pitying justifications and pleading with her to leave her husband—*she* wanted to get off the phone.

She never denied the incest. That was the saddest part.

Initially, uncovering the truth felt good. At last, I felt blameless. Then the misery of knowing commenced. The horror of what it meant for my little girl body to be sexually exploited by *my father* drove me to the farthest reaches of shame. I was going insane, the pain of my childhood rushing to the surface of my awareness, certain it would kill me. Frightening images flitted through my mind like wispy ghosts stuck in limbo with unfinished business. Memories of my father came to me in snapshots on a slide show—latex condoms burning and chafing me, though he never penetrated my tiny vagina. He was required to save me, for what I did not know. And I did not want to know. My father was supposed to teach me about men! No wonder I didn't trust them.

I believed my life was done. And Elsa's, too. That death would be our only means of escape. This thought terrified me.

My childhood "dreams"—which weren't dreams at all—tilted precariously on the edge of consciousness, impatient to show themselves.

In the meantime, thoughts of Marjorie, the woman who told me they were only dreams, swelled the banks of my psyche, spilling once more into my conscious mind, this time helping me understand more about my mother, and the complexities of a life . . .

Springtime. 1967. Our father informs us that our mother has been taking the wrong medicine for her thyroid problem. The doctor is taking her off of it so he can give her the right medicine.

Our father says our mother will be very sick, and we are not to disturb her.

The next day, we hear our mother moaning in the bedroom. When Emma and I peek in, she's groaning and moving around in pain and maybe dying. She doesn't seem to recognize us, and won't even look at us. She's far away in another world that must be like burning in hell. We take her hands and pat them. She calms down, but still doesn't see us. When our father finds us in the room, he shoos us out. We run to the kitchen table. He stands over us, smiling, like it's no big deal, our mother sick like that. He says she's fine and tells us to go outside to play. I don't want to go outside. I can't play. I think my mother is dying, and I don't understand. Groaning in pain happens when people stop taking medicine for thyroid problems? I sure hope I never get a thyroid problem.

She's calling out from the bedroom, begging for the medicine. Grinning, our father shakes his head and says, "Sheesh!" as he walks toward the bedroom, chuckling. He tells us again, flipping it over his shoulder, to go out to the backyard and play on the swings or something. We guess she must be okay if our father finds it so funny. Are we supposed to laugh?

We go outside, but we don't play.

. . . Christmastime. Two years later.

My mother sits at the dining room table filling out Christmas cards and wrapping presents. Such a busy time of year. So much planning for her elaborate Christmas dinner.

I must admit, my mother does put a dash of magic into Christmas, all the whoop-de-do about presents and Santa Claus. She has a flair for lovely gift wrapping. But those pretty packages, when unwrapped, are often as much of a disappointment as I am. Sometimes they do contain what I've dreamed of, such as the white go-go boots Emma and I got one year, and the Barbie with blue hair I got another year, still playing with her on our family's summer vacation to Wisconsin.

My mother sets her elegant Christmas table with fine china edged in gold, delicately painted Christmas trees filling the center of each plate. Her Grandma Inga's 1800s sterling silver place settings glint in the centerpiece's candlelight— a red wooden candelabrum painted with the traditional Swedish rosemaling *flower design. After dessert, my mother lights and relights the candles so Lorain, Emma, and I each get a turn snuffing out the light with her silver candle snuffer.*

This year, my mother's adult table, seating for ten, will feature her new red tablecloth and napkins, embroidered with rosemaling. She embroidered them herself last year, over months of painstaking care, in the evenings, while she watched her favorite television programs.

I sat with her, watching her stitch the design onto the rich linen cloth, her hand moving in a rhythmic sweeping motion, lulling me into a sense of comfort. I took her kindness toward me as an expression of love and appreciation. She even let me help embroider the napkins—I've been sewing since I was five, when my mother taught me and my twin sister how to cross stitch on squares of blue and white checked cotton, using yellow embroidery thread, of course, to make Swedish colors. I'm waiting for the Christmas when I'll be old enough to sit at the adult table instead of the kids' table, set with silver, yes, but only plain white linen, and no candles.

Those months of embroidering our revered Swedish rosemaling onto our Christmas tablecloth created treasured memories of my mother, when she included me in the magic of creating beauty amid her chaotic household. United in a secret, we conspiratorially waited for Christmas Eve, the night we would unveil our handiwork, the final touch to her celebrated Christmas table.

And then it was over. In one sweeping motion of linen over the expanse of her table.

I couldn't stand the sadness, thinking of Marjorie.

As far as I was concerned, my life was over. And Elsa's, too.

Ray disagreed, of course. "Elsa needs you. Alive! To protect her and show her the world. I *promise* it'll get better," he declared.

Thoughts of checking out, permanently, persisted. It seemed the logical solution. I had to talk about it because Elsa was part of that solution. With my abuse issues, I didn't see how I'd provide a good, happy life for her.

"The abuse is not happening *now*," Ray reminded me for the millionth time. "You simply have Post Traumatic Stress Disorder, like other kids raised in abusive homes. Everyone who experiences trauma can develop PTSD, even survivors of hurricanes and tornadoes."

"What do you mean 'simply'? I see nothing simple about these horrible things I'm remembering."

"I'm not trying to minimize your abuse, Hanna." He rolled his chair over and clasped both my hands in his. "I'm hoping you'll feel better knowing you are not alone."

"Well, I don't know if I care right now."

"I know," he said, his hands wrapped around mine. "But hear me out, okay?"

I looked at our hands and nodded.

Ray released them and continued. "Post Traumatic Stress Disorder, PTSD, was coined after the Vietnam War to describe trauma experienced by post-war soldiers. It was called Shell Shock or Battle Fatigue during World War I and II. It's all the same, just that we call it PTSD now. The symptoms of PTSD become acute when the sufferer remembers the traumatic event, or events, which had been blocked from the conscious mind. In order to survive. Manifested in the reliving the trauma, like what's happening with you and your sister."

I knew about Vietnam vets. My brother-in-law Rick was a marine on the ground, twice enlisted. He came home a heroin addict, switching to cocaine when he saw the needle was going to kill him. Rick was more than Lorain's husband. He was a big brother to me and we loved each other as siblings. He made me laugh, teased me relentlessly, and listened to my problems. I was twenty when Rick turned me on to cocaine and taught me how to free-base. And even that was brotherly. One Sunday afternoon, Rick showed me a photo album he'd put together of his years in Vietnam. We inhaled deep snorts of cocaine between the pages of gruesome photographs of his wartime activities.

The guilt Rick suffered for having lived through two stints in the jungles of Vietnam ravaged his life. Lorain often woke up to his screams, sometimes with his hands around her throat. Once, she had to knee him in the groin to wake him up. He woke up disoriented, unsure of where he was.

Ray's explanation of my condition in terms of PTSD made sense. Rick's drug habit, guilt for atrocities he took part in, surviving when so many died, and his nightmares, were all manifestations of PTSD. I saw the same symptoms in myself. Listening to Ray, I realized I had been experiencing them my entire life.

"We remember when it's safe to remember, sometimes months or years later. Yes, *we*. Including me," said Ray, a Vietnam veteran. Tears rimming his eyes, he shared a combat experience of arriving on a scene via helicopter to find every man dead. I felt connected to him, and more deeply connected to Rick.

Ray talked about similarities between victims of child abuse and prisoners of war, describing me as a prisoner of an abusive family, locked in a system I could not escape. "Think of yourself as a veteran!" Ray cheerily proclaimed, as if it would ease my pain. Which it did, sort of. I didn't feel so alone anymore, me and Emma against the world.

Relieved I wasn't going insane, or maybe remorseful that I wasn't—I would have preferred a pill to make the pictures go away—I proceeded to educate myself on PTSD in relation to childhood abuse. As a result, I discovered a phenomenon in the late 1980s. For the first time in modern history, people were disclosing the truth about incest.

At the downtown Austin library, I found a book, *Assault on the Truth,* by Jeffrey Moussaieff Masson. It was about Sigmund Freud's popular theory in the late 1800s, asserting that women alleging they'd been raped were "hysterical," that they harbored sexual fantasies rather than suffering from sexual assaults. Masson wrote that although Freud believed his patients' maladies indeed lay rooted in sexual trauma, particularly from childhood—his original Seduction Theory—Freud recanted to appease his psychiatrist cohorts who'd shunned him, refusing to recognize sexual abuse in any form.

Well, that motherfucker.

I saw the grave consequences of Freud's decision to hide the facts, and its tremendous influence on the field of psychiatry. How many suicides and trips to the insane asylum would have been averted had Freud stuck to the truth?

I was fortunate to relive the horror of incest in the 1980s, when Freud's false theory was supplanted with a blossoming recognition of the reality of incest and other sexual abuse, as well as the mental health field's search for appropriate psychological treatment for its long-lasting effects.

Still, I remained glum.

Emma corroborated what I remembered in quick phone conversations, though we never discussed the details, as we hadn't discussed them when we were kids sharing a bedroom and a bad dream.

Ray used light hypnosis when anxiety overtook me, and counseled me to remember, remember, remember every minute detail of abuse, stressing the importance of feeling the emotions attached.

"That's all you need to heal!" With a jaunty smile and clap of his hands, Ray rose from his chair to escort me out.

Oh, how wrong he was.

My mind's filing cabinet of unwelcome memories didn't slide open. It blew apart, scattering memories hither and yon. Imagine the Hoover Dam cracking and splitting, the damage when the floodgates crumble. Pressure would release, yes, but then havoc would rush forth. That was me.

With nothing to hold it back, an unsettling notion flowed out in the floodwaters. I stopped looking at myself in the mirror, detesting my white skin and pointed Scandinavian nose I'd inherited from my father and his mother, Grandma Elsa. I wanted brown eyes and black hair to replace my blue-eyed, blonde-haired Nordic features, repulsed by my heritage. I wished for a bloodletting to exhume all traces of Swedish blood from my body. I couldn't understand my obsession to recant my Swedish ancestry.

Aching with guilt for being white, I attempted to erase all attributes of Scandinavia from my life. I threw away everything from Sweden: several Bode crystal figurines, a crystal clock, a teakwood Swedish horse.

I hated and wanted to throw aside my Swedish relatives, too, even my beloved Grandma Elsa, regretting naming my daughter after her. I could not quite discard the afghan she crocheted for me when she was ninety-two, though. I hid it in a closet, out of sight.

Things were not getting better, as Ray had promised. I woke up every morning between 3:00 and 5:00, gasping for air as if submerged underwater. I'd run to Elsa's room, thinking she was dead in her crib, hoping I wouldn't find her dangling from the ceiling fan. Ray answered the phone, never angry that I called.

Anxiety smothered everything but fear. One evening, at dusk, someone knocked on the door, three sharp raps. A young man—tall, slender, white-blonde hair fringed across dark blue eyes—asked in a Swedish sounding accent where Josef lived, pronounced "*Yosef*." I slammed the door in his face.

A long-lost dread crawled from the bowels of my soul, penetrating every cell of my being. *Who was that guy?*

The following morning, startled awake with fears of Elsa being dead, I woke up Ray and told him about the man at my door, blurting out what I'd suspected for several days. "They're going to kill my baby and make it look like I did it so I'll have to suffer knowing it was them, because nobody will believe me. It sounds crazy, and I don't know why I'm saying this. I just know it's true."

112

"It's okay." Ray yawned. "Keep talking and don't censor your words."

"Or they'll make me kill her, and myself, and everyone will think I'm crazy or suffering from postpartum depression or something. And because I told you I thought we should both die a few weeks ago, you'll think I killed us.

"But Ray, I don't want to kill my baby. Listen to me, please. I love her and want her safe. Alive!"

"Shhh, it's okay. Calm down. I know how much you love your daughter and you don't wish her any harm. Hanna, listen to me carefully. Who are *they*?"

"I don't know! *They. Them.* My father and my brother? And I don't know *why*. Ray, if my baby ends up dead, it's not me! Okay? It's not me!"

"I hear you."

"What is going on? I don't understand it, but I know it's true. They'll kill us and make it look like I did it. Please help me. Please believe me."

"I *do* believe you. Take a deep breath. . . Good, now another one. . . That's right, now one more. Feel calmer now?"

"A little."

"Listen to me carefully. I have to be honest. I've never worked with this before."

"Oh no! You *don't* believe me!"

"Yes, I do. Hold on now. Just because I haven't dealt with what you are experiencing, I know it's related to your childhood. Not being experienced with this does not mean I don't believe you. Of course I believe you. And your twin sister remembers the abuse, too. Right?"

"Yeah. That's right. I'm scared, Ray."

"Take another deep breath . . . good. I believe you, I want to help, and of course you are upset. I'm trying to find help for myself, to help you better. I'm waiting for a call, in fact. Come into the office this afternoon at 3:00. Okay? Can you do that? And bring the baby."

I had grown to trust Ray unequivocally. He made himself available to me twenty-four hours a day. I needed someone I could rely on. Ray gave me that.

I called in sick for the third day in a row and counted the hours until 3 p.m. By now, I'd confided everything to my boss, Candace. She was sympathetic and supportive.

At Ray's office, he told me he'd found an inpatient treatment program in New Mexico specializing in sexual trauma. With Ray's gentle pressing over several days—I needed his urging to allow myself to get the help I didn't believe I deserved—I consented. Thus, in early July 1988, my sister Lorain flew in from Chicago to take Elsa home with her while I went to New Mexico for treatment at Cottonwood de Albuquerque.

Eleven

The plane landed in Albuquerque in the brightness of midday. Dar held up a sign at the gate, a smile crumpling her middle-aged face. Crossing the walkway to the parking lot, I took a deep breath of the dry New Mexico air, a hint of fresh mountain coolness to it, even in July. I liked it.

"I'm a tech at the treatment center," Dar said on our twenty-mile drive to Cottonwood de Albuquerque in Los Lunas. "Not a counselor. A helper. Someone who hangs out with clients to make sure everyone feels safe. Cottonwood prefers the term client over patient because we aren't sick, just suffering from childhoods we didn't ask for."

I looked at her sideways.

"Yes, I'm an incest survivor, too."

That she'd admit to being a survivor of incest was quite shocking. Especially the "survivor" part. I liked it. And I liked the idea of client versus patient, survivor versus victim. I felt understood, respected, hopeful.

Nearing the treatment center, we drove through a neighborhood where every backyard housed a large, beehive-shaped earthen object with a small square door at its base. "What are those things?" I asked.

"*Hornos*. Adobe ovens for baking bread," said Dar.

"That's cool."

"Yeah. The Native peoples of this region are the Pueblo people. There are nineteen Pueblo tribes in New Mexico, and it's mostly Isleta Pueblo families that live around here. We buy bread from them, made in those hornos, so you'll get to taste it. It's delicious."

That sounded nice.

Beyond the last house was a dirt road leading to the entrance of Cottonwood de Albuquerque. Colossal cottonwood trees surrounded the buildings, giving the center its name. The terrain stretching out beyond was a vast prairie landscape of tall grasses and short mesquite trees. The mountains on the horizon drew me to them, a fringe of majestic protectors ringing the flatlands. Several people milled about, watching us approach. Timid, I wrapped my arms across my chest. Dar patted my shoulder and reassured me I was in the right place.

A woman in admissions assigned me to a room with three roommates, in a long, single-story building with rooms strung together like a pearl necklace. Dar gave me a tour of the center, and then we walked over to the dining hall for dinner, cafeteria-style. I met my roommates—Lara, Emily, and Janice. We sat outside after dinner, talking about how we'd gotten there. They told me that everyone in our program was a sexual abuse survivor, including the men. I was flabbergasted. I'd been thinking incest was an isolated occurrence—my sister, me, the woman from the codependency program in Austin, Dar, and perhaps a few other women and girls here and there.

Breakfast was at 7 a.m. I met more clients in the dining hall, including those in the drug and alcohol program on the other side of the facility. Even a few of them admitted sexual abuse as kids, and would be coming into our program when they finished their treatment for drugs and alcohol.

I felt okay for the first time in several months, reassured I wasn't alone. Maybe I'd be able to recover my dignity.

The rest of my morning was spent with the psychologist, Guy Peterson, PhD. We talked about why I was there and I filled out a lengthy questionnaire called the Minnesota Multiphasic Personality Inventory, MMPI, designed to measure depression and anxiety levels, defense mechanisms, and possible underlying psychiatric conditions. Upon completion, Guy sent me to my first one-on-one session with my counselor, Sharon.

Sharon pulled the MMPI from the file Dr. Peterson handed her, perused my answers, and then got right to the point. No small talk.

"Your results show you use confusion as your primary defense mechanism. In your case, that means you blocked your childhood abuse by using confusion to diminish or deny reality. You repressed what you didn't want to believe in the form of Traumatic Amnesia, a fancy term for forgetting."

I laughed. "*That* sounds confusing."

Sharon smiled. "Confusion is a component of both denial and repression, two of the primary defense mechanisms used to cope with trauma. That's how you survived it. That's how many of us survive. By forgetting," she said, admitting that she, too, had survived sexual trauma. "You'll learn more about defense mechanisms in group therapy and lectures."

I liked that my counselor had also been sexually abused, and survived. It helped me trust her and gave me confidence in her ability to help me.

"Don't worry," she said. "You'll figure it out."

The first ten days of treatment were to observe group treatment methods, and to learn about the many ways abuse shaped our lives. Daily lectures stressed identification and definitions of the primary unhealthy defense mechanisms we used to cope with life: denial, passive-aggression, withdrawal, repression, projection. According to Freudian theory, denial and repression were the two most common strategies to distort unpleasant reality and defend delusional ideas about what we wanted reality to be.

Denial was the defense mechanism most often discussed in group therapy.

After our sessions, smoking cigarettes with our counselors on the upstairs deck of the counseling building or the patio below, one of us would inevitably claim, "My abuse wasn't *that* bad."

The rest of us would pounce with accusations of "minimizing" their abuse, a form of denial. I, however, never minimized incest—from the moment I remembered my father coming into my room at night, I knew sexual abuse was the worst thing that could happen to a person. But, unlike me, many clients drifted back and forth, in and out of denial, one day freaking out about sexual assaults inflicted on their child bodies, the next day wondering, "Did it really happen?"

"Jeff, you did *not* make it up," Sharon said to a man who flip-flopped hourly.

Jeff's family had accused him of lying. He said he hoped he'd only imagined an uncle's seductions, an uncle he always liked. He came to treatment hoping it wasn't true, that he'd find out why he would imagine such a thing about his uncle.

"Sexual abuse is not something people are inclined to make up. Or imagine," said Sharon. "Why would you? Why would anyone?" Sharon waved her arm out across the deck, displaying Jeff's support system. "See? You're not alone."

Everyone nodded their heads with great enthusiasm.

"Anyone can be a child abuser. *Anyone*," Sharon said. "Uncles, fathers, grandfathers, cousins, neighbors, mothers, brothers, babysitters. Even teachers, police officers, ministers, priests, rabbis. I had a client who was sexually abused by a boy scout leader."

"Me too," said Charley, looking down, face red with shame. We huddled around him, enveloping him in our arms, assuring him he was blameless.

We learned how pedophiles operate in lectures given by Garry Giles, the program director.

Garry described the typical pedophile as an insecure, socially awkward individual who convinces themself it's okay to have sex with children by using various techniques to coerce child victims into appearing to be willing participants.

"Pedophiles 'groom' their victim for months or years before approaching them sexually," explained Garry. "They do this by slowly, methodically, manipulating the child into acquiescence with candy, gifts, money, special attention, declarations of love, and other favors. By the time the pedophile makes his move, he has created a relationship wherein the victim believes he or she cannot say no. Once the sexual encounter has begun, the abuser continues the sex with more favors, or switches to force and threats."

Garry cleared his throat, took a swig from his plastic water bottle, and looked around the room. I looked, too. Every person stared wide-eyed with mouth agape. I shut mine.

"Typically, but not always, the abuser manipulates the victim to believe *they* seduced the abuser," continued Garry. "That type of pedophile is an expert at emotional blackmail, cornering the child into taking responsibility for the sexual act; exonerating himself, or herself, from any wrongdoing and turning the blame on the child. And the child, of course, takes it on."

I understood what Garry was saying. Pedophiles had to convince themselves of the normalcy of their acts, even though they knew it was against the law.

In my case, my father wasn't one of those. He was a pedophile who believed he was unjustifiably superior, above the law. He didn't need to pretend his victims were agreeable to his assaults, which allowed him to be as physically and psychologically violent as he cared to be. Which also made it easy for me to drop him from my life.

"And to keep the victim quiet," Garry added, "some pedophiles threaten to kill pets, friends, or family members if their victim tells. Or the victim themself."

A gasp went up as the survivors around me recognized how they'd been coerced and manipulated. Every face in the room shone with tears.

At Cottonwood, joining a legion of adult survivors who had also outlasted the sex abusers of their childhoods, my shame subsided. A new sense of strength penetrated my bones and soul. I savored the solidarity I found with these other survivors. Strength in numbers.

Garry called pedophiles "perpetrators" of a crime. Hence, when referring to our abusers, we shortened it to perps. "My perp was such an asshole," I'd say. It felt better than saying father.

Another lecture suggested that sexual abuse severely compromised our psychological, emotional, and social well-being. And the enablers who supported the perpetrator were equally to blame.

It helped explain my distrust of people, especially authority figures. My rebellious nature, I surmised, was a militant reaction to distrust, a survival mechanism packed with pride.

Garry lectured on the significance and importance of spirituality in one's life, how the nature of sexual abuse destroyed it.

"The manipulative and controlling behaviors of your perpetrators replaced your innate sense of a loving, benevolent God," he said. "In effect, your perpetrators—people you couldn't trust—became your gods."

Whoa! That blew my mind.

"A spiritual sense of God," he continued, "or a Higher Power, if you like, *will* heal trauma. I appreciate the difficulty in accepting the idea of God for some of you. Be assured that spirituality does not equal religion. Spirituality encompasses the common ideals of love and helping others that are the basis for all religions, with a Higher Power who loves you. Call it whatever you want, in whatever form you'd like to see a Cosmic Entity you want to trust—God, Creator, Jesus, Great Spirit, Mohamad, Buddha, Higher Power. Deep inside every person is a fundamental idea of God." He looked us each in the eyes, adding, "Think about it."

I did.

Garry's lecture introduced me to the idea of spirituality versus religion, a concept I had never considered or even heard before. I'd shunned God and religion as far back as I could remember. The notion of "God" was the last thing I expected to hear about in treatment. Yet, I suspected Garry might be right. A shadowy presence awakened and surrounded my vault of secrets with a misty blanket of comfort, protecting me. I tried to unwrap my Protector and shove it into the vault, terrified of that love. Thus, my steps toward accepting the spiritual damage caused by my abuse were meager, fraught with questions I didn't understand enough to even ask.

By the end of those ten days, Garry and Sharon had ripped off the band-aids of defense mechanisms I'd used to cover my trauma. Without them, it was easy to believe what I was never supposed to tell.

Eager to move forward, I asked Sharon, "Now what?"

"You're right where you need to be. And now It's your turn for experiential psychotherapy. We'll start tomorrow. With role-playing," Sharon said with a grin.

Role-play was a Gestalt therapy technique, as were all the methods used in our group therapy sessions. To role-play, I sat in a chair facing an empty one in which I imagined my father sitting. Even though I'd observed other clients do it, I felt silly talking to an invisible person. With my friends' encouragement, I started speaking to the chair, which quickly turned into yelling everything I'd always wanted to yell: "You sonofabitch pervert! You destroyed my life! You're a sickening excuse for a man! I hate you! I hate you! I hate you!"

It felt so damn good. I felt strong. Powerful. Everyone hugged me, which was difficult to accept.

Robert took a turn next, placing his uncle in the empty chair.

"I'm not angry with my uncle," he said. Then, in a quieter voice, added, "I've always loved him. I still do." And he broke down in gulping sobs.

Robert, twenty-one, admitted he'd been having sex with his uncle since age eleven and was beginning to see that maybe it was inappropriate for his uncle to have sex with an eleven-year-old, who also happened to be his nephew. "But with me," he claimed, "it was different, because I wanted the sex."

To Robert, their relationship was merely a twisted love affair. When he decided to tell his family, there were repercussions, resulting in Robert's sole purpose in coming to treatment to appease them. His family believed counselors at Cottonwood would force Robert to "admit" he'd lied about having sex with his uncle so they could all return to the status quo.

Garry, overseeing role-playing that day, said, "Robert, if it's truly a love affair, has your uncle told your family?"

"Um, no." Robert glanced at his hands in his lap.

"What kind of relationship is that, if it's a secret?"

Robert looked up at Garry with a gasp, turned to everyone, and began sobbing.

"It's okay, Robert. We're here for you," said Wendy and Charley in unison.

Robert stared at the empty chair and cried. For a long time.

I was thankful my father never pretended to love me; it made it easy for me to divorce him and his enabling supporters from my life, such as my mother, Marjorie. Though a few other clients had also cut ties to their offenders, some of them clung to relationships on the periphery—family members and friends who supported the offender, not believing the client or accusing them of overreacting.

After lunch, my counselor, Sharon, led us in another method designed to address anger. I went first.

I held one end of a towel and asked Emily to take the other end. Envisioning my father in the middle of it, together we twisted that towel into a tight knot. I felt silly until the twisting sensation—like cranking the handle of a bench vise—erupted a volcano deep inside me, hot and dangerous, oozing with pent-up, burning hatred. I screamed in rage. A wordless, ravaged, primordial soul scream.

At the end of ten minutes, Sharon took the towel. I was hoarse with grief.

Everyone huddled around me, hugging me. I resisted, wanting to push them away, but they held on tight. "It's okay. We're here for you, and we want to be here for you. You're safe now," my new friends said, declaring, "We love you," until I collapsed in their arms, sobbing.

How could someone like me, whose *father* sexually assaulted her, deserve love or have the nerve to ask for help? The love of these new friends hurt. A pain deeper than the truth of my loveless childhood. I think we all felt that way. It was easier to give each other the love we longed for than to accept it.

After a long break, Garry sat on the floor with us. It was Nancy's turn to beat a large pillow with a plastic bat. On her knees, the pillow on the floor, Garry placed himself behind her and to the right, urging her to release all the caged words and memories needing to be freed.

Nancy had arrived at Cottonwood two days after me, laden with four enormous suitcases. Sharon, also Nancy's counselor, assigned her a room down at the far end of the women's quarters. I was smoking on the upstairs deck with Sharon on the day she told Nancy to move into my room, replacing Janice, who'd left that morning. I watched Nancy struggle with heavy suitcases, shoulders slumped with the burden of her luggage. Sharon's stare streamed down from the balcony in a river of intense deliberation, flowing back and forth with Nancy's many trips from one end of the women's quarters to the other. I sensed Nancy's humiliation and wanted to help. Sharon placed her hand on my arm and said, "No, let her do it herself."

Nancy had been a prostitute in a former life, and had married one of her customers, a wealthy Texas rancher. She had taken on the air of an aristocrat, her hordes of clothing of the highest quality. I think Sharon, also a former prostitute, wanted to remind Nancy whence she'd come. Sharon cut her no slack. Thus, Nancy requested Garry as her guide when it was her turn to beat the pillow.

I watched with fascination the unpacking of Nancy's story.

Half-heartedly, she tapped the pillow with the plastic bat. Garry urged her, "Come on, Nancy. What are you angry about?"

"I don't know," she said.

"Yes, you do," he urged.

"We were poor. Sometimes there was no food," Nancy whispered.

She hit the pillow, picking up pace and force. Guttural sounds began to emanate from deep within her, growling louder. She lifted her arms high over her head and pounded the pillow, Garry beside her, urging her to put words to her rage.

I pulled my knees into my chest and rocked. Nancy's anger was an ancient rage I could relate to. I wanted to wail with her.

"Daddy chopped up the dog," she shouted. "And they buried the baby in the backyard!"

"Who buried the baby?" Garry asked, kneeling at her side.

"My mother had the baby at home, screaming and screaming. The baby was already dead. Right?" She looked pleadingly into Garry's eyes. "Right? The baby was already dead, wasn't it?"

Nancy fell to her side. "They buried her in the backyard. My baby sister."

She threw the bat across the room, collapsing in heaving sobs. I noticed Sharon standing by the door, arms crossed below her breasts. The intensity of her stare was an electric current. She grinned, almost imperceptibly, but I saw it. I saw, too, the pain in her dark brown eyes, with unspilled tears.

Garry opened his arms in a hug, beckoning us.

We crawled across the pea soup carpet to embrace Nancy with soothing caresses. And tears, for all of us. We held onto each other, Nancy in the middle, the child within us each momentarily quenched of our thirst for attention and love.

I looked at Asher, also a prostitute, knowing without a doubt that he deserved love. He looked back at me and mouthed, "I love you."

I looked at Jeff, Roger, Mary, Lara, Charley, Robert, Emily, Wendy, Alice. They deserved love, too. We all did. The energy of releasing our buried feelings of lovelessness heated the room. Metallic. As if we'd created a new earthly element.

* * * *

1975. Something bad is going to happen. Something sad.

A couple of months ago, before school let out, I found out I was pregnant. I don't know what to do. I'm sixteen, just finishing sophomore year. I know I don't have much time, so I went to an abortion clinic this morning, all by myself. But I couldn't do it. I ran out of there, scared to death, not wanting to abort the fetus.

I have to tell my parents. I'm scared, so I talk to my sister Lorain first.

She yells at me in a whisper, like she does—lips pursed in a sneer, deep lines furrowing her upper lip like an old lady who's been smoking for sixty years, even though she just turned eighteen in May. Lorain jabs her pointed finger in my chest and says, "You have to get an abortion, you have to."

But I don't want an abortion.

There's no way my parents are going to allow me to have this baby. After all, they can't let their friends find out I'm not a virgin. I reluctantly tell them I'm pregnant and don't want an abortion, but they harass me so much about it, I can't refuse.

I'm almost five months pregnant now, so I can't get an abortion at the clinic. I secretly waited so it would be too late. But no such luck. My parents are arranging for me to have an experimental abortion, a brand-new procedure being performed on humans for the first time, and only at one hospital, in Chicago.

My parents originally planned to send me to New York for a saline-injection-miscarriage-abortion, and are so happy to have found something closer to home. This forced-miscarriage-abortion in Chicago is performed by a hormone injection—estrogen or progesterone, I don't know which. Could be testosterone for all I know.

I can't believe how much time and effort my parents have put into this abortion. It's the most attention I've gotten from them since . . . well, it's probably the most attention I've ever gotten from them. Not exactly the type of attention I'd like, though.

The day has come and I'm not happy about what's going to happen.

I leave this morning and run to Jim's house, whom my father has now forbidden me from seeing.

To my utter astonishment, he shows up at Jim's door! I had no idea my father knows where Jim lives. Did my sister Lorain tell him because she's also dead set on me having an abortion?

My father drags me to the car, acting as if I've caused him the greatest inconvenience ever.

I look out the back window at Jim on the sidewalk as we drive away.

. . . The nurses are nice to me. There are two other girls in this room with me, fellow guinea pigs.

I'm begging for drugs to make me sleep. I want to be totally unconscious for this. They consent with a morphine drip, I think it is, from an IV bag. I keep waking up, talking, but have no idea what I'm talking about, or to whom.

Too bad for me I can't go fully under, so I'm half-awake when the cramping starts, but mercifully in and out of consciousness for the next several hours it takes for the fetus to die.

Die!

The moment has come. I wish, wish, wish I was unconscious. I don't want to listen to the nurse and doctor talking about how much it weighs. I will myself not to hear, humming "lalalalalalala" under my breath.

It has been difficult to admit my relief for that abortion, thinking of the abuse that child would have been exposed to in my family. Some people may think it is not for me to make that decision. However, if I'd gone full term, that child would have been sexually, psychologically, physically, and spiritually abused, as had I. Why haven't we, as a society, put money and energy into campaigns to stop child abuse and all the societal ills that come with it? Maybe then the need for abortion would cease.

Twelve

My desire to distance myself from Swedish heritage persisted. I felt the shame of my whiteness down to the pink beneath my finger and toe nails.

Growing up, I'd never thought much about my father's racist comments. People in the community where I lived used racial slurs all the time, words I hated to repeat: spic, wop, dago, pollack, kike, nigger, dirty Mexican.

Alone in our group therapy room with my journal, a memory from fifth grade appeared on the page . . .

There's a new girl at school, Teresita, the only kid in our school from Puerto Rico. The rest of us are white, so she stands out with her brown skin and foreign accent; foreign to us. Nobody likes her, not even the teachers. She is kind of annoying, trying too hard to fit in. Even though I'm not crazy about her, for the above reason, I suspect the number one reason everybody else dislikes her is because we've never had Puerto Ricans living in our neighborhood.

Kids are mean to her on the playground. They taunt, "Go back to Puerto Rico, spic!" One kid, a boy, shoved her to the ground the other day.

I couldn't stand it. "Leave Teresita alone!" I screamed and pushed Danny.

Everyone *on the playground stopped and stared, mouths gaping, shocked that I, or anyone, would come to Teresita's defense. Danny glared at me, shaking his strawberry-blonde bangs out of his face.*

I helped Teresita get up. She ran into the building, sobbing. I started crying, too, and ran after her, rushing into the girls' bathroom. She was crying in the stall farthest from the door, so I ducked into the first stall, away from her, and sobbed my eyes out.

How can humans be so nasty? Especially the Jewish kids, with their *history of persecution. Why do people hate her just because she has darker skin, and an accent I quite like? I fell apart over it—the cruel looks on those kids' faces.*

I walked out after I heard Teresita leave. I didn't want to talk to her.

Mr. Pearson was waiting for me in the hallway.

"What are you crying about?" he chuckled.

"Nothing," I said, and tried to get past him.

He grabbed my purse and wouldn't give it to me until I told him why I was upset. He thought it was funny. Funny!

Mr. Pearson is such an asshole. I hate him, and this school, and everyone in it.

Teresita never came back. Her parents changed schools.

I kept writing, a passenger on a time machine dialed to the 1960s, piecing together my disjointed memories. One piece held my father's statements about Jap this, Jap that, from his proud World War II days, "when the United States stopped the scourge of those nasty little Jap hornets," he called them. Funny thing is, he never, and I mean *never,* said one negative word against the Germans.

And though I never heard my father say anything overtly racist about Black Americans, I felt his hatred when he disdainfully referred to them only as "those Blacks." Not Black *people*, "those Blacks."

Like tumblers lining up on a safe, a memory clicked into place . . .

Today, our father is taking me, Lorain, and Emma to the Barnum and Bailey circus in Chicago. Lorain just turned nine. Emma and I turned seven two months ago.

I've never been to the circus. There's so much going on—ladies on horses, lions doing tricks (in cages, of course), elephants with fancy ladies riding them, and I love the high-wire acrobats. We get popcorn and sodas, a treat, and my favorite, cotton candy.

At the end of the show, a clown gives us each a balloon. Mine is blue. We leave the giant tent and walk into the afternoon sunshine toward the parking garage.

A group of Black people in African clothing is walking towards us. Our father drags us across the street. "Walk quickly," he says.

I've never seen anyone dressed this way, except in books about Africa. The women's long dresses are like scarves fluttering about them, designed with brightly colored geometric shapes with matching turbans wound around their heads. The men's wide-legged pants and geometric patterned tunics flutter like scarves as well. Their faces are chocolate, with high cheekbones. The loveliest people I've ever seen. I don't understand why our father wants us to be afraid of them.

"What's wrong?" Lorain asks.

My sisters and I crane our necks to watch the Black people gracefully glide down the sidewalk, the women's hips swaying.

My father says, "They're Black Muslims," and leaves it at that, as if we're supposed to know what he's talking about.

I turn around to look where they're going. My father grabs my wrist. I open my mouth to cry out, watching my balloon soar up and away from me. A breeze catches it and floats it back the way we came, following the beautiful people.

Click. And the safe opened . . .

Emma and I are with our parents today, visiting the Vikssons, family friends we've known our whole lives. We just ate lunch on their patio that faces a little lake. We're bored now, so we play in the bathroom sink, giggling and splashing water. Eunice, the Vikssons' housekeeper, was in there before us. We slipped in as she stepped out, wiping her hands on her apron.

When we come out, our mother is waiting with her arms crossed over her chest. The thin-lipped, straight line of her mouth means we've done something wrong. I turn back to make sure we wiped up the water.

"Never use the bathroom after the maid," she says loud enough for Eunice to hear.

Eunice's friendly face fades, shame tugging the edges of her eyes, pulling her eyelids into sagging eaves. I feel terrible. She is always nice to us, slipping us cookies with a warm smile. We love her.

I'm embarrassed for Eunice, but more so for my mother's rudeness toward her. I don't understand, yet I do. It's because Eunice is a negro.

I kept writing. The scene changed. I saw the distasteful look on my father's face whenever he said anything referring to "the Jews," his derogatory tone echoing across my mind. It made no sense. We lived in a Jewish neighborhood. At school, some of the kids' parents and grandparents had concentration camp numbers tattooed on their forearms. And besides us, only two or three other non-Jewish families lived on our block of around twelve houses. My sisters and I played with two families of gentile kids.

Thinking it over, I realized I knew only two of the Jewish families—the Graces at the end of the block, and the Levin family next door.

Our next-door neighbors on the other side of our house were Mr. and Mrs. Verva. I remembered playing in their yard, and sometimes I'd ring their doorbell but couldn't recall why or what I'd say when Mrs. Verva came to the door. Mr. Verva was a musician. He played the clarinet in a well-known jazz band. We'd hear the band practicing at their house once in a while. I didn't know if the Vervas were Jewish, only that my parents didn't speak to them.

The WWII atrocities committed against the Jews were common knowledge, yet my father had nothing derogatory to say about Nazi Germany, the country that tortured and murdered those Jews. He was an army intelligence officer in London during the war; he must have known first-hand the extent of Nazi crimes.

A faint photograph snuck out of the safe . . .

Emma and I stumble down the steps to the basement in front of our father. This isn't the first time he's taken us down here.

I don't know where our mother is.

My father arranges us on the far side of the basement, where storage shelves line the wall. He walks slowly back and forth, looking us up and down, hands on hips. He stops before us and yells "Achtung!"

This means "Attention!" in German, as in a military command. It means we are to stand with our arms glued to our sides like soldiers.

I fidget because I have to go to the bathroom and he won't let me. He shoves my arms to my sides and stands back.

"Achtung! Achtung!" he shouts in German.

I turn into a sculpture of stone.

Another dimension of my father's cruelty had crept up the steps of that dark basement of long-lost memories. I tried to shove that photo back into my mind's safe of lost memories, but it no longer fit. I turned it over, but my father's army satchel materialized in my mind, flipping the photograph upright, and then turning into a movie . . .

I watch my father pull a uniform from that old duffel bag, stored on one of those shelves. The trousers are blue. I watch him slowly pull the sleeves of a long woolen overcoat with large gold buttons over his arms, and a military cap such as an officer might wear completes the ensemble.

> Generals gathered in their masses
> Just like witches at black masses
> Evil minds that plot destruction
> Sorcerer of death's construction
>
> "War Pigs"

In my mind, I turned the photograph face down again and again, hoping not to remember more. Yet, I could not unknow what it had already revealed.

Now, in addition to accepting that my parents harbored a superior attitude toward people of different skins colors, I had to face what appeared to be a superior attitude toward religions. Specifically, the Jewish faith. I linked this new knowledge to my desire to change my Nordic features, wanting a new body and clean blood more than ever.

In my next session with Sharon, I relayed the events at the circus and the Vikssons' house, finding it difficult to retell what happened with my father in the basement.

At the end of our hour together, I shoved aside my shame and told her, adding, "I'm pretty sure my father was reenacting something from WWII, from concentration camps." My body stiffened with panic as I recognized the truth. "He was in army intelligence in London during the war," I said. "He would have known what happened in the camps. I wish with all my heart this wasn't true, and I don't want to believe it."

Sharon looked into my eyes. "Believe it, Hanna. You have no reason to make it up. Why would you? Does it help you understand where your recent abhorrence of your white skin may have come from?"

"Yes," I said, uncertain how to feel. "It hurts."

"I totally understand."

"My father hated American Indians, too, of course. He called them 'dirty savages' and 'stinkin' injuns.' It makes little sense, because I'd never even seen a real Indian when I was a kid, except at the Wisconsin Dells, though they were probably white men dressed up as Indian chiefs. In elementary school, our teachers led us to believe that Native Americans were practically extinct, relegated to the pages of history books."

I sat back in the chair and stared out the window.

"Oh yeah, I remember watching protests on TV with my father, out west somewhere. Indians with guns marching in the streets. I was a young teenager wasted on drugs, so I can't remember what it was about. I was supposed to be afraid of them, though."

"Lots of Native Americans protested in the 1970s. The feds had files on members of the American Indian Movement, AIM," said Sharon. "AIM staged a protest up north of here after three white boys, high school students, brutally tortured and murdered several Navajo men. The boys stripped the men, tied them up, and set off firecrackers in their anuses. Despicable."

"Oh, my God! Why?"

"Who knows? Filled with hate. Those white boys, by the way, got off. The judge sent them to 'reform school' or some bullshit."

"And white people call *Indians* savages," I said.

"Yeah, right?"

"Why are people filled with hate, Sharon?"

"I don't know. Maybe they're afraid." Sharon shook her head. "But Hanna, *we* can let go of *our* hate."

"Do you think I can do something good with my white skin one day?"

Sharon nodded. "Sure. Why not?" She picked up her pack of cigarettes. "Come on, let's grab a smoke," and we moved our session out to the deck.

That night, more came . . .

It's Wintertime. I'm nine. Under a gray sky bearing a future snowstorm, I'm frozen to the ground, lost in the woods. Soon it will be nighttime and the darkness will surround me in a shroud. I look down in my lap, pretending if I can't see scary things, they can't see me. I've given up hope someone will rescue me, searching instead for a reason to go on. Why was I left here?

My broken spirit leaves my body and flies away, free, soaring above the treetops.

Last summer, when it was warm, I saw a newsreel on TV of white policemen in helmets with shields, like ancient warriors, swinging bats at weaponless Black Americans marching on a Chicago city street. Police officers hooked up hoses to fire hydrants and sprayed the Black people—even kids and old people—sending them flying across the pavement. Other policemen ordered German Shepherds to attack and bite them.

I wept in horror. "Mother, why are they doing that?"

She said nothing.

In walked my father.

"Why are those policemen beating Negroes?" I cried.

He huffed with disgust and clicked off the television set.

I knew not to ask my parents about it, but couldn't stop myself. I don't understand. It was terrible to watch.

Now, I sit on the forest floor now, wondering . . .

Snow falls, erasing the trail they'd brought me in on. I suck my thumb for comfort and peek up at the vanishing path. The sensation in my eyes is of stinging shame and bewilderment. What crime did I commit to deserve abandonment? Do I ask too many questions? Was I born unlovable? I said it was wrong for those policemen to put those fire hoses on those Negroes. I know I was supposed to keep my mouth shut, but I couldn't help it. It's just not right!

Is that why they've left me here?

As my blue woolen overcoat accumulates a layer of powdery white glitter, I feel myself disappear.

Circling high above, my spirit watches the speck of my pathetic child body shackled to the earth below.

Reluctantly flying back to me, I am whole again.

> And I dreamed I was flying
> High up above my eyes
> Could clearly see
> The Statue of Liberty
> Sailing away to sea
> "American Tune"

Los Lunas weather was delicious. Perfect. Not too hot, even in July. The air was crispy clean, void of humidity. I loved the dry air, the cool nights. We liked to sit outside in the evenings. We'd cry about our sad lives of incest, laugh about our sordid antics while drinking and drugging, and write out our treatment homework in three-ring binders, chain-smoking cigarettes long past the splendid sunsets and into the starry nights.

I'd never seen the sky so black and lit with stars, layers upon layers of them; a deep river of stars streaming along the Milky Way, spilling over its banks. I saw a shooting star one night, the first shooting star I'd seen in my whole life, and I was twenty-nine years old. I wondered if nature was where God had been hiding. I felt hopeful.

Family week was coming up soon. We prepared by practicing effective communication skills with each other—positive ways to include our families in our recovery, to inform them of our sexual abuse and how we'd been affected. The idea was to build better relationships. We'd also tell them, in a positive way, all the ways they'd hurt us. Conversely, our family members' program would teach them how to communicate, too, and we'd listen to how we'd hurt them.

Neil, despite his insistence that he loved me and didn't want a divorce, declined my invitation, as did my sisters Lorain and Ellyn. Emma accepted. And it dumbfounded me that Marjorie and Evert also agreed to attend.

Several other clients also planned to confront their perpetrators, which would take extra work with Garry Giles, the program director. Separated from our abusers until we would confront them, we watched them arrive through a glass door in a darkened room—we could see them, but they couldn't see us.

Evert showed up in plaid Bermuda shorts and a white T-shirt, walking briskly up the path as if he owned the place. He looked ridiculous. Marjorie, dressed in pink pedal pushers, tagged behind him. My face reddened in embarrassment for them, a weight of sadness weakening the anger in my heart.

Family week didn't go as planned, of course.

Garry Giles took me into the yard next to the counseling building the day before I was supposed to confront Evert and Marjorie. Garry sat in front of me on a matching lawn chair and patted my hand. He said, "I'm sorry, but we had to ask your parents to leave."

"What? Why? I'm ready to confront them."

"Your father refused to cooperate with the family program. During breaks, he went around to the other family members and tried to enlist them in a revolt against this treatment facility."

"My father, Evert, led a *revolt* against Cottonwood?"

"Pretty damned near. He told the other family members that we were brainwashing you and the other clients and that the sexual abuse is a lie we've planted in your heads."

"I don't care. I still want to confront Evert. I want my day in court, to tell him, *publicly*, how much he fucked up my life. And Marjorie, too."

Garry took my hands in his and looked into my eyes. "Listen to me. We had to do it. Your father got some of the other family members, especially the other accused sex offenders, to rally with him. Some people wanted to leave."

"Oh no! You're kidding, right?"

"No, I'm not."

I pulled my hands away and stood up, wanting to run. He gently pulled me down into my chair.

"We spent some time with Emma after we figured out she was your sister," he said. "She wasn't happy either, when we told her we had to send your parents away, and why."

"Is Emma okay?"

"Yes, she's okay. We took care of her. She said that on the day your parents arrived, they didn't even acknowledge her, and that she felt very uncomfortable in the room with them and avoided them at breaks. When we told her what'd gone on in their small group and during breaks, she said she felt validated."

"Garry, I'm sorry."

"Why? It's not your fault."

"I know, but . . ." I felt incredible shame, a reflection of my parents.

"No 'buts' about it. Your father's behavior is *not* about you. It's about your father. Period." He held my hands tighter. "We've never experienced anything like this during family week. Your father is a violently sick man. He exhibits an insidious, um, intelligent violence that is truly frightening."

"What do you mean?"

"Although your father is, how should I put this, not as urbane, not as sophisticated as he might like to think—have you seen the Bermuda shorts?—he has an influential air about him. It's strange. Although he appears to be socially inept, he successfully persuaded a roomful of people to question their reasons for coming here. And, more importantly, to question why you survivors are here."

I felt too humiliated to cry. Too angry.

My parents' behavior was too validating. I had been holding out hope that my childhood hadn't been that bad.

"We put your mother and father in separate private offices to talk to them," Garry continued. "We didn't hold out any hope for your father, but we thought if we could get your mother away from him, we might reach her. But we couldn't. I talked to her myself, and she wouldn't budge an inch. She supports your father one hundred percent. There was something in her eyes, though. Apprehension, maybe. Fear? I saw tears in her eyes, but she would not allow herself to cry."

A tear in my heart.

"Emma watched them leave, your father stomping off in anger with your mother passively trailing behind. It was quite stirring." Garry cleared his throat as if holding back tears. "We're changing our family week program because of this. And we'll have to do a better job of screening accused sex offenders."

More validation.

Garry assured me it was not my fault. He said family members had settled down and we would proceed with family week as planned, minus my parents. I hoped this validating experience would help improve my relationship with Emma.

Two days later, we all gathered in the big conference room for our family sessions.

Mary was up first. Her mother took complete responsibility for not protecting her daughter from her husband's sexual assaults.

Then Roger. His wife agreed to marriage counseling and admitted she'd also been molested as a child, by a much older cousin. They wept together.

No one from Asher's family came, but he sat with the rest of us for support.

When it was my turn with Emma, her most significant issue with me was when I left her and Lily in Chicago without saying goodbye. She told me how terrified she'd been, not knowing where I was.

"We had to wait three days before the police would take a missing person report on you," she said. "Lorain, Linda, and I were frantic. We searched for you everywhere we could think of. We even went down to the beach several times looking for you. We thought maybe you pissed someone off at a bar and they killed you or something."

"I honestly didn't think anyone would look for me," I said. "I was so out of it, it didn't even occur to me to call until Jerome insisted. But it was only a few days before I called Evert to send my clothes."

"No, it was more like . . . it was at *least* ten days."

"I'm sorry, Emma," I apologized. "I didn't mean to hurt you. I felt I had to run for my life and wasn't thinking about anything else."

Then it was my turn. My resentment with Emma was her demand that I get rid of my cat, Casper. Michael gave him to me when I lived with Emma and Lily. He was a white, furry fluffball shedding his coat all over the orange sculpted carpet.

"Michael gave me that cat," I cried. "I loved him so much, and I still miss him." I realized as I said it that I meant Michael as much as Casper.

When Emma left for the day, we hugged for the first time since childhood.

Family week ended the next day. When Emma came to say goodbye, we hugged for the second time since we were kids.

Without my twin sister, it would have been easy to stay in denial forever, for the secrets to remain locked inside my mind's vault of lost memories. Were it not for Emma and the childhood survival games we played, I surely would have died, or at least stark raving mad.

* * * *

2nd grade. Springtime. I just turned eight. I wrote a story about a squirrel family for my sister Emma. I've written other stories, too. I read them to her, and then I hide them in a box with a pink lid that has white polka dots all over it, tied closed with a hot pink ribbon.

4th grade. Fall. Emma painted a beautiful picture of an eagle soaring over mountaintops in southwestern colors of coral, turquoise, ochre, and rust. It won an award and is hanging up at an elementary school in another neighborhood. I walk over to see it and wonder at all the parents admiring their kids' artwork. I admire Emma's eagle all by myself.

When the art show ends, Emma rolls up her picture and hides it with my story box. We must hide my stories and her drawings; if our mother finds them, she'll take them.

Thirteen

The date was set for my departure. My mind, however, had other ideas.

It began with a meditation tape Lara played while we fell asleep. She found it in a box we borrowed from the "library," a small closet filled with recovery books and cassettes. The sound of water trickling over river rocks grated on my nerves, keeping me awake in aggravated anticipation of the click at the end of the cassette.

On the third night, I felt I would suffocate from anxiety grabbing me by the throat. Gasping for air, I plummeted over the edge of a cliff inside a dark cavern, falling into a blackness of screams. The screams were mine . . .

A tempestuous bonfire blazes, obliterating the light of the stars overhead. Young women twirl in place while slowly dancing in a circle around the fire, arms swaying above their heads, eyelids flickering like flames. Their wispy white dresses flow about them as they dance.

I became insane with terror, fearing my three roommates were witches and that Lara, in particular, had been planted inside the treatment center to get me.

To get me for what? I didn't know. An old feeling of betrayal resurfaced as, alas, the witches of my past flew into my consciousness on broomsticks, sweeping away the lock on the drawer marked "Witches' Circle" in my mind's filing cabinet of lost memories.

My roommates gathered around me, but they were no help. They wore wispy, light-colored summer nightgowns, like the witches. And their smiling faces became those of a witch—sinister grins that would trick me into believing they wanted to help me. The trickling water on the meditation tape reminded me of tinkling little bells from my past, which I couldn't place. I pulled the cassette from the player and threw it across the room.

Lara tried to calm me down by telling me where she lived. "In a small town, up the road from Purgatory, in Colorado."

I freaked out. "*Purgatory?*" I wound into a ball as my roommates loomed over me, talking in the soothing voices of tricksters.

Lara's long, wavy hair, the color of muddy water, reminded me of my sister Lorain's hair. Even their names were alike. Then I saw my sister dancing with the witches around the fire burning in my mind.

Dar was on tech duty that night. She coaxed me outside with sheltering arms and walked me to the night nurse's office, where I curled in a chair for two hours before the fear subsided and I regained rational thought.

Garry Giles persuaded my insurance company to approve five more days for treatment, in which he scheduled daily counseling with him, and with Sharon. Terrified of the witch memory, not wanting it to be true, yet knowing it was, my last week at Cottonwood was dominated by a PTSD stupor from which I did not fully recover for many years. And even then, it lingered.

On the morning of my departure, several of us went outside with letters we'd written to our Higher Powers, which we attached to balloons. Mine was blue. Releasing our balloons would symbolize letting go of our childhood trauma, putting our lives into the care of God as we understood God. I rolled my God letter around a yellow flower I'd picked from the garden. Asher helped me tie it to my balloon.

On the count of three, we liberated our balloons in a gesture of spiritual freedom. Fittingly, mine hesitated. I was about to retrieve it and remove the weight of the flower when it drifted upward and lazily followed the others. The blue balloon the circus clown gave me when I was seven came to mind—it had escaped my grasp and blew away toward an unknown destination. This balloon, with my God letter, was supposed to reach God and release all my pain and confusion.

High above us, the wind blew our balloons eastward toward the Manzano Mountains, dots of purple, blue, orange, red, and yellow fading into the distance. I wanted to fly with them, imagining their journey, wondering who would find them. Would they make it to God?

Lorain and I coordinated our flights to meet at the Austin airport. They were already there when I arrived. "Thank you, Lorain," I said, trying not to picture my sister dancing around a fire. Elsa's outstretched arms were medicine as I grabbed her to my heart, forlorn for our future.

"We love Elsa *so* much. Rick and Gina wanted to keep her," Lorain said. "She's the *sweetest* thing. We'll take her anytime you want."

"That means a lot to me, Lorain." I hugged her, wishing she could stay forever—to face the truth and heal together. I relished every moment of the light-hearted chatter and delicious dinner she prepared that night. In the morning, Elsa and I took her to the airport for her flight back to Chicago.

Ray Gunn, PhD, resumed our counseling sessions with the continuation of reliving details of my childhood, which now included unabated memories of witchcraft, which I called Occult Abuse—abusing occult knowledge for evil—because I discovered in extensive research at the Austin public library that not all occult practices were evil. Benevolent worshippers of the moon and nature called themselves white witches. As did Wiccans.

Since the unveiling of Occult Abuse, the latest complex twist to my story, I felt a loss of confidence in Ray. I suspected it might be too much for him, that he wanted to get rid of me. But I didn't want to be rid of him. I loved Ray. Truthfully, I was a bit obsessed.

My boss greeted me with a hug, happy to have me back at work. I did the best I could to get out payroll, file employee insurance claims, and design spreadsheets for the budget.

At home, I sang a new bedtime song to Elsa, "Song of the Soul," which we all sang at Cottonwood after group counseling sessions: *"Open mine eyes that I may see, glimpses of truth Thou hast for me . . ."* by Cris Williamson.

After placing Elsa—asleep like a sack of rocks—in her crib, I'd trudge to my bedroom to lie wide awake, hiding under the covers, fearful of every bump in the night, the reality of my life repeating over and over like a skipped record.

I dragged myself to work in the mornings, rushing to my office to close the door and stare out the window at the University of Texas students walking back and forth along Guadalupe Street below. My boss rapped on my door every hour, each knock frazzling another nerve.

In my mind, I replayed the ugly truth day and night. There was no glamor in a childhood such as mine. No heartfelt, lingering memories to pass on to grandchildren. No chronicles of a youth well spent. I didn't have a heart-warming Hallmark story of the beautiful pain of adolescence. Instead, I would leave a legacy of a tragic, disgusting, unmemorable childhood of sexual abuse at the hands of my *father*. Added to incest, the fact that my parents had initiated me into a coven of black witches was hard to take.

Elsa's first birthday came at the end of August. Pamela and Ted invited us over to celebrate. Pamela had become my best friend by now. She made a white cake with chocolate frosting and placed a single candle in the center. We clapped and cheered when Elsa's pursed lips on her radiant face blew out the candle.

By September, the flashbacks had become debilitating. The hallucinations weren't like LSD hallucinations—psychedelic-colored paisley patterns and cartoon animals beckoning me to follow them on cartoon trails at night. No. My PTSD hallucinations were a reliving of my past as if it were happening again. I'd hear chanting outside my windows in a language I didn't recognize, yet did. Big, dark shadows of robed figures loitered in the corners of my eyes, vanishing when I turned to look at them. Scenes from my childhood exploded in my head, in no particular order . . .

I'm lying on a metal table, naked, the light so bright it hurts my eyes. I don't know what I'm doing here. People are walking by the open door.

I was three, in the hospital having my kidney removed. I wanted my sister Ellyn to stay with me, but hospitals didn't allow that in the 1960s. This led to other memories of lying naked on stone altars—three, four, five years old. The child I had once been took me back to watch . . .

I'm in a room with lots of stuff: paintings and tapestries hanging on walls; large, heavy, dark furniture with porcelain figurines on tables; satin textiles thrown on dusty-red overstuffed chairs; a winding staircase in the center of the room. This place has an ancient feel to it, as in medieval times. A man is wearing a black cape with horns on his head. An altar stands near the spiral staircase. That's where I am, lying on top of it. The man talks to me, but I can't understand him. I do not move or speak. I must obey or suffer, just short of death.

There's blood everywhere, all over me. It's awful, sticky, with a horrible smell. There are other adults here, standing in a half-circle around me. They're swaying in black robes, chanting something in a whisper. A bright light comes

146

shining from somewhere, a spotlight obliterating everything but me on the altar and the man with horns standing above me. I know the horns aren't real. Is the blood real?

Me, the altar, the chanting, the blood—it's a game for them.

Why are adults playing this ridiculous, scary game with a child?

"What's happening to me, Ray?" I cried in our next session. My whole body trembled, even my teeth. I imagined how the filing cabinet inside my mind's vault of memories might look—drawers open wide with files of memories strewn about, the papers inside fluttering here and there, dark witches on broomsticks sweeping them into a tornado.

Ray kept assuring me we'd get it all out, together, and I'd be fine.

That night, my recollection was of boyfriends, when I was fifteen . . .

Summer. Finally! 1974. I just finished freshman year. My grades aren't that great, except English, the only class I liked. I already know two classes I want to take sophomore year—Earth Science instead of Biology, and Psychology, a new course they're offering. It should be interesting.

A few weeks ago, leaving the grocery store on Oakton Street, I saw Michael in the parking lot. He must have seen me go into the store and waited. He pulled up and asked if I wanted a ride. I said no and walked off. He followed me, driving very slowly, crooning, "Come ooon, get in." But I refused again and again. Then I ignored him, looked straight ahead, and kept walking. My heart cracked when he gave up and drove off.

Sometimes I see Michael at Kostner Park, but he's usually with Robin, *and she acts like she's too good for us. I try not to think about him, but always hope he'll drive up when I'm there, minus* Robin. *He doesn't come to the park as much as he used to, now that* she's *back from vacation.*

Adrienne, Alex, Emma, and I still hang out at Kostner Park with the other guys. We pile into their souped-up cars and drag race down Highway 41 on our way to the ruins of McCormick's mansion; the McCormick spice family's demolished estate on Lake Michigan, called Villa Turicum. All that's left is the cracked cement swimming pool, an archway, and two winding cement stairways going down to the beach.

We trip on acid out there sometimes. It's pitch dark, with no streetlights, so the darkness acts as a negative canvas upon which to paint any LSD reality our minds wish. Friendly little psychedelic rabbits and squirrels wave and beckon me to follow them down trails painted in Day-Glo cartoon images. I experience the psychedelic paths, not just see them, because when I trip on acid, everything is an experience—every thought, emotion, idea, even what I hear, see, touch and smell. Each acid trip is a wild, mind-expanding journey to Ixtlan, like Carlos Castaneda's adventures with don Juan Matus. Another reality.

This guy named Jim has been coming with us to McCormick's mansion. He drives a 1969 navy-blue souped-up Camaro, and he's cute. He's got long red hair, a clean-shaven baby face, and small, bright eyes the color of an afternoon summer sky, the season right now. Naturally, all the girls are after him.

Yesterday, we all met at Jody's house so Jim could pick one of us. I'm serious. It's true. And guess what? He picked me!

The other girls are so jealous. I'm acting extra nice to them because I don't want them to be mad at me.

In Ray's office the next day, I told him about my drug overdose a couple months after meeting Jim . . .

Dianna and I drive to St. Paul Woods in her cute little Triumph Spitfire to buy Angel Dust, a dime bag—ten dollars. We snort some and then head over to Kostner Park. I keep snorting on the way. Dianna says she's already too high.

148

"A dime of Angel Dust is nothing for me," I gloat.

"I don't know, Hanna. I think this stuff is cut with something."

I claim I don't care and keep on snorting.

Hell yeah, that Angel Dust was cut with something!

I only remember bits and pieces of the rest of the night, at some point ending up with Adrienne and Jim. I broke up with Jim a couple of weeks ago, after we went to the car races with Michael and Robin, *because I wanted Michael, not Jim—not like that's going to happen. I don't know how I ended up with Jim tonight. We're back together now, I guess.*

The ambulance ride to the hospital is completely erased from my memory, but I'm starting to come down from the Angel Dust now. My father's walking into the hospital room, lumbering toward me through waves that distort him like carnival funhouse mirrors. He looks so round and fat, like an oversized, bulbous helium balloon, that I laugh and laugh. I can't stop, pretty sure I comment on his rotundness. Then he shrinks to an hourglass, and I laugh harder.

A few hours later, I guess, an orderly wheels me to my father's car. Adrienne is in the hallway talking to a police officer. I don't know where Jim is.

As soon as I get out of bed this morning and stagger to the kitchen, my mother says, "You're grounded!" trying to sound all authoritative and shit. I'm like, "Yeah, right," though I do kinda feel like I might need to dry out for a while.

I have been doing a lot of drugs. I'm still high from that Angel Dust.

Disregarding my mother, I stroll over to Kostner Park. Adrienne's here.

"What happened last night?" I ask her. "Besides the hospital, I remember you and Jim propping me up on your shoulders and walking me around a parking lot. On Howard Street?"

"Yeah, we were trying to walk you down. You were talking about God and Satan all night. We walked you around that parking lot, and then over to Jim's

house, and you went completely berserk in the backyard, certain you were going to die and Satan would take you away."

"Shit!" I bark, and then, "Oh, yeah, I sorta remember that part, rolling around in Jim's backyard, totally freaked out. But I don't remember saying anything about God or Satan."

"Well, you did. It was really creepy. We didn't know what to do. We had *to call the ambulance. We thought you might be dying. I'm sorry. I'm sure you're in big trouble."*

"It's okay. Yeah, my mother tried grounding me, but here I am." I spread my arms out, palms facing upward.

I'm still high. And humbled, though I'm not going to tell anybody that. *When I go home later, I'm gonna stay in the house for a few days. I need it. To dry out.*

"I was such an idiot!"

Ray rolled his chair over to me, sitting on the couch, and took my hands.

"How old were you?"

"Fifteen."

"You were only a child, Hanna. Fifteen-year-olds are still children."

Ray glanced at the clock. Our session was over for the day.

At work, my boss, Candace, came into my office several times a day to check on me.

Candace had shared her own story of childhood abuse and that she, too, was in counseling. She missed a lot of work, mostly Mondays and Fridays, due to *her* inability to function up to par. Thus, we supported each other. Once, when I was especially afraid, she spent the night.

On the day Candace found me hiding under my desk, I had completed no work for several days. She closed my office door and gently helped me into my chair. "I'm sorry, Hanna," she said, "but I have a job to do, and so do you. If you want to keep yours, you'll have to get more help, either back in New Mexico or someplace else."

Ray agreed. He set another thirty-five days at Cottonwood de Albuquerque, including arrangements for Elsa to go with me this time. A woman who worked in the Cottonwood business office offered to take care of her and bring her to see me on Sundays, visiting days. I took another leave of absence and thanked my boss for understanding.

Ray's car broke down a few days before I left for New Mexico. I offered to lend him mine while we were gone. "Okay, great! I'll take you to the airport and take your car from there," he said.

Fall was just beginning on the October morning I bundled up Elsa and drove to Ray's brand-new house in a brand-new, upscale Austin subdivision. A young son, waddling around in a diaper, greeted us at the door. He looked just like his daddy, who came up behind him and invited us inside. He motioned us into a furnitureless room filled with boxes and walked away, shoes clicking on ceramic tiles. I heard muffled voices—Ray and his wife talking. When he returned, with a harried, "Come on, we're gonna be late," he shooed us out of the room and ran out the front door.

I hustled to catch up, placing Elsa in her car seat while Ray jumped in the driver's seat. I hopped in the passenger seat, barely buckling my seatbelt before Ray sped off to the airport, hardly stopping to drop us off at departures.

I threw Elsa in her stroller, checked our luggage at the curbside check-in, and ran at top speed to the gate, Elsa giggling with glee. We missed the plane.

Ray huffed and said he couldn't come back for us when I finally reached him on the phone an hour later.

Pamela picked us up and took us to her house.

In her son's bedroom, where Elsa and I were to sleep that night, I moped all afternoon, steeped in self-pity because Ray had refused to return to the airport.

Pamela came in and asked, "How are you doing?"

"Eh, not good."

"Hanna, are you sure you want to get better?"

"*What?*"

"Don't be upset. I'm just asking."

"Why?"

"This chaos you're experiencing has been going on now for *months*. I'm just wondering how much longer you're going to allow it."

"Allow what?" I snapped defensively.

"Please, Hanna, don't get mad at me," she said, taking my hands in hers. "I love you so much. You're a sister to me. I hate to see you in this dark place. I want you to live. Do you understand? Do you think antidepressants might help?"

"Oh, because I told you I wanted to kill myself."

"Well, yes. I don't see any improvement at all. You seem worse now than before you went to Cottonwood last July. Will it help this time? Do you think maybe you should try another therapist?"

Pamela didn't understand the treatment model popular at that time, which neglected to include a respite from remembering every dark secret of one's life.

. . . Well, perhaps she did.

As far as medications were concerned, that same therapy model believed in addressing the issues rather than medicating them. Pills were band-aids, the wounds festering beneath.

I didn't speak to Pamela until she dropped us off at the airport in the morning. "Thanks for everything," I said sarcastically, refusing a goodbye hug.

Fourteen

Dar greeted us at the Albuquerque airport. She grinned and cooed over Elsa all the way to Cottonwood, where we deposited her at the business office with the woman who assured me she would provide the best care. I kissed Elsa goodbye and hesitantly walked over to the counseling building.

"Hi, Sharon. Good to see you. But not good." I smiled. "Ya know?"

"Good to see you, too, Hanna. I'm glad you came back."

"Thanks. I've been having a rough time."

"I heard," she said and got right to the point, her typical style. "Dr. Gunn and I have spoken frequently about your case, and we're concerned about your intense PTSD symptoms, especially the hallucinations that accompany your flashbacks."

Dr. Gunn? I wasn't used to hearing Ray referred to as a doctor, though the PhD after his name meant Doctor of Philosophy.

Sharon said she and Ray Gunn, PhD, weren't sure how to help me in my current state of meltdown.

"Our concern is that you might have a psychotic episode," she said, without explaining what that meant.

They hadn't considered their therapy technique—drawing out every detail of my childhood—as a contributing factor to my evocative PTSD symptoms. Instead, Sharon admitted, "I've consulted a psychiatrist. Your appointment is tomorrow morning."

Sharon hadn't asked for my consent to discuss my case with a psychiatrist, much less make an appointment for me. I assumed Ray knew and hadn't mentioned it either. It didn't feel good to know my case had been discussed with a third party behind my back. I could have refused, I suppose, but I didn't.

After dinner, I met my roommates. We sat outside until a tech sent us to our room at midnight, where I spent the remaining hours until daylight curled in my assigned bed in restless anxiety.

In the morning, after breakfast, a tech drove me to Albuquerque for my appointment. To my astonishment, he pulled up at a psychiatric hospital.

"What are we doing *here*?"

"This is the address Sharon gave me for Dr. Dumass," said the tech.

Sharon had failed to mention the psychiatrist was located in a psychiatric hospital. Surely, they weren't thinking of dumping me there, were they?

Too surprised to protest, I reluctantly, defensively, entered the psychiatrist's office. The rebel within me took charge. I was on high alert, ready to fight, sarcasm my weapon of choice.

Dr. Dumass had ghostlike white skin, made even more so by his contrasting dark hair. He was my height, around 5' 8" or so, with a thin, boyish body. His jade eyes were rather attractive, though, behind stylish glasses.

"Hello. I'm Dr. Dumass," he said. "Please, have a seat."

He didn't offer to shake hands. I quickly withdrew mine.

Dr. Dumass took a seat in his comfortable-looking leather chair behind his mahogany desk, his chair positioned slightly higher than the narrow, straight-back chair he offered me. I perched rigidly before him, facing a *psychiatrist* from across the span of his desktop. A green-shaded lamp, a stack of books, the back of a picture frame, and several file folders covered the expanse between us.

He began grilling me as if conducting an interrogation. Having never been to a psychiatrist before, I was quite taken aback by his strange questions.

"What is your name?" The psychiatrist's first question.

"Hanna."

"And how old are you, Hanna?"

"Twenty-nine. Isn't it right there on that piece of paper you're looking at?"

Disregarding my question as if I hadn't asked it, he continued. "Do you know what year this is?"

"Uh, 1988?" *That's a weird question.*

"Good, good. Do you know where you are, Hanna?" His syrupy voice oozed with condescension. His superior, distant persona reminded me of a picture of Sigmund Freud, minus the goatee, and I half expected him to pull out a pipe of sweet-smelling tobacco.

"Uh, yeah. Do *you* know where we are?" Unnerved, I was cynical.

The good doctor smiled. "Who is the president?"

"President? You mean of the United States? What the hell kind of question is that?" How was this guy going to help me by asking these stupid questions?

"Yes, Hanna. Who is the president? Of the United States." He half smiled, but I sensed a slight irritation.

I was irritated. "Ronald Reagan. And I'm in New Mexico, being asked a bunch of ridiculous questions. Oh, maybe I better specify. I'm in Albuquerque."

Dr. Dumass smirked. And after several more absurd questions, asked, "Does the radio or television ever speak to you?"

"What do you mean?" *Someone is nuts here, and I don't think it's me.*

"Do you ever think there are messages on the radio or TV, telling you to do things?"

"No. Like, what kind of things?" *Where is this cat going with this?*

"So, your answer is no."

"Are there people who believe the radio and TV speak to them?" I asked, seriously, without sarcasm.

Dr. Dumass looked at me as if I knew the answer and was playing dumb.

Ignoring my question, he asked, "Do you hear voices in your head telling you to do things?"

My fright jumped up a few notches. *Had* the plan been to lock me up there?

"What's this all about? Why are you asking me these questions? Do you think I'm some kind of nutcase or something?"

"I'm just trying to ascertain the nature of your hallucinations, whether caused by your obvious PTSD or an underlying psychiatric condition."

"Oh. Okay. I get it. So, after all the therapy talk of getting to the *root* of my troubles, all the talk about PTSD symptoms, which include hallucinations, are you now going to suggest I'm some sort of lunatic?"

"No, no, nothing like that. I've been told you are in an almost constant state of flashbacks, and we are trying to help you." The tone he used chilled with iced arrogance.

My heart sank. *We?* A conspiracy with Ray and Sharon? With such authority they'd assured me the key to recovery from childhood abuse was dropping defense mechanisms to get to the core of the trauma. They promised that after re-experiencing *all* the emotions associated with the abuse, I'd be healed. Yeah, right. Now this.

I chose not to tell Dr. Dumass about the time little green men sat on my shoulders—one telling me to go this way, the other to go that way. Granted, I'd smoked a whole ounce of marijuana with a friend, but still. Then there was all that acid I ingested in my teen years. But those LSD hallucinations—cartoons and swirling paisley patterns—were different from what I was experiencing now.

"The PTSD hallucinations are mostly auditory; I hear chanting almost all the time," I said. "But sometimes I also see shadowy figures in my peripheral vision, and when I'm driving at night, sometimes I see people in dark robes along the roadway that disappear when I look directly at them. It's creepy. I know it's not real, but sometimes I think it is. I'm afraid. All the time."

"Uh huh," Dr. Dumass muttered, taking notes.

At the end of our interview, Dr. Dumass's diagnosis was Post Traumatic Stress Disorder, the same diagnosis I'd received from Ray Gunn, PhD, and Cottonwood psychologist Guy Peterson, PhD.

"I see no indication of mental illness," he said. "PTSD is not a mental illness, it's a disorder that can be treated with psychotherapy counseling. However, I am prescribing a drug typically used for psychosis. called Haldol, which will stop the hallucinations."

He walked me to the door, handing me prescriptions for Haldol and a drug to alleviate its side effects, benztropine. *A drug for side effects of a drug?*

The tech who'd driven me there escorted me to the on-site pharmacy to fill the prescriptions, and then watched me swallow a tablet of Haldol.

By the time we made the trip back to Cottonwood, the Haldol side effects had taken hold: I felt simultaneously sleepy and hyper, my left eyebrow lifted up and down, and my right shoulder twitched. When we got back to Cottonwood, I took the benztropine; within minutes, the drug knocked me out.

For the next several days that I consented to take the Haldol and benztropine, I could hardly wake up in the morning. Staff members berated me for being late for breakfast and early morning group therapy sessions, where I sat gaping at my fellow trauma buddies, unable to speak. The daylight hours were a muffled blur. I laid down right after dinner and fell into a stupor.

In a rare lucid moment one night, my roommates expressed their concern and convinced me to stop taking the drugs.

I agreed, to the chagrin of the night nurse who tried to force me to take them.

Off the drugs, I participated in group and individual therapy, though I kept my memories to myself, jotting them in my journal instead. No longer incessantly talking about my Occult Abuse lessened its intensity. In place of heaving emotional flashbacks of witchcraft, I felt sad, but not devastated.

Cottonwood de Albuquerque's core philosophy opposed psychiatric medications, even antidepressants. Their admission procedures included an evaluation of clients' prescriptions, weaning them off the antidepressants and psychotropic drugs many had been taking for years. Counselors explained that the mainstream medical model was heavily reliant on pharmaceuticals, that it had not yet gleaned a full understanding of the manifestations of PTSD. Thus, typical psychiatrists and physicians often misdiagnosed the symptoms of PTSD as depression or mental illness, prescribing antidepressants or heavy-duty drugs such as Lithium and Haldol.

I was lucky I hadn't come across one of those doctors, even though some part of me would have liked a pill to make the pictures disappear. Still, I wholeheartedly agreed that it was better to face the truth than to drug it, despite the intense pain and remorse—the price for meeting memories unmedicated.

Free from the effects of Haldol, I enjoyed my next Sunday visit with Elsa.

Although my preemie was over a year old, she hadn't started walking, but she was trying. My back ached from stooping over her with my fingers in her tight grip, walking her around the yard. To everyone's delight, she led me from one person to another, smiling and laughing with joy, showing off her monumental accomplishment of putting one foot in front of the other. It was the simple things of being a mother that kept me going. One step at a time, one moment at a time, one day at a time. I saw several staff members loitering in the area, people who wouldn't normally be there on a Sunday afternoon. I presumed they were watching to see if I was a good mother.

A few days later, a bald man showed up for drug and alcohol treatment, on the other side of the campus. I noticed him immediately—his eyes were a penetrating blue, and he had an aura about him, an energy field that was palpable, and not good.

He seemed familiar, but I couldn't think of when or where I would have met him. I sensed him watching me, and he tried talking to me several times. Terrified that people from my past had sent him to scare me into silence, I begged staff members to check him out.

After interviewing the bald man, Garry asked him to leave, refusing to tell me why. I observed an increased hypervigilance among counselors and staff, carefully scrutinizing every new client admitted.

I spent my time quietly studying new clients as well. And continued to keep my memories to myself, writing them down in my journal instead of talking about them.

Ironically, it wasn't the bald man who scared me into silence—it was the fear of being forced to take those meds that would have put me back in the stupor wherein I wouldn't have even noticed that bald man. I felt less vulnerable being aware of my surroundings, rather than drugged, regardless of the fear and paranoia which was perhaps what I needed to stay safe.

My second thirty-five-day stint at Cottonwood de Albuquerque came to an end the first week of November, 1988. Again, I was sent home with instructions to keep remembering my childhood trauma, sans coping skills. This time, Sharon invited me to attend Cottonwood's aftercare group counseling with their Bastrop facility, located thirty-five miles southeast of Austin. Conveniently for me, aftercare met in Austin, within walking distance of my apartment. Sandra, an Austin artist, would be graduating from treatment two days after me. Sharon and Garry urged us to continue role-playing and anger work together, and with others we'd meet in aftercare. We agreed and exchanged phone numbers.

I signed my aftercare plan and collected the unused bottles of Haldol and benztropine. Dar drove me and Elsa to the airport.

I dumped the bottle of Haldol in an airport trash bin as soon as Dar left, but kept the benztropine because I knew it'd make me sleep.

Satisfied, I boarded the plane, snuggling Elsa against my heart.

Within days, occult memories flooded just about every waking moment of my post-Cottonwood life.

Without the structure and community of the treatment center, I was a stripped-down version of myself. A naked little girl who still needed to be taught about life, *my* life as an incest and Occult Abuse survivor. I didn't know how I was going to do it, but I would survive.

I called my boss several days after we got home. She said, "Sorry, Hanna. If you'd contacted me as soon as you'd gotten back, you'd still have your job," and fired me. I didn't blame her. Truthfully, it was a relief, allowing me to devote more time to reliving the events which had brought me to this point in my life—a total wreck.

I registered with a temporary employment agency so I could take days off when I needed to put together more pieces of the jigsaw puzzle scattered across my mind. I was willing to face the financial hardship coming, believing I would finish the puzzle, even if I had to dig under sofa cushions to find all the oddly shaped missing pieces invading my thoughts; some dark, some light, and some just messed up.

In a moment of clarity, I snapped together a string of puzzle pieces depicting a poignant crossroads at age sixteen, when I quit dropping acid—one of my attempts to have a normal life. Maybe the LSD had opened my mind to a new perception of possibilities, propelling me to think about what I wanted to do with my life: study anthropology or become a writer. I looked at the picture taking shape out of those LSD-laden puzzle pieces . . .

It's Wintertime. 1974. I started high school last September. Can't believe Christmas is over and the new year has begun. Seems like a long winter this year, with at least *another two months. Damn, most of my* life *is winter. Cold. Snow. Icy, snow-packed roads that crunch with the weight of cars rolling by, the crunch louder than the cars' engines. But wintertime is my favorite time for tripping on acid, which I've been dropping ever since my sister Emma's old boyfriend turned us on in the seventh grade. Windowpane, Blotter, Orange Sunshine, Microdot. It's all the same, creating multicolored, swirling, paisley-patterned paths in the snow, lighting up the night with psychedelic colors of neon pink and green.*

Sometimes I buy acid at school. We have twenty minutes free between fourth and fifth period and about twenty of us girls hang out in the bathroom down the hall from the dean's office, smoking cigarettes and lighting up joints or passing around a hash pipe. A straight-looking girl, who never wears blue jeans, opens her school folder to show sheets of Blotter stuffed behind her algebra homework. I swear! It's crazy! In another bathroom upstairs, a teacher comes in and smokes with us—cigarettes though, not pot. We don't smoke pot in that bathroom.

Last weekend, I went to a party at Anne's house. She lives across the street and kitty-corner from Dianna. Dianna was grounded, as usual, and couldn't come to the party. Anne's parents were out of town, so everyone at the party stayed all night, piling into Anne's finished basement, furnished like a den, with couches and a bar and windows up above at street level.

Anne, Jodi, and I drop some acid. Purple Microdot. Around midnight, the three of us snuck over to Dianna's house and talked to her through her bedroom window. The colors in the snow were so beautiful, the night lit up in LSD Land.

When we got back to Anne's house we listened to Emerson, Lake and Palmer's new album, Brain Salad Surgery. *Everyone drank and smoked pot, and we partied until daylight.*

That acid-trip night marked a turning point. Something shifted in my mind and I have a deeper understanding of life and human nature. I know it's a personal voyage I cannot explain or try to make anyone else understand.

Anne experienced something that changed her thinking, too. It was as if our minds became one and we didn't need to speak. We were on a higher thought plane, way beyond the material world. Jodi wasn't there with us, but she sat and observed us, seeming to understand.

Late the next morning, after we came down off the acid, I told Anne we shouldn't talk about it because people might not get it. But she's so freaked out by our shared experience, she can't stop talking about it. Everyone thinks she's nuts. I told her that would happen, but did she listen to me?

Come inside, the show's about to start
Guaranteed to blow your head apart
"Karn Evil 9: 1st Impression, Part 2"

. . . January 1975. Will winter never end? My second semester of sophomore year just started. I'm turning sixteen soon.

Mark, aka Eagle, is picking me up for a party at Julie's house. I'm wearing my new plaid jacket with a fake fur collar and double-breasted round buttons, which is "in" this year. I've got on crisp new blue jeans and boots, feeling very fashionable.

I drop a hit of acid as I walked to Eagle's car—Blotter, a perfectly round droplet of LSD dripped carefully onto the tiny square of paper I swallow. By the time we reach Julie's house, I begin experiencing the colors of whirling paisleys that light up the winter night. The paisley patterns swirl in psychedelic pinks and greens, like a Peter Maxx poster, illuminating every detail of every snowflake, creating a wonderland of beautifully colored paths that only exist in LSD Land.

I haven't completely found my voice, but am well on my way, at least in the house I live in. I'm smart now; I leave when I feel like it and don't return until I'm good and ready. No one asks where I'm going. No one asks where I've been. If they do, I tell them to fuck off.

Tonight, Eagle decides to freak me out while I'm on acid, which I didn't share with him. He does this by staring at me the entire night. No words. Just staring. As my paranoia increases, I glance furtively towards him. He does his he, he, he *laugh with no sound, pointing a finger at me.*

The room is shrinking, growing smaller and smaller. All the kids milling about become nothing but blurred shapes and muted, indecipherable sounds. I am only aware of the sharp outline and image of Eagle, the intense penetration of his blue eyes, even his glass eye that doesn't move, and I wonder how they were able to match that exact midday-sky-blue color.

Why are you doing this? *I plead with my dark blue eyes.*

The silent he, he, he *and pointing finger is all I get.*

Eagle isn't my boyfriend or anything. I just like him so much as a friend, or at least I did. He's been the boyfriend of both my friend Dianna and my sister Emma. I could never think of him any other way, even though I think he is exceptionally good looking with those sky-blue eyes and long black hair. You know how you meet or see someone you find so attractive you can't stop looking at them, but they just aren't for you? Well, that's how I think of Eagle. Except now, after tonight, when he's deliberately trying to freak me out, maybe I don't like him so much anymore. What does he want from me?

Acid freak-outs force you to face yourself. You question everything.

Who am I? What am I doing at this party? Why am I wearing this jacket with a faux fur collar? What's going on? Really *going on?*

Things like that. You analyze everything. Eagle knows this and I sense he's trying to teach me a lesson about LSD, maybe thinks I should stop?

163

I will myself not to look at Eagle. I feel like I'm moving through thick plasma that jiggles as I weave around the other kids to find a dark corner far away from him. Sitting on the floor, I try to hide within the little ball I've made of my body, curled over my bent knees. My mind wanders, and I think about school. . .

I like Earth Science so far, and of course, English. Last semester, I got an A+ for my book report on Ape and Essence *by Aldous Huxley. My teacher wrote on my paper that I have great insight and asked me to stay after class to talk about it. I was so surprised. I have that same teacher for English this semester, and am really happy about that.*

A new course offered this year, Psychology, is unusual. The teacher talks about things I've never thought about. She's kind of weird, though. She chews on her tongue, twisting it sideways in her mouth.

I like what I'm learning in school.

But I also like LSD. Sometimes I act like a guru when I'm on mind-blowing, mind-expanding acid trips. A few friends sit in a semicircle around me while I tell them about the teachings of don Juan Matus, the Yaqui shaman that Carlos Castaneda writes about in his book, Journey to Ixtlan. *My mind has expanded on acid, and I play a game with it, seeing how long I can keep myself from peaking—the height of the acid trip when the hallucinations take over. It's a challenge to see if my mind is stronger than the drug. LSD opens my mind to new ways of thinking about and analyzing the world—the* real *world—a reality so different from my usual thoughts that drown me in self-doubt and uncertainty.*

But I've been taking LSD since I was twelve. It may be causing me to over-analyze reality; I've noticed I talk backwards sometimes, as if my thoughts are way ahead of my words. I don't know how else to explain it. Maybe I'm getting burnt out.

A couple of weeks ago, Dianna and I wanted acid so badly we drove all the way to Old Town in Chicago in her beige VW bug. We asked everyone we saw if they had acid until a guy on a corner sold us what he said was Pink Microdot, but wasn't. There were indents in the tiny circles of pink, which were all different sizes, but we were so desperate we bought them anyway, willing ourselves to trip on pink pieces of plastic.

So, yeah, maybe Eagle is intentionally freaking me out because he cares about me. And maybe he's right. Maybe I should quit dropping acid. But if I do, what will become of reality?

. . . Summertime. 1976. I finished my junior year in May. Traffic's Low Spark of High Heeled Boys *is always on the stereo at Howie's place. Howie turned me on to this album, and I really like it. Howie has turned me on to lots of things. Music. Ideas. Lots of reefer, though it's not my favorite.*

I met Howie last winter, back when I was still taking acid trips, lots of them. I'm having a lot of trouble talking to people since I stopped dropping acid, after that fucked-up abortion my parents forced me to get. Howie seems to understand, and I don't have to try to make sense when we talk. I don't have to talk at all. It's cool with him. He lives across the alley with his mom, and helps me get through the day by always being there, offering an open invitation to their apartment with the old-fashioned glass door knobs that look like giant diamond-cut crystals. I can always count on Howie's happiness to see me when I come knocking on the door. We float on his waterbed listening to music, getting high, and talking forever, or not talking. He offered to marry me when I was pregnant last year, before that fucking abortion. He was so sweet and genuine about it. Now why don't I fall in love with him?

Howie fell in love with me, I think.

And I'm beginning to see, with alarm, that other guys may have really liked me, too, more than just a friend. Guys I could be myself around, like with a brother. I'm always disappointed when they want more, because I've so much enjoyed their friendship. . . well, maybe they fall in lust *for me.*

165

Whatever enlightenment I had gained by putting those pieces together, like every other independent thought I'd ever had, slunk beneath my mind-fucked perceptions instilled during my upbringing, activating a crushing reversion to self-doubt.

Yet, seeds of awareness had been planted, left to germinate in the soils of future experiences that would nourish the truth.

Fifteen

No longer able to afford my two-bedroom apartment, Pamela and Ted helped me move our furniture into their garage. Judith and Denny invited us to stay with them until I got another job. We put Elsa's crib in Augustus's room with him, Judith gave me the guest room, and I registered with a temporary employment agency first thing in the morning.

The temp agency placed me on a long-term assignment in an accounting office. Judith and I took turns getting the babies ready in the morning, and then one of us would take them to Augustus's babysitter, Mrs. Lopez. Judith and I shared clothes, too, but I mostly borrowed hers for work because I had to look more professional for this job than at jeans-on-Friday KLRU-TV, which I missed terribly.

Losing my job at KLRU-TV meant losing my health insurance. Ray offered to pay for COBRA insurance coverage, which would extend it for eighteen more months. Although I questioned his ethics, paying a client's medical insurance, I still needed help—lots of it—so I allowed him to pay the monthly premium.

Ray upped our therapy sessions to every day after work, which would more than cover his out-of-pocket expense for my COBRA premium.

We continued as before—Ray assisting me on a journey back in time, me ending up a slobbering mess on his office floor.

Angela, a co-worker at my new temp job, befriended me on the first day. She talked about her life and asked about mine while we smoked cigarettes outside the back door, shivering in the pre-Christmas chill. Whatever I said or didn't say, she must have sensed something was wrong because she took it upon herself to do both our jobs. Stuck as I was in another dimension, reliving my horrific childhood, it was too much for me to concentrate on anything not related to the care of Elsa; the numbers in the accounting ledgers looked like a foreign language. Shrouded in shame for accepting Angela's help, I avoided her compassionate eyes when she'd walked over to gather my account ledgers. Thanks to her, I earned enough money to get a one-bedroom apartment, a fraction of the cost of a two-bedroom.

Fleeting glimpses of a Christmas tree at Judith and Denny's house, in the den next to the kitchen, are all I remember of Christmas 1988. Whether Elsa and I moved out before or after, I can't say, but we were definitely in the new apartment in January, because that's when my life turned sideways. Again.

Judith helped me set up Elsa's crib in the single bedroom, along with the bed Marjorie and Evert bought for me after Elsa was born. It didn't matter that we had only one bedroom now; I didn't sleep in that bed Evert bought. Instead, I spent nights in the living room, listening with hypervigilance for the tiniest bump, thankful when daylight grayed the sky.

I was so tired I couldn't think straight, distracted by bubbles of memories popping to the surface of my consciousness like little plastic buoys on a fishing line. The tormented fishes of my soul kept trying to pull them back down, deep into the unseen darkness, while Ray kept snapping their hooks.

I could no longer tell myself I was doing okay at that temp job. I started missing work, unable to circumvent my growing fears. The temp agency fired me, which meant I was eligible for unemployment checks. Relieved, I said goodbye to Angela, one of the many angels I met along the way. I hope I thanked her for doing my job.

Unemployed, I retired to my living room and Ray's office. I'd drop off Elsa at Mrs. Lopez's in the mornings, then drive to my psychotherapy sessions as if reliving my childhood had become my new full-time job. Ray continued counseling me to recall every trauma-driven event of my life and experience the emotions. "Regurgitating your feelings, a purging of the pain," he would say with zealous conviction. Sometimes I'd be at his office all day, sitting with a magazine or staring into space in the waiting room between clients. "You *will* overcome your past one day," was his daily refrain.

I needed extra support many weekends, meeting Ray at his office to weep in despair. Even then, he looked well-manicured in his cardigans, jeans with an ironed crease, and loafers. I hated to watch him get in his car and drive home to his wife and kids. One weekend I told him about my "dreams" . . .

My mother takes me and my sisters out of the house late at night after she makes me swallow a horrible drink. She takes us into the forest, where my father waits with the others. Emma and I are three, four, five, six, seven. Lorain is two years older.

We return at daybreak and get into our beds. I lie still, trying really hard to be waking up from a dream. Early morning sunlight glows through the paper shades my mother pulls down over the windows in the bedroom I share with my twin. She whispers, "Shhh, go back to sleep," as she tiptoes out and quietly closes the door with a soft thump. "Was that a dream?" a twin will whisper, the other one replying, "I don't know."

As strange childhood wanderings in the forest slid open the mystery drawer in my mind's filing cabinet, I recalled a game I played with Emma. We made up the game to help us remember what the witches instructed us to forget . . .

It's my turn to sit stock-still, looking straight ahead like a zombie. Emma sneaks up and jumps in front of me, splaying her fingers right up in my face, barking a loud "Rah!"

The purpose is learning how to not flinch, not even blink. We take turns in these roles, imitating the test our abusers perform to see if we've gone into a trance after wafting sweet-smelling, pungent smoke under our noses, waving slowly and steadily with a white hand. The whiteness of the hand is important.

"Ray, I think that game helped us resist the drug so we could stay in reality somewhat."

Ray rolled over to me in his chair, our knees touching. He looked into my eyes, listening intently to every word I said.

"We cheered each other on, telepathically, to fight the trance," I sobbed. "What a lovely kids' game, huh? Emma says we had our own language. I don't remember that, but I believe her." Ray nodded his head, cheering me on.

"We had another game, pretending to be asleep on the nights it was our parents' turn to host 'Vacation Club,' their monthly dinner party with their friends to plan our summer vacation to northern Wisconsin." . . .

After our father looks in to check if we're asleep, we sneak out of our room and sit on the floor in the hallway, out of sight of the dining room. We listen to their conversation and take quick peeks when they start singing an old Swedish drinking song:

Helan går
Sjung hopp faderallan lallan lej
Helan går
Sjung hopp faderallan lej
Och den som inte helan tar
Han heller inte halvan får
Helan går!
Sjung hopp faderallan lej

"Skål!" *they shout at the end, clinking their glasses in a toast to their proud* *Viking lineage. The song means you better drink the whole drink, or you won't get anymore, something like that.*

Tonight, we creep into Donald's closet when they get settled in the dining room. We saw someone hanging up black capes earlier, hoping it was only our imagination. Yep, the capes are real, and they are *hanging in the very back of Donald's closet.*

In the morning, we sneak back to the closet to make sure we weren't really asleep last night, only dreaming the black capes were in Donald's closet. Nope, not a dream.

We hear someone and throw ourselves to the back of the closet. We curl into balls on the rough carpet, peeking under the capes. We see the shadow of a man who opens the closet door. "Get out of there," he shouts in the gruff voice of an old man. Grandpa John? Why is our father's father here so early?

We crawl out, look up, and the shadow extends both arms to yank us up.

"I can't remember anything else. But the number '8' keeps flashing on and off in my mind like a neon sign."

"Interesting," says Ray.

"Which could be important, because I'm almost positive we were eight years old that night. It was a turning point, when our relationship and lives changed forever."

"I am utterly fascinated by you and your twin sister's ingenuity," Ray said. "Don't worry, we'll get to the bottom of it."

"Thank you, Ray." I got up and hugged him, wanting to linger.

I pulled myself away and looked into his eyes. "Survival goes back to the beginning of our lives, does it not? What would have become of me without my devoted twin sister to play those games of endurance?"

"You were fortunate you had each other." Ray escorted me to the door. "I'll see you tomorrow."

Amidst flitting memories buzzing in and out of my mind like hummingbirds in search of nectar, a vision of the attic above my parents' garage landed in my mind, in the house in which I'd survived my childhood and where my parents still lived. Into my consciousness a knife climbed each rung up the ladder Evert used to stash it up there, under Marjorie's watchful gaze. A long, sharp knife, sterling silver, with symbols or pictures ornately carved into the handle. I saw it lying on purple velvet inside a mahogany wooden box.

I asked Emma if she remembered the knife. She said it rang a bell, but she couldn't say for sure. Lorain and Ellyn still claimed they had no contact with Marjorie and Evert, so I asked them too. They didn't remember anything like that, but they believed me. Telling my sisters made it real. An idea came to me. Why not go to my parents' house to look for the knife? I talked it over with Ray.

"You wanna do *what*?" Ray rolled across the room so fast his chair almost flipped. He got right in my face. "Go to your *parents'* house?"

"I'm going nuts, sitting around with all these memories swirling around my brain. I've got to know if it's true. Wouldn't it be great if I found evidence?"

Ray sighed. "I can understand that. But I'm not sure you're up to it. You'd have to stay in their house with them. Can you do that? Long enough for your parents to trust leaving you alone in the house. Do you think they'd allow that?"

"I have to try. I can put up a good front for a while, pretend I want to reconcile. Hell, I learned from the best." I laughed.

Ray chuckled. "You sure are brave, Hanna. You sure are brave."

"What choice have I got? Go on like this forever, never knowing the truth with any certainty?"

"Well, to tell the truth, I'd like to see myself. I wish I could go with you."

"I wish you could, too."

We plotted for several days how I would gain Marjorie and Evert's trust. Then I mustered my courage and picked up the phone.

Marjorie answered and gave the phone to Evert. Before I could implement my scheme, it backfired—instead of going to Illinois to snoop around in their attic, I'd agreed to let them come to Austin.

* * * *

I try to talk to my mother about the strange things that happen in the forest at night. I'm confused. She's in the forest, too, so why won't she talk to me or even look at me? Instead, she looks down at her ironing and snickers. "Oh, that's your imagination. You were only dreaming."

Even though I'm older now—I turned twelve five months ago—my mother still insists everything is my imagination.

Or a dream.

"It's not my imagination, mom," I say this morning. "Look at this dress. What is that?"

She gasps with a dramatic intake of breath, eyes bulging, arms thrown up in the air. "What are you doing with that dress?"

She grabs it out of my hands, a heavy white dress with a deep brown stain.

Frantically, she walks in circles with it, finally wadding it up and shoving it into the garbage can.

"What is that on that dress, mom? What happened last night? I thought it was only a strange dream, but there's the dress, right there!"

I gesture with open hands to the trash can, walking over to dig out the dress. My mother grips my arm so tightly she leaves nail marks.

With a straight-lined grimace and round, angry eyeballs, her stare bores straight into my soul as she hisses, "Put that dress down, and never mention it again."

I freeze. Seldom does my mother mean business. I drop the dress.

Quickly regaining her composure, her face transforms into her day-to-day, oblivious, bright-eyed, grinning, devil-may-care mask. Turning her gaze from me, she shoves the dress to the very bottom of the garbage can and casually says, after steering me away, "You have such a wild imagination, Hanna. Nothing like that happened last night. You had one of your crazy dreams. Ask Donald . . . Donald!" she yells, "Come in here."

I never said what happened last night. I simply showed her the dress.

And I don't know why Donald just happens to be at the house this morning. When did he come home? He and our father haven't spoken since Donald dropped out of college to flee to Canada to avoid the draft. My father is furious. He says Donald should fight for our country, as he did in World War II. Donald insists the war in Vietnam isn't ours.

Careful to avoid my eyes, my mother resumes ironing with straight-lipped seriousness. She brusquely slides the iron back and forth across a sheet, sprinkling water here and there. Hissing steam and the rattling of the ironing board accompany the ticking of the wall clock, waiting for Donald.

In disbelief, I sit at the kitchen table. I want to talk to her, *not* Donald.

Here he comes. And it starts.

They're treating me like I'm a complete idiot; laughing, insisting I had a "crazy dream," regardless of the fact that the dress is in the trash can.

I prefer to believe their fantastical stories about what really happens; I'd rather be imagining things and having nightmares. Right now, though, I can't pretend I don't know the truth. I want to say, "There was a man on a cross last night," but I don't want to believe it.

But it comes back to me. And I think it's true.

I was wearing that white dress. I was in the forest.

And this is what happened . . .

I am a puppet, not on strings, all limp and docile, more like a cutout of a girl made from a heavy material someone's hands must manipulate. That's what I am. I am a cardboard cutout of a life-sized, twelve-year-old girl.

There's a black presence behind me. A giant, hooded vulture. Large white hands protrude from the black robe he's wearing. My puppeteer. My controller. At least, that's what he wants me to believe. I sense it's my father by the anger pulsing through my resistant cardboard arms. I feel his bulk behind me, his flabby stomach. (How often that bulk forced itself behind my little girl body at night). I imagine my father's grimace of loathing inside his black hood, violently shaking my wrists to loosen them, make them pliable, make them yield to him.

Don't you know, Father, that cardboard will crack before it bends?

He forces a knife into my hands. And I dance before the man on the cross.

Please, God, if You exist, don't let this knife be real.

The man.

He looks down at me each time I pass before him on my circular journey around him, twirling and spinning in a dance I was taught years ago. His erection extends upward and slightly away from the surface of his naked body. Without any touch, it has erupted on its own. His sorrow is shame for his arousal. He can't resist the dance.

Please, God, make this not be real.

175

The vulture, my father, grabs me, ending my dance. He shoves his erection into the small of my back, holding my cardboard hands around the shaft of the knife in a vise grip.

He slides the knife under my white dress, between my legs. Onto the flat edge of the knife blade, he smears my first menstrual blood.

With his vulture talons, my father holds my hands around the shaft of the knife. I watch in horror the stabbing motion, my blood on the blade.

The eyes of the man on the cross fill with sorrow. For me.

One thing's for sure, I'm not telling this story to my mother or my brother. I don't care how much they pump me. I'll make something up if I have to, but I will not let them know I remember what happened. I will not give them the chance to twist the truth with a fantasy I'll prefer to believe.

Sixteen

Thunder echoed across the sky as a storm moved in, escorting Evert and Marjorie into Austin. It was January 12, 1989, Evert's sixty-seventh birthday. I strapped Elsa into her car seat and, windshield wipers on the highest high, drove to their motel, mumbling, *Shit! What am I going to do with them?*

We climbed the stairs to their room under an umbrella, a birthday card crammed into Elsa's little hand. Evert's smile brightened his blue eyes when I told her to hand it to him. I felt sick. It gave them the false impression that I might consider going back to Chicago with them, which was what they said they wanted.

We dined out on Texas barbeque to celebrate Evert's birthday. I didn't feel good about it.

The next day, Friday the 13th, they came to our apartment. Our *home*. At least I had taken Elsa over to Judith's house first. "I sure hope you know what you're doing, Hanna," she said. She kissed Elsa's nose, scooped her from my arms, leaned over to kiss my cheek, and closed the door.

I motioned for Marjorie and Evert to sit at the round table they bought after Elsa was born.

I started right away, confronting them about my whole life, disallowing interruptions, declaring I wasn't interested in any of their bullshit. No more Ms. Nice Gal like the day before, when I took them to dinner. I couldn't allow myself to pity them, so I didn't even offer a glass of water.

Surprisingly, they remained quiet and listened.

My monologue was a shiny, clean magnifying glass with which to examine the truth. I voiced my thoughts and feelings with confidence, spewing out everything disturbing over the years of my youth, especially the abortion they forced me to have when I was sixteen.

Marjorie looked at the ceiling, the floor, the front door—everywhere but at me—undoubtedly disappointed there was nothing to iron or fold. Evert's jaw twitched, and he held his threatening, oh-so-familiar, icy glare on me.

I kept my cool. I, the orator, lectured them on the evils of their parenthood. I described a memory of my brother sexually abusing another of their daughters, Ellyn, my sister. Evert shifted his gaze when I tried to make eye contact, fueling the truth. Doubtless, he'd known.

Eventually, my oration reached the incest perpetrated by Evert.

"Do you really believe your father did that to you?" Her voice quavered.

In disbelief, I replied, "Yes, Mother." Regretting the word, I revised my reply. "Yes, *Marjorie*. You know it's true. Stop denying it."

The muscles of her face drooped like a withering house plant, the sadness in her eyes unbearable. She looked devastated, like waking up to a destroyed home in the aftermath of a tornado. Her hope that I'd admit I was crazy crumbled into rubble, her last effort to get me to recant shattered into shards of truth.

The ice in Evert's eyes turned into glaciers. His twitching jaw went wild. Fists formed as he stood up and over me, glaring. I stood, too, glaring back. He was not going to win.

He panicked. "That's it! This family is over! Come on, Marjorie, let's go."

178

A stillness came over me as the weight of pretending lifted. Confidence in the truth blossomed like a wilted desert rose in a rainstorm.

"Why don't you stay, Marjorie? I'll drive you back to the motel later."

She looked at Evert.

"You don't need his permission," I said calmly.

Evert stomped to the door and opened it with a gruff, "I'll wait for you in the car."

Marjorie declared her intention to stay, shocking the hell out of me. Evert didn't listen to her. He walked out, slamming the door behind him.

Marjorie started shaking. She fidgeted, pulling on a cigarette, about to stand up to follow him. I placed my hand on her knee to stop her, feeling incredibly relaxed and confident. I bent forward in my chair, elbows on knees, staring at her eyes, which were diverted from mine, staring as she was at the slammed door.

"Stay, Mom. For a couple of days."

I felt a serenity I'd never known. It is said that the truth shall set you free. I wanted my mother to experience that freedom now.

Evert honked the horn. Three sharp beeps.

"Oh," her voice quaked, "I don't think I could do *that*." Light from the window shone silvery-white on her face, illuminating fear and worry buried deep in her pale blue eyes.

"You know, you don't have to go with him." I wanted to save her. "Please stay, Mom," I said, trying to appeal to any motherly feelings she might have for me. "I'll drive you to the airport in a few days."

I believed if I could keep her with me, alone, she might tell me. Everything.

In a shaky, faraway, defeated voice, Marjorie said to me, her daughter, "No. I've got to go." She didn't even look at me, so intent was her spellbound gaze beyond the door.

Another toot of the horn.

Marjorie walked to the door.

Her hand hesitated on the doorknob, then she opened it and looked out. Evert honked again, laying on the horn this time. She turned to me, opened her mouth to say something, and stopped. She put her head down, closed the door with a soft thump, and came back to sit beside me.

Evert hauled ass out of the parking lot, screeching tires down the street. I smiled. I'd never seen him that angry.

I looked for life in Marjorie's eyes, the silvery light shining ghostly against her face.

"How could you make up such a terrible lie about your father and hurt him so, after all he's done for you?" she practically whispered, staring at the door with worried eyes.

"Mother, you know me. I know you do. I am not a liar. Why would I make up such a disgusting thing? What motive would I possibly have?"

From head to toe, her body trembled. It was pitiful to watch.

"Don't you remember all the good times we had sitting around the kitchen table laughing?" Even her voice trembled.

I tried to get her back on topic. She refused. She talked over me with a tremulous laugh, trying to recapture our merriment around the kitchen table. It was heartbreaking.

I let her talk.

I drove Marjorie back to the motel, listening to her fantasies about our so-called family.

"Aren't you coming up?" she cheerily asked when I pulled up to drop her off.

My heart ached. "No."

A couple of hours later, Marjorie called to say they decided to go home early because of the weather—it was raining—emphasizing that it was her idea.

In a sad, sick way, it pleased me to triumph over Evert.

It eased the pain of realizing I'd probably never have another kind word with the only mother I'd known. And doubted I'd ever see her again.

Elsa fell asleep in my lap that night, rocking in the rocking chair.

I held onto her, feeling her warmth, listening to her breath, smelling baby shampoo in her hair. Marjorie's eyes, the fear in them, played across the movie screen of my mind. How could a mother, I wondered, not protect her children? What had happened to Marjorie that caused her to choose a pedophile over her children?

After placing Elsa in her crib, I stared at a TV show, telling myself I felt nothing. Until the phone rang. Pamela asked if Marjorie and Evert were still there and I fell apart in heaving sobs, my pain rising straight from hell.

It was for my parents that I cried. Or so I told myself.

The muted television kept me company all night. I couldn't stop thinking about them, especially Marjorie. So sad, her life. Fond memories of her, blended invariably with sorrow, made it more painful . . .

"Girls! Time for supper!" My mother's first summons to our evening meal is joyfully called out in her sing-song voice, a soprano lilt.

Emma will be reading or something in the bedroom we share, and I'll be talking to my boyfriend, Michael, on our avocado-green princess dial phone. We ignore our mother's call to dinner.

Knock. Knock. Knock.

"Girls!" She claps her hands. "Supper is ready. *Come on! Now!"*

She isn't really angry. *Just impatient because we're not accommodating her punctual routine, expecting everyone to be on her schedule, so she always knows, minute by minute, what to expect. It's the only thing she can count on, I think.*

"Okay, we're coming! Geez!" I yell. "Michael, I gotta go. See ya later."

I rush to the kitchen table, my mouth watering.

My favorite dinner—pork chops floating in buttery, tomatoey, barbequey goodness, served with mashed potatoes and corn. It's one of the recipes my mother made up, like her dry stew she's so proud of, which isn't dry at all—tiny cubes of beef, potatoes, carrots, celery, corn, and peas roasted in a sauce she makes from onions. She's usually a rather mediocre cook, many dinners a flop. But occasionally she hits it big, like her Heath bar coffee cake we all love, her savory dry stew, and her pork chops.

"Save some for your father." Her daily refrain, first thing when we sit down to eat.

Where is my father all the time? Working? I think my mother feeds us early to avoid the arguments that erupt when he eats with us, which make no sense and send us girls flying from the kitchen table with angry, stomping feet.

My mother serves supper—her old-fashioned word for dinner—a couple of hours after Afternoon Coffee, an event among us girls in the house. When we were very young, I vaguely remember Great-Grandma Inga, my mother's grandmother, sitting at the kitchen table with us. It fascinated me to watch her drink coffee through a sugar cube held between her teeth like a sieve. My mother says Great-Grandma Inga would sometimes come to stay with us for several days. "Every afternoon, Grandma Inga would ask, 'Isn't it time for ficka?'" *says my mother, imitating Great-Grandma's sing-song Swedish accent, her eyes sparkling, gazing off into memories of her grandmother.*

Ficka *is the traditional coffee time Grandma Inga brought with her from Sweden. But my mother doesn't call our coffee time ficka. I don't know why she changed it to Afternoon Coffee. She just did. Tea is not condoned at Afternoon Coffee. Oh, no. Only the dark, robust coffee my mother brews. I love the delicious aroma and swirling sound as she pours it into porcelain cups. Mmmmm . . .*

In the center of the kitchen table, my mother places the silver creamer from which to pour half & half, a vital necessity, with a bowl of sugar cubes beside it,

182

also vital. Next to the sugar is the tiny bell-shaped silver container for saccharin, with elfin-sized silver tongs to lift out elfin-sized tablets of sugar substitute. I prefer sugar cubes, plunking three squares of delectable sweetness into my coffee, which I drink with more half & half than coffee. Plates are spread with cookies and table wafers, perhaps, but Swedish Coffee Bread is the star of Afternoon Coffee.

I capitalize Swedish Coffee Bread in reverence to its importance as the main staple in our lives, homemade by Grandma Elsa, my father's mother. She prepares her bread dough every Friday evening, covering it with a muslin cloth and a plate, letting it rise in the refrigerator overnight. On Saturday mornings, she punches down the dough and fashions her coffee bread into braids, setting them aside to rise again. Like magic, they puff up into braided loaves of a spongy texture, distinguished by their principal ingredient of tiny black cardamom seeds.

Grandma's toasted coffee bread tastes delicious with lots of melted butter for breakfast. However, at Afternoon Coffee, we cut into a fresh loaf, eaten with thin slices of pale-yellow Bond-Ost cheese loaded with caraway seeds, imported from Sweden by my father's gourmet import business. The Bond-Ost is always, without exception, sliced with a teak-handled Scandinavian cheese slicer, also imported by my father's company.

Most special of all at Afternoon Coffee is my mother. Her aquamarine eyes sparkle, her laughter is contagious. In her joyousness, she makes me feel like I have a real mom. I smile to think of her this way, tears streaming down her face as she covers her eyes and bows her head, trying not to laugh (as she so often tries not to cry). We sisters living in the house—Lorain, Emma, and I—love our mother's laughter.

Sometimes our oldest sister, Ellyn, comes for Afternoon Coffee, and the laughter becomes riotous; she's hilariously funny, with an uproarious laugh. I am in awe of her. Eight years older than me and Emma, Ellyn possesses the unknowable mystery of a much older sibling from another decade. It's on the afternoons when Ellyn is here that our mother overflows with eye-sparkling, cheek-throbbing glee. Our make-believe Norman Rockwell painting. Mother at her most charming. I wish I could say it's her true nature, and hate to invite you to open the cabinet above and to the left of the kitchen sink to reveal her pharmacy on the bottom shelf.

Oh well, such are the realities of life we try to deny, such as the summer my mother's doctor cut her off cold turkey, only to accumulate, over time, a new stash in her sacred cabinet. Why can't life among the people I love be joyous and uncomplicated all the time?

I wish every day was an Afternoon Coffee Day.

Sleepless, I contemplated the human complexities of Marjorie's life. She didn't drive, so she was a prisoner to that house. I hadn't thought of her that way before. Maybe her prison sentence in my father's jail shaped her ideal of what a normal family home should look like. On the surface . . .

My mother likes to decorate and rearrange the kitchen and living room. But, quite frankly, her taste in decorating isn't any better than most of her cooking. I suppose my father's stingy funding is a contributing factor. Recently, she decided to paint the kitchen cabinets avocado-green, a popular 1970s color, and plans to hang ruffled white curtains with tiny yellow flowers in the single kitchen window. The cabinets are already thick with years of her attempts to color a sense of . . . joy? happiness? Her avocado idea will cover the blue and yellow Swedish kitchen she wanted a couple of years ago.

What would we find at the base of those cabinets if we peeled away the layers of paint? Fine oak, pine, or cheap plywood? My heart tells me the foundation of my mother's kitchen cabinets is a fine, solid, beautiful wood buried beneath the stratigraphy of her longings to alter reality.

184

With smiling enthusiasm, my mother plows forward with her living room make-overs. Often, she simply moves the furniture around, employing the help of me and my sisters, ignoring our complaints as we push and pull pieces of furniture back and forth across the carpet. She stands back with a sigh of satisfaction once we achieve her vision. Her most recent furniture grouping— gold lamé sofa, atrocious puke-brown coffee table, and two gold-and-white upholstered wingback chairs we've had for years—does not match the pastel-blue shag carpet she had installed a couple of years ago.

Her dismal taste in decorating is in odd contrast to her graceful movements, such as the refined way she holds her petite figure when entertaining: legs elegantly crossed, tapping a delicate arched foot, toes pointed in stylish high heels. She possesses graciousness with people, too, perfect strangers confessing their entire life stories when stumbling upon her warm smile and pale blue, twinkly eyes.

My mother's charming personality and distasteful decorating renovations show the incongruity of her life, of all *our lives in that house. Yet, despite the chaos and confusion, I learned how to laugh and hold my head high— sometimes—by observing my mother with strangers, while entertaining guests, and during Afternoon Coffee.*

I stepped into the night. The January chill penetrated my bones, rousing me to the present moment. A light gust rattled a cedar tree near the door as if to shake me awake. My life belonged to me now. I could construct a new reality for myself and my daughter. But I'd have to face my old reality first. And believe it . . .

There's a dark side of my mother, the side I don't like to think about, and try to deny. It's the side of her that comes into my room in the middle of the night and parks a straight-back dining room chair beside my bed, waiting until I swallow every drop of an awful tasting drink. I was four or five when it first began. I'm nine now. There is no laughter in her crystal eyes, no pretense of ignorance as she awaits my final swallow. Oh, no. During her night visits, my mother's eyes are pure ice, shining with intelligence that belies her day-to-day passive demeanor. It isn't easy to accept that this really happens. Sometimes I think I'm making it up.

But deep inside, it's as crystal clear as my mother's eyes that the horrid drink, served in a silver cup, is what causes the bouts of "stomach flu" that plague my childhood. My mother's remedy for the puking is pink Pepto-Bismol, which makes the puking worse.

The concoction, whatever it is, makes me lightheaded and spacey, followed by vomiting several hours later, after we've been out of the house somewhere I can never remember.

Daylight framed the living room window, and still I was awake, pondering the mystery of Marjorie. She was indeed an enigma, a mix of personalities—light and dark, graceful and awkward. I never knew which mother I'd wake up to or end the day with. Once in a while, she'd turn her eye-sparkling charm on me. Other times, her tight-lipped annoyance. Most of the time she was passive and easy to push around.

It was the intelligent nighttime mother that I feared.

I recalled what may have been the last time she forced that puke cocktail on me, on a school night when I was in sixth grade. I became dizzy and didn't know what was going on, except that we went somewhere deep in a forest.

In the morning, I was violently ill when it was time to leave for school.

I stayed home, puking, and tried to read my Pepto-Bismol-pink hardcover book about Isadora Duncan, a famous ballerina. My mother's repeated tablespoonfuls of Pepto-Bismol made the vomiting worse, and I spent the day retching into a bucket.

186

Ever after that day, I associated ballet with vomit, my dream of becoming a ballerina flushed down the toilet along with the pink.

I still feel queasy whenever I see a bottle of Pepto-Bismol, or that particular shade of pink.

I had never forgotten this incident. I thought it must not have been real, even though it had always hung out in my mind's filing cabinet, in the file marked "Things that Cannot be Real." It would take many years to accept it was a midnight witches' brew that Marjorie had me drink from a silver chalice, with drugs to make me unconscious yet mobile, like an alcoholic in a blackout—pliable for rituals.

Marjorie sent me a letter a few days after they left. She wrote about inane, nonsensical things, such as her beauty shop appointment and what the neighbors were doing. She wrote that their abrupt departure was due to Evert not feeling well and apologized for not saying goodbye. *What?* Her original explanation had been bad weather, which wasn't even bad, only raining.

Neither scenario, of course, was the truth. Did she think we would forget what really happened and make up?

Poor Marjorie, pretending everything was hunky-dory.

If I had bothered to press a discussion of their visit, she would have denied that Evert stormed out of my apartment in a rage, perhaps adding something like, "Gosh, Hanna, you sure have a wild imagination."

I dropped the letter onto my lap and stared out the window, reflecting on the "truth" stories Marjorie concocted over the years, suspecting she half-believed the fables she authored. I couldn't help feeling sorry for her, for the life she had chosen, feeling sorrier for her after reading her pathetic letter.

Marjorie needed to believe her substitute versions of reality, and had spread her disease to me. But no more.

Not with her and Evert, anyway.

Flashbacks of my life with my family increased in frequency. Memories came randomly, a bitter-sweet mix that included some that were quite nice . . .

August 1965. Ellyn, fourteen, went to see the Beatles with some of her girlfriends yesterday. She can hardly talk because her throat is hoarse from screaming. Her friend Dawn is over and even though they can barely speak, they can't stop talking about the concert. Dawn says Ringo Starr looked right at her and smiled. "It's true, I swear," she croaks, and crisscrosses an "x" on her chest and holds up two fingers in a "v"—that's supposed to mean she's telling the gospel truth.

We've been hearing a lot about the Beatles. When they appeared on The Ed Sullivan Show, Ellyn sat right in front of the TV set and screamed her lungs out. Not even our father could get her away. He laughed and walked out of the room with a "pshew" and a wave of his hand as if batting away a yapping puppy.

Still pumped up on the concert, Ellyn and Dawn run into the backroom to play Beatles records on the built-in turntable underneath the long countertop that lines almost the entire length of one wall. Emma and I, six, sneak in behind them. Ellyn flings open the cabinet where her records are stashed and flips through them. She makes a stack of 45's, placing her favorite Beatles record, "Twist and Shout," on the bottom so it will plop down first, then fumbles with the automatic record changer, jumping from side to side like she's on a pogo stick.

They giggle and squeal when John Lennon rasps, "Come on and twist a little closer now, and let me know that you're mine . . ."

Ellyn and Dawn do the Twist, Mashed Potato, Pony, and the Jerk, grabbing our hands to dance with them. They've been teaching me and Emma all these dances since we were five. We're pros now.

Our mother stands in the doorway laughing, slapping her hands on her knees. Ellyn tries to get her to dance, but she refuses,

Smiling from ear to ear she says, "Oh no! I'm just going to watch you girls."

But Emma and I take advantage of their goodwill, letting us dance with them, and we Twist our way through every record Ellyn owns.

. . . Holidaytime. Another 1960s winter has set in. I'm in Chicago with my sisters, parents, and grandparents at the Swedish restaurant on Ashland Avenue for a holiday smörgåsbord.

The food doesn't taste as good as Grandma Elsa's, but everything looks pretty, long tables set with candles and Swedish Christmas decorations tucked in among the dishes smelling of Sweden. I eat limpa bröd, a brown bread with small squares of orange peel, and Potatis Korv, heavily seasoned sausage made of potatoes and pork, although I prefer the Potatis Korv my father makes with his Swedish friends down in our basement.

After dinner, my mother, sisters, and I go to Grandma Elsa's church with her for Santa Lucia Day. Since my mother and grandmother don't drive, my father drives us over, telling us he'll be back in one hour. Santa Lucia Day is a Swedish holiday tradition borrowed from Sicily. My grandma doesn't know how the festival migrated to Sweden, or when, but it's been an important holiday celebration for hundreds of years, altered to fit Swedish customs.

We take our seats up toward the front, on red velvet pews. Several pews in the back are empty, but there are still a lot of people here, mostly old women. Grandma says that "back in the old days," church was packed with people on Lucia Day. She sighs. "The younger generations aren't so interested in their Swedish customs anymore." Then she tells us to sit still as the lights go dim.

Santa Lucia leads the procession, her attendants trailing behind her—little girls in white dresses with wreaths of tinsel and glitter ringing their heads, *followed by little boys looking like miniature wizards in white tunics with dunce-cap-shaped hats decorated with stars on their heads.*

This year a granddaughter of one of Grandma's friends is playing the role of Santa Lucia, and I can't take my eyes off of her! She looks so beautiful flowing up the red-carpeted aisle of the church with her crown of white candles set in lingonberry leaves and her heavy embroidered robe, edged with white fur, dragging behind her like a wedding gown. I wish I could be one of the little girls following behind her.

This is a special part of our Swedish holiday time with Grandma Elsa. She's so happy.

Grandma told me that when she was a girl in Sweden, winters were long, with only a few hours of daylight. Everybody would be tired of the endless darkness by the time Winter Solstice rolled around in December. People in her village of Trädet *(The Tree) looked forward to Lucia Day, which began the final twelve days of celebrations before Christmas, when each night the villagers would gather at a different house. Villagers each brought a log for the fire, plus food and gifts. They sang songs and told stories about* Jul Tomtar, *tiny Christmas elves who take care of the horses.*

When I ask about Grandpa John's village, she says his upbringing was different from hers, but won't divulge the difference, only that he was raised in Dalarna, Sweden. I know Grandpa John was sent to live on a farm when he was only twelve, and wonder more than ever why his parents would send him away.

Grandma Elsa speaks only Swedish with her friends at church. She's proud to be from Sweden and I can tell she misses her home. I feel proud to be Swedish, too, when I'm with her.

I suspected my father of sending Neil money when he started handing me a hundred-dollar bill each week, the first money he'd ever given me.

I had to take it. My unemployment would eventually run out, and the continuous flashbacks of mind-fucking Occult Abuse kept me busy, too busy to work a regular job. Consequently, I did not ask Neil where he got the money. Instead, I dug through my bag of defense mechanisms and pulled out *Denial* to pay the rent.

Nonetheless, I still had to stand up for our baby. Neil flatly refused to discuss a divorce, threatening to commit me to an "insane asylum" if I pursued it. He demanded that I allow him to move in and let my parents see Elsa.

"I do not understand how you can even *consider* allowing my parents to see our daughter. I've told you everything. The incest. . . Good God, Neil, they practice black magic!"

"It's not true," he said with chilling composure.

"Why the hell would I make up such a thing? About my own *parents*!"

"You are a very sick woman," he said coolly. "Your parents are wonderful people who should be able to see their granddaughter."

Incredulous, I gaped open-mouthed. "What the hell are you thinking, Neil? It's not like you have a *relationship* with them. You barely know them."

My parents lived twelve hundred miles away. During the two years Neil and I lived together, he only saw them two or three times. To my knowledge, Neil hadn't seen them in the past year since our separation. What was his motive for aligning himself with sex offenders?

"Your refusal to discuss my parents, rationally, is my number one reason for wanting a divorce. I'm begging you to listen to me. We *must* protect our daughter from them." Distraught beyond words, I added, "Why won't you help me?"

Neil stared at me with an unblinking coldness that replaced my blood with ice water. "You know, Hanna, as your husband, I *could* have you committed to an insane asylum. Do you want that?"

"*Why* are you doing this?" I shrieked.

191

"You are insane, Hanna. Your parents are fantastic people who want to see their granddaughter." Neil's calm, monotone voice was unnerving, each "s" an exaggerated hiss, adding, "You're sick." On the couch he sat, staring down at me genuflecting before him like a groveling masochist.

His eyes were the murky green waters of Emily Park Lagoon, where my friends and I walked to as kids, traveling far from home over the train tracks and along a narrow dirt path.

Elsa cried, waking up from a nap. I got her from the bedroom and held her close, her knees wrapped around my waist. "Hush, little baby, don't say a word. Mamma's gonna buy you a mockingbird," I sang. "Neil, look at our precious baby. We need to protect her."

He replied, "She needs to live with *both* of her parents."

I gave up on him. For that day. He'd become an enemy in the fight for our child's safety, and my sanity.

As was the strange woman who was about to show up.

The rhythm of my life became synchronized to a pendulum slashing out a metronomic beat:

—Swoosh   Swoosh   Swoosh   Swoosh—

A warning of trials to come.

Seventeen

I was stunned to find a woman in my apartment.

I'd just stepped out of the bedroom into the darkened living room, the only light streaming in from the light over the stove in the kitchen. She was sitting in my rocking chair, appearing quite relaxed. She looked familiar, someone from my childhood I had forgotten until the moment I saw her, thought I couldn't place her. A thin, aging woman, slightly past middle-age with pearl-white skin and shoulder-length black hair that was thick, wavy, and streaked with wisps of white. I didn't know her name or what significance she'd played in my past, only that she had.

"Who are you? What are you doing here?" I asked.

She watched my every move, saying nothing. She crossed one knee over the other in black tights beneath a shin-length dress, slate-gray, and no shoes, which somehow accentuated her authority. Her tight-sleeved arms were bent at the elbows, propped on the arms of my rocking chair, fingertips touching to form a pyramid. Her pale lips curved in a playful smile, enjoying an amusing game. She stared into my very being with luminous aquamarine eyes brimming with mischievous intensity. Those crystal-blue eyes were the only color in what seemed a black-and-white noir film of her, rocking back and forth ever so slightly, sitting straight-backed in elegant confidence, never once averting her penetrating gaze.

"May I help you?" I asked.

She bent her head slightly, drawing her pyramid fingertips to her odd smile. Still, she said nothing.

"You will never have my daughter," I said, and everything went black.

Later—a few minutes or a few hours, I didn't know—I wondered if I'd imagined the woman. I didn't know how she got in, and I didn't remember her leaving, whether she walked out the door or disappeared. I had a sense even then of what was real and what was not, and the woman's presence in my apartment had elements of both. It wasn't like PTSD hallucinations, which were auditory and sensory. She was there. I saw her rocking in my chair. Yet, she seemed to appear by magic, which wasn't possible.

The malevolent witches *would* send a voiceless messenger from my past. Yes, that would be their style, so I wouldn't know for sure and could only guess why she'd come. Their unspoken, implied message, I believed, was their intent to take my baby.

That's how it was with them. Their mind-fuck to make me question my sanity. I didn't even think to check the front door to see if it was locked. If the woman had walked in and out of the door, she would've needed a key. . . Did she have one?

I raced to the bedroom, relieved to see Elsa asleep in her crib, clutching her stuffed pink bear. Fearing I might be imagining *her*, I placed my hand on her warm tummy, feeling the up and down motion of her breathing.

When I told Ray about the woman, he said, "You're safe now. I'm here."

I had heard him say I was safe so many times it had lost its meaning. Because I wasn't safe. Haunting oddments of my history never left me, relived in incessant PTSD flashbacks: eerie chanting I heard outside my window; black-robed figures

I glimpsed lining the road when I drove at night, and sometimes during the day in my peripheral vision; nightmares filled with guns, knives, bloody wounds. And night terrors—acting out my nightmares in my sleep.

Ray wasn't interested in hearing about my flashbacks at the moment. "About that woman," he said. "Think hard. Did you let her in?"

"I don't know, Ray. I'd like to think it was some kind of crazy hallucination. But maybe she *was* there."

"In deep depression, sometimes people can experience a psychotic break in which—"

"Are you saying I'm psychotic?"

"No. Please, listen. I do not believe you are psychotic. I'm only trying to explain, so you know I support you and am concerned for your daughter's safety. And yours."

"Okay." I was terrified of what he would say next.

"As I was saying, it is possible for people to go so deep into depression t that they can break with reality for a brief time. Whereas PTSD hallucinations are a reliving of past trauma, psychosis hallucinations seem very real—you can see and have conversations with people who are not really there. That type of psychosis, brought on by severe depression, may occur only once, or intermittently over time, usually when stress levels are high." Ray crossed his arms over his chest, leaning back in his chair. "Unlike schizophrenia, in which psychosis is the norm."

"So, you don't think I'm psychotic or schizophrenic, correct?"

"Absolutely correct," said Ray. "Though I must be honest and admit I've been concerned you might break. However, in this case, I do not believe you were having a psychotic episode, nor do I believe you were experiencing a PTSD hallucination. In fact, I see no indication that you are even suffering from severe depression. I'm certain the woman was there, Hanna. Think. Did you let her in?"

"Ray, I'm telling you, I have no idea how she got in my apartment, and none whatsoever of her leaving. How can this be? If she had really been there, then why can't I remember how she left?"

"Traumatic Amnesia. A common manifestation of PTSD. We've talked about this before. I think you don't want to believe your parents and their 'friends' may have sent her to scare you. Therefore, you blocked out what you don't want to know."

"It's true that I don't want to believe she was real. But I don't get why her arrival and departure are completely gone from memory." Tears stung my eyes. "I wish I were insane and could fix it with a pill. Not *Haldol*, but something without side effects, that would make me normal."

Ray chuckled. "Sorry Hanna. The only thing wrong with you is your unfortunate upbringing in a fucked-up family. You are *not* mentally ill. You're suffering from Post Traumatic Stress Disorder. Period. There aren't any pills on the market for that. And even if there were, or a pharmaceutical company comes up with something one of these days, you know I don't believe in medication unless absolutely necessary. I'll help you learn how to deal with the effects of PTSD. I promise it'll get better."

"I'd rather be mentally ill," I said, half laughing.

Ray patted my hand. "But you're not. You just need to remember your abuse," he cheerfully said, grinning. "I'll see you tomorrow. Until then, try to remember the woman's name."

He stood up, the cue that our fifty-minute hour was over.

Dissociated when I left Ray's office, a sensation of a band tightening around my head distracted my driving. A bizarre thought crept into my consciousness—maybe I couldn't remember because my memory had been erased.

I quickly dismissed that idea, banishing it from my mind. I didn't consider it long enough to even wonder how memories would be erased.

If, in fact, they could be.

Years later, Ray told me he bought a gun that afternoon, which he kept in the glove compartment of his car for several months.

The pendulum swung faster and lower when the phone calls began:

—*Swoosh Swoosh Swoosh Swoosh*—

"Hello." No answer. "Hello?"

Nothing. I hung up.

That first call was in the morning. There were several more that day and night, including one at 3 a.m., which pissed me off.

On the third consecutive day, I noticed a pattern of three—three rings at 9 a.m., noon, 6 p.m., and 3 a.m. If I didn't answer, there would be a pause (three minutes?) and three more rings, continuing until I answered.

I imagined myself stuck in The Twilight Zone, Rod Serling introducing the next episode of my life at the beginning of his TV show:

The phone calls. Began. In patterns. Of three.
Act three. In the strange. And curious.
Three-ring circus. That was. To become.
Her life.

Regardless of the pattern of the day, my phone rang without fail at 3 a.m. I tried not to pick up the receiver, but couldn't stop myself. I *had* to answer, knowing the silence on the other end meant something.

Ray's idea was to unplug my phone. "If the calls are associated with your past, which I'm assuming they are, you need to be cautious. Shut off your phone and stop giving them so much power."

"I can't keep it unplugged all the time. I do use it."

"Yeah, but turn it off at night, so you can sleep."

"I can't unplug the phone. I feel *compelled* to answer it, especially the 3 a.m. calls. I think the calls mean something about the number three, signaling me to do something or think something." Hearing myself say it, I knew, from the depths of my unconscious mind where I'd shoved all unpleasant knowledge, that this was true.

"Who do you think it is?"

"I don't know."

"Well, that's a ridiculous question, I suppose," said Ray. "You gave your parents your phone number, and they *have* been to your apartment."

"True. I know it was a mistake to let them come, Ray. And if it's not them calling, then they must have given my number to a henchman."

"Yeah. If it's not Marjorie or Evert, they gave my number to a henchman."

"Possibly. So, I'm suggesting you unplug your phone. At least at night."

I did not enjoy jumping at the sound of the phone ringing like a jolt of electricity. Still, I listened for that ring, waited for it, fixated on its changing patterns of three.

I knew the truth, but I didn't know the truth. I wanted to know, but I didn't want to know. Answering the phone was my way of taking my power back. It was a challenge. I wanted to fight, to show them—my parents, their friends, whoever—that I was tougher than them.

Not yet aware of the cult's mind-control strategies, I couldn't articulate my struggle to fight triggers that had been implanted in my mind via brainwashing techniques begun early in my life. I did the best I could, imagining myself the triumphant winner by picking up the receiver. Which, of course, I was not. The calls drove me into a frenzy, precisely as the caller or callers designed.

"If you want to try antidepressants, I'm acquainted with a psychiatrist you can see for a prescription," said Ray.

"What? You've said hundreds of times that you don't believe in meds. And how the hell will that help with the phone calls and all my questions?"

"We'll have to address the phone calls with the police if they continue. But maybe antidepressants would calm your mind, help *you* answer your questions, rationally."

"Well, Hanna, the answers are deep inside you somewhere, waiting to express themselves. Antidepressants might help with that."

"Hmmm . . . I'll think about it," I said.

Time ticked on, day after day, night after night.

Ray called early one morning to ask, in an accusatory manner, if I'd called him at 3 a.m. and hung up when he answered, to "prove" the calls were really happening.

"What the hell? No, Ray. I would never do that." Concerned, I added, "How did they get your home phone number?"

He hung up.

Ray's tone had been changing for some time. I heard his irritation and couldn't blame him. It must have been quite challenging to wholly listen to and consider a person who presented herself with the obsessive, repetitive, defensive, hysterical, wide-eyed rambling I'd been exhibiting. Especially when I sensed someone didn't believe me, insisting everyone unconditionally listen to me, becoming irate when they did not.

In Cottonwood aftercare, the other survivors of childhood sexual abuse helped me see that the more extreme the trauma, the more intensely the victim seeks validation. That was me.

I ate and slept out of necessity, sickened by food and terrified of nightmares. The only moments I felt put together were with Elsa, watching her grow. She was trying to say words now and was walking with confidence. She was sweet and happy all the time, her open-mouthed, delightful smile like medicine. Having long since lost my favorite job at the public television station and unable to keep another, the unemployment checks and cash from Neil provided an opportunity to devote myself to motherhood.

I leisurely made breakfast for Elsa in the morning, then we played and took long walks in the apartment complex or went to Town Lake to feed the ducks.

Most days, I took Elsa to Mrs. Lopez's house at lunchtime, and then spent two or three hours with Ray. In late afternoons, I watched The Oprah Winfrey Show, having become a devotee. Oprah was my second therapist. Her courage in confronting the Ku Klux Klan inspired me, and she publicly admitted she was sexually abused as a child. Despite the three-ring circus of my life, I felt hopeful.

After Oprah, I'd pick up Elsa for our relaxed dinner and nighttime routine.

That was on a good day. The bad days, which were many, took a turn for the worse when a 3 a.m. phone call asked, "Is Mary or Joseph there?"

Someone had spoken. For the first, and only, time. A woman.

"Who the fuck is this?" I demanded, her chuckle cut short as she clicked off.

My heartbeat sped, then stopped. I slunk to the floor, clutching my chest, breath shallow.

My thirtieth birthday burst like a firecracker into my mind—the third decade of my life would be over in March—the third month of the year.

Suicidal thoughts intensified.

The pendulum picked up the pace, slicing mercilessly through my illusions:

—*SwooshSwooshSwooshSwoosh*—

Neil continued his refusal to grant me a divorce, wanting to move in with us instead. Regardless of how much I begged, *pleaded* with him to support me in my recovery and help protect our baby, it was useless.

His eyes became a menacing storm when he'd shamelessly declare, "I am your husband, so I can have you committed to an insane asylum," stated with chilling, unemotional self-assurance.

Neil's bullying worked to instill fear in me. I was afraid to pursue a divorce. It worried me to think Neil might actually be able to have me committed to an "insane asylum" or "mental institution"—his favorite terms for psychiatric hospitals. Plus, he had my father's financing and influence on his side, the most frightening fact of all. I barely had enough money to pay the rent, which Neil knew, of course, and I was a still writhing in agony over my childhood.

Dealing with Neil was an agonizing, frustrating, useless endeavor. I wanted to unzip the top of his head and rearrange his appalling thinking.

Added to Neil's constant pressure were the constant memories of Occult Abuse. Haunting specters day and night, relived in torturing PTSD flashbacks, pictures from my past snapped on and off in my mind's eye, gathered speed, turned into a slide show, and rolled on into a film version in which I no longer viewed the scene from a distance, but became part of the movie. To believe and not want to believe the truth was exhausting, wishing I could file my history back into my mind's amnesia drawer.

Yet, to forget the truth again could never be. Even if I closed the door on reality, a window had already opened, if only a tiny crack, wide enough for darkness to slip in, leaving Elsa susceptible to the abuse I had suffered as a child. Maybe that's how that woman got into our apartment—she slipped in through that metaphorical window.

I vowed to use every ounce of fight I had left in me to keep Elsa safe, which meant facing more truth. And believing it.

That meant forcing myself to accept a memory I'd never forgotten, but discarded from my thoughts whenever it came to mind, believing it must have been my imagination.

Out of the vault now, I didn't want to wait to tell Ray. I called him before our therapy session and wept, "There's more."

Ray asked to wait until our afternoon session in the safety of his office.

He was standing in his office doorway when I arrived, arms crossed below his chest, left knee bent with foot crossed over his right ankle. He waved me in and closed the door.

"What's going on, Hanna?"

"It sounds so bizarre, you're never gonna believe it. *I* don't believe it."

"Try me," he said gleefully, as if I were about to tell him a wonderful story. Which, in some ways, my story *was* one of wonder.

"It's always been hazy, like a fog surrounding the scene," I said. "But I've never forgotten it."

I closed my eyes and willed the fog to lift . . .

There's a little girl in a cage. I know her name is Michelle because I'm singing a song to her called "Michelle" by the Beatles: "Michelle, ma belle, sont les mots qui vont très bien . . . "

I want to make her feel better, but someone starts making fun of me for singing that song. I stop immediately, my face burning red hot.

"She was in a cage, Ray!"

I paused for his reaction.

Encouraged by his nodding head, I continued. "It was bright daylight, so there must have been windows, or maybe we were outside. Her big eyes were frozen open like two huge black saucers, like maybe her pupils were dilated."

Ray rolled his chair over, as he often did, to look into my eyes, hypnotizing me into telling the whole story, which I'd told no one, except maybe Emma when we were little.

"I know I was at least six years old, because 'Michelle' came out on the Beatles' Rubber Soul album in 1965. I found the album at a record store before I came today, to look at the date."

"I remember that song. It was in English and French."

"Yes. And I think that's why someone made fun of me, for singing the French part. I felt humiliated and embarrassed, I think partly because I really cared about Michelle, and I wasn't supposed to. I must have known her before she was put in that cage, because I felt like I knew her, and I got 'caught' trying to make her feel better. About being in a fucking *cage*! And now that I'm saying it, it seems strange for a little girl of six to feel love for another child."

"That little girl of six was you, Hanna, feeling love and caring for another child. Why would that seem strange?"

"I don't know," I wept, engulfed by relief to admit I cared about Michelle, whoever she was. Ray took my hands and held them tight.

"I can't believe I'm saying this. For all these years, every time I hear that song the image of that little girl in the cage pops into my mind. But I've always brushed it aside, telling myself it wasn't real." I cleared my throat. "I think there were other cages with kids. But I can't really see them, and I don't want to."

Ray leaned over, placing his elbows on his knees. His eyes flickered intensely and his jaw twitched, grinding his teeth.

"Do you believe me, Ray?"

He looked into my eyes and slowly nodded his head. "Yes, I do."

A few days later, in early February 1989, Emma told me our parents were selling their house. The house they'd lived in for nearly forty years. She said Ellyn told her. The two of them were going to pretend to be prospective buyers so they could look in the attic for that silver-handled knife.

That night, somewhere between awake and asleep, I saw my father . . .

1977. I'm in high school, thinking about quitting and moving up north with my boyfriend, Jerome. Of course, I haven't told my parents yet, but, hey, I'll be eighteen soon, so I can do whatever I want.

Out of the blue, my father places a book in my hands, The Omen, *by David Seltzer, and suggests I read it. I wonder why my father wants me to read this book about parents who adopt the Antichrist. The movie came out recently, starring Gregory Peck. Why would my father even be interested in this story?*

A week later, my father is home from work early, actually eating dinner with us. When everyone scatters after eating, he gleefully asks, "Have you read it?"

I say, "Um, The Omen? *Yeah, I read it." Weird. He wants to discuss it.*

My father and I don't talk. Why does he want to chat about Damien, *the Antichrist? Plus, this is the creepiest book. I felt very uncomfortable reading it, and I do not particularly wish to have a discussion about it with my father. I make an excuse and walk out of the house, practically running to the library, where no one will know where I am, to choose a hundred other books to read.*

This was one of those memories I hadn't forgotten, but it was so odd I'd pushed it out of my mind.

Now that my father's sexual assaults were out, the drawers of my mind's filing cabinet of unwanted memories would not close. The survivor in me was thrilled, having been waiting a long time to talk about Evert's strange book club . . .

1980. I broke up with Jerome and moved out. I'm staying at my parents' house for a while.

I walk into the kitchen for a coke and my father follows me with a book, shoving it firmly into my hands. It's Smiley's People, *by John le Carré. He says, "Read this. And then tell me what you think."*

He smiles like a teenager, young and alive. I don't think I've seen my father so animated, except for a few years ago, when he wanted me to read The Omen.

I look at him quizzically, like what? *This is quite perplexing. We never talk.*

I say, "Okay?" just like that, as a question.

He nods, turns, and walks off, heavy feet lumbering back to his recliner and TV set in the backroom.

Smiley's People *is a complicated story about World War II spies searching for a Russian KGB spymaster who uses a woman's daughter (missing somewhere in Russia) to fake the identity of his own daughter, whom he's had committed to a sanitorium for the mentally ill.*

Why does my father want me to know this story?

Combined with his desire for me to read The Omen, *about the Antichrist, a creepy feeling penetrates and distracts me from my daily life. A vague memory comes to mind of my father instructing me to memorize Psalm 23 from the Bible:*

The lord is my shepherd; I shall not want. He maketh me to lie down in green pastures: he leadeth me beside the still waters. He restoreth my soul: he leadeth me in the paths of righteousness for his name's sake.
Yea, though I walk through the valley of the shadow of death, I will fear no evil: for thou *art* with me; thy rod and thy staff they comfort me. Thou preparest a table before me in the presence of mine enemies: thou anointest my head with oil; my cup runneth over.
Surely goodness and mercy shall follow me all the days of my life; and I will dwell in the house of LORD forever.

I don't remember how old I was when he sat me down with a stern warning that I was to memorize Psalm 23. But I remember feeling that it meant Jesus would maketh me lie down in the presence of Evil. Like force me to lie on the grass and Evil would lie on top of me? Or Jesus? I'd suffocate under the weight in a valley of shadows. Black shadows of death. And I was not *to fear Evil.*

If I was not supposed to fear Evil, was I supposed to fear Jesus?

To what LORD was my father referring I lie down for?

Eighteen

Emma called at dinnertime. I switched off the stove and peeled a banana for Elsa. She kicked her feet in her highchair, stretching her arms across the tray, calling, "*Bamma! Bamma!*" I handed it over, turned a chair at the dining table to face her, and sat down to hear Emma's story.

Emma and Ellyn gave the realtor fake names when they arrived at our childhood home, pretending Ellyn was the potential home buyer and Emma was helping her find a house.

"After looking around a while, we asked if there was an attic or something to accommodate Ellyn's storage needs. The realtor said yes there was, with two convenient openings—one in the garage and one in a bedroom closet inside the house; you know, Donald's old bedroom."

"Yeah."

"So, the realtor took us into the garage to get that tall ladder."

"The same ladder that was always hanging on the wall?"

"Yeah. Our father hasn't moved out all of his garage stuff, so it was still there. We pulled it off the hooks and dragged it into the house."

"Ellyn held the ladder, and I climbed up. It was dark, and we didn't have a flashlight, but I saw a rolled-up carpet, probably that old Oriental rug of Grandma Elsa's. It was the only thing up there."

"An Oriental rug?"

I'd remembered something about an Oriental rug, hoping it wasn't true.

"Did you tell Ellyn about the rug?" My throat and upper chest constricted. It took great effort to stay calm.

"Yeah, I told her. Why wouldn't I?"

"Just curious. Go on," I said, adrenalin pumping through my body.

"We moved the ladder to the attic in the garage to look for that knife you told us about." Emma cleared her throat. "Ellyn insisted on going up this time while I held the ladder. I was sweating in fear, afraid mom and dad would show up, trying to hide my face from the real estate lady standing right next to me."

"What did Ellyn see?"

"She stuck her head up into the attic really quick and came back down, shaking her head when the realtor turned to put the ladder back against the wall. Then the realtor insisted on showing us the backyard, so we *had* to go back there, you know, acting like we were still interested in the house, trying to hurry up and get the hell out of there. We were scared shitless. Like, what if mom and dad were down the street watching or something? That's how paranoid we were."

"We? You *and* Ellyn were afraid?" I asked sarcastically.

Ellyn, the notorious liar. Although she claimed she'd broken ties with our parents, I wasn't so sure. She was the one who told Emma about our parents selling their house. How did she know? Yet, neither of us had questioned Ellyn, wanting to believe she was *our* ally.

"Yeah, both of us were afraid," Emma replied defensively. "Back in the car, Ellyn told me there wasn't anything in the garage attic."

"Did you believe her?" I asked.

207

"Yeah. Why wouldn't I?"

"Just curious. You know how Ellyn is." Elsa had been playing with the banana peel and flung it across the room. I smiled.

"No, Hanna, she was just as scared as I was."

"All right. Forget it," I said. "Thanks for telling me what happened. I've got a hungry little girl here waiting for her dinner. I'll call you later. Okay?"

I tickled Elsa's bare little feet, kicking away in her highchair, and then finished cooking chicken in mushroom sauce, Elsa's favorite. We ate it with wild rice and peas.

Elsa and I did our nightly routine, beginning with a walk after dinner. Then bath time, followed by books and bed.

After Elsa was off in dreamland, I lolled on the couch, pondering my conversation with Emma.

Oriental rug. A knife blade in my chest when she mentioned it. Thoughts gathered, demanding I connect the pieces: the dream about Michael when I was pregnant; the vision of Jake holding the gun, surfacing a few months before in the codependency program; and a party in an old apartment building in the city. Even though Michael wasn't at that party, I suspected it was related to my dream. I paced the living room. A crazy scene projected onto my mind's movie screen. It had been coming in bursts of snapshots, now a film. I was fourteen . . .

Music is blaring. I think this is supposed to be a party. In east Rogers Park.

From the room's doorway where two guys just forced me to perform a sexual act to get them off, I see the couch, shaped like a comma, with a large square coffee table. A bunch of stoned people are sitting on it, a crescent moon of fucked-up kids. Low light comes through the windows in the room to my right, a narrow room with a fireplace called a piano room in these old apartment buildings. The light of a muted-gray, stormy, summer Chicago day illuminates a crazy scene. And the music is so loud! Are the neighbors deaf?

208

To my left is a long hallway leading to the kitchen, and the back door with a window framing dull, gray light outside. That door seems so far away, the gray light from its window a beacon beckoning an escape. I want to dash for it, but there are people back there. The front door, a solid wooden door with a brass doorknob, is right in front of me, just to my left. But I know that door is not a means of escape, either, nor are the windows in the narrow piano room with the fireplace.

I wish I could be sucked out the chimney to the roof like Santa Claus, where a sleigh pulled by reindeer would whisk me away to a faraway fairy tale land. Or maybe beautiful flying horses would rescue me. My only means of escape, ever, are in my fantasies, hiding deep inside my mind. Nightmares make me a prisoner. So, is this a nightmare imprisoning me here?

I pray it is, so I can wake up. Because a girl is screaming and I can't help her.

Standing in the doorway of the bedroom where I was just molested, the girl is to my right, her agony drowning out the loud music. Two people are holding her. I can only see their silhouettes, framed by the dusty light coming through the window of the piano room beyond them. I see a knife, the black shape of its blade. The scene is unreal, simply a charcoal drawing of someone's nightmare.

The girl was fourteen, like me, screaming in terror. I thought I recognized her, had maybe met her a few weeks before at a place Michael took me, but I couldn't remember where. I saw blips of a hill, trees, and water.

As I tossed and turned between asleep and awake, the girl rose out of the embers of my burning memories . . .

I'm standing against a living room wall with the girl. Karen? Yes, I think that's her name. It's her turn to be raped.

209

I tell her not to cry or scream and it will be over quickly.

She is a sheltered girl of wealth, I see. I hate her. She's a goodie-two-shoes, too special for all of this. She didn't want to take the acid they forced her to swallow earlier, and she's shaking now, terrified. I sense that the most deranged guys here are reacting to her fear. I nudge her with my elbow to shut her up.

She's begging and pleading. It feeds their frenzy and their guilt—they don't want to see how fucking crazy they are.

Hoping to get on their good side, I turn to Karen and shout, "Shut the fuck up!" I want to get this over with so I can leave. I don't even care about her anymore. I want out and she's prolonging it, intensifying it, making them frenetic, igniting their perversions, their violence.

"Shut. Up!" I screech, glaring into her eyes.

The kids on the horse-shoe couch only stare at the scene.

I'm starting to peak on the acid and everything gets really confusing. The silhouettes become real people. Wait. No. Now they are caricatures of people. Do I know that cartoony guy holding the knife? He's older than the rest of us.

Later, I don't know how much later, I'm in a basement, waking up from a nightmare. It's quiet. I'm lying on the floor. A yellowish ceiling light is sharply defined through the trails and paisley patterns of my acid trip, now on the other side of peaking. I still have hours more to go before I come down, but I'm more alert. Above me I see the sun setting through a narrow, horizontal window at ground level, just above a washer and dryer. Or is it the rising sun?

Where are the people who live in this building? Didn't they hear Karen screaming? Didn't they hear the music? Isn't someone going to come down here to do laundry?

I look around.

That girl, Karen, is rolled up in an Oriental rug. I wonder why, because they're so expensive. I know it's her because her long brown hair and a porcelain hand hang out of the end as if she's trying to crawl out. But she can't. She's dead. But I really, really don't want to know this. People drag the rug up the steps to a door opening out to the backyard. I look down so I don't have to see who they are. This can't be happening, it just can't.

I bolted upright on my sofa. Scenes flooded my mind from isolated storms scattered across the landscape of my brain. Pacing the room like a caged tiger, I suddenly remembered wearing blue jeans and a gray hooded jacket. I saw myself in those clothes being shoved up basement stairs, out the door into daylight . . .

The daylight is too bright. I wish to hide my shame in darkness.

Someone behind me pushes me up the stairs and through the basement door, and keeps shoving me across a bright green lawn to a small, tannish-yellowish car—a Toyota sedan, I think. It belongs to Jake, Maria's boyfriend. He shows me a gun and tells me to get in the car. I say nothing, sliding into the back seat with Maria.

Maria? Jake? What're they doing here? What's going on?

I was confused, because I saw myself in that gray hoodie and those jeans. I hadn't seen Maria and Jake at the party, but that didn't mean they weren't there. Maybe I'd spent the night on the basement floor, and they came the next day? Was this a different time I was wearing those same clothes, a different memory? Was Karen in the trunk of that car?

Jake.

The guy with the gun from my memory in codependency treatment . . .

They're discussing what to do with me—Maria, Jake, and someone in the front passenger seat I can't see because there's a fog obscuring him. I'm not sure if it's a natural fog or one I've created to not see the truth, like Chief Bromden did in the book, One Flew Over the Cuckoo's Nest. *I know it's a man in the front seat because I hear his voice but will myself not to know him. Maria talks fast in her thick Polish accent, trying to get us out of the car. "Look at her," she says, referring to me. "She's almost comatose. Hanna won't say anything. I promise."*

Then she slips into Polish, I think because she's scared.

This pisses off Jake and Fog Man, who shouts in what might be a familiar voice, "Speak English, for Chrissake!"

Maria turns to me and says, "Hanna, tell them you won't say anything."

Jake taps the gun on the steering wheel. We're driving north on Sheridan Road, past Northwestern University toward the North Shore villages of wealth and prestige. Bumping down a cobblestone street made of red bricks, I gape at Maria, unable to speak. She pleads with them to turn around.

Yeah. Jake had a gun . . .

With disgust, Jake makes a sharp U-turn and guns the engine.

Fog Man says, "Slow down. We don't want to draw attention." Even his voice is foggy, but I think I recognize it. So, I turn off my hearing.

Finally, they let us out at the entrance to the alley behind Maria's house. She yanks my arm, pulls me from the backseat of the car, slams the door, and we run without looking back. We enter the basement door into her bedroom. She pushes me down on a chair.

Maria's twin sister comes running down the stairs and whispers harshly in Polish. Their mother soon follows, talking loudly and gesturing with her arms, wanting to know where Maria has been and who I am, I suppose, but I'm only guessing that's what she's saying because it's in Polish. Maria goes upstairs with her mother. I hear them arguing in Polish as I drift off to sleep.

I'm awakened by a thud, like someone dropped a 10-pound weight. I feel drained and burnt out, as I always do after I come down from an acid trip, as if my soul has been away for a long time and has finally come back to my body. I don't know how long I've been asleep. Maria's twin sister sits in a chair beside Maria's bed, where I'm lying. I still can't speak.

Their mother, yelling in Polish, comes down the stairs with a police officer. Maria's twin nudges me to stand up. I look down at the policeman's shiny black shoes, refusing to look in his face. I say nothing. I can't speak. I can't hear either, his voice foggy and indistinct. He eventually leaves and I know I must go home.

I walked to the bathroom to splash water on my face. That first dream I'd had, the one of Michael in the gray room, drenched my mind. I saw him bending over the girl from the party, Karen, lying unconscious over his knees, her face ghostly white. Did Michael know what happened? Was that the secret we forgot? I was certain he hadn't been at the party. Perhaps that dream, unlike any I'd had before, symbolized the secret between us, though I didn't know how Michael would have known about the murder or if he really did. Why the gray room?

Maybe that dream came the way it did to shake me awake to the truth about my life, so I could save the life of the baby growing in my womb.

I circled the living room, carving a ring pattern in the carpet. I wanted to run out into the night, but Elsa was asleep in the bedroom. I peeked in on her, arms and legs sprawled across her crib. Watching her, my love for her strengthened me to keep going. I gently closed the door, walked back to the couch, and plopped down on it with a sigh of acceptance. Yes, I'd met Karen somewhere Michael had taken me—a hill, trees, and a creek below.

In the morning, I dropped Elsa off at Mrs. Lopez's and picked up a beer on my way to Ray's office.

I told him everything.

213

"I know I was tripping on acid at that party because of the paisley patterns linked like a fence between me and everyone else. Huge!" I demonstrated the size of the paisley patterns with my hands, about half the size of my body from head to waist. "I wish I could blame LSD, write off the murder as a hallucination. Oh my God. I said it. Murder!"

I wanted to believe I'd hallucinated the whole thing.

But that wasn't how LSD worked. Acid hallucinations were cartoon animals and psychedelic-colored paisley fractals, *everything* in colors of neon pink, orange, yellow, green, and sometimes white. The rabbits were always cartoon white. This murder—yes, murder!—was performed in harsh reality, not in make-believe psychedelic hues, though the details may have been skewed during the hours of peaking, when the acid trip is most intense and chaotic. Like a train moving so fast the scenery is a blur outside the windows, while the train rumbles and shakes down the tracks.

Ray rolled his chair over, took my hands, and looked into my eyes, as he always did when making a passionate plea. "God doesn't give us what we can't handle. Believe that." He gripped my hands tighter and shook them. "You are a strong woman. Being on drugs certainly obscured things, but trust that you recall what you need to recall. *And* you were only fourteen. Just a kid."

"I didn't feel like a kid."

"Maybe you didn't, but you were. When you see fourteen-year-olds, do you see them as adults?"

"No, I guess not."

"Pay attention now when you're at the grocery store and the mall. Look at the kids. Watch their behavior. Fourteen-year-olds are still children. You were one of them. You were no different, Hanna."

"Yes, I *was* different."

He looked deeply into my eyes, gazing into my soul. "No, you were not. You were no different than anyone else would be in that situation, no matter the age." His eyes, brimming with tears, looked glassy, like people on acid. But instead of enlarged LSD-induced pupils, Ray's were pinpricks, heightening the color of his greenish-hazel eyes. I peered into them, hypnotized.

"Ray, do you remember when we met in the outpatient codependency program?"

"Of course!" Ray declared with customary exuberance.

"Jake, the guy with the gun I just told you about, who was driving the car down Sheridan Road? He was the guy with the gun I remembered in treatment, when my counselor dismissed it, saying I was 'only seeking attention.'"

"I remember that," he said. "*I* didn't dismiss you."

"True. That's why I asked you to be my psychologist. And now I realize the memory of Jake was a part of remembering this murder." I cringed at the word. "And the dream about Michael, when I was pregnant, was also related, and began everything."

Ray nodded.

"There's something else about that apartment. Or maybe another apartment in the city. I think it was a different time, maybe in the fall. People I know were there, a neighbor and maybe one of my sisters. We were sitting in a circle in candlelight, passing a silver chalice. A bunch of teenagers." I felt myself crumple like a wadded-up playbill after a Broadway show. Ray's hands around mine held me up. "How could that be? It's so crazy. How could so many insane things happen to one person?"

"I don't know. But I promise we'll figure it out. Together." Ray spoke with a seriousness divergent from his usual upbeat, motivational speaker tone. A single tear fell over the edge of his left eye. I watched it slowly slide down his cheek, where it rounded beneath his chin and slid down his neck, disappearing behind the collar of his crisp, white dress shirt.

I wanted to be far, far away.

Ray's grip on my hands kept me from slipping off the cliff of despair I'd slid off of as a kid whenever I was left with "only my imagination," abandoned in a dark forest or building, or that dark cave-like room of rough rock walls and cold floor—the place of my occult teachings. I'd persistently been telling myself that my flooding memories were indeed only in my imagination, repeating the refrain from my childhood. I hated Ray for making me see the truth.

Ray was speaking, but I couldn't hear him. I saw his mouth shape the word "Hanna!" and he shook my arms. His tear-brimmed, shining eyes spilled more tears. The ridges outlining his mouth deepened.

I snapped back like a rubber band. I could hear again. I pulled my arms away and sat on my hands.

"I'm fine," I said.

Ray looked at the clock, sighing. "Ok then. I'll see you tomorrow."

Oh, yeah. There were time limits in this office.

I stood quickly and grabbed my purse, feeling the pain of rejection, surmising he'd shaken me and called my name to end our fifty-minute session.

When I got home, I called to cancel the next day's appointment, which I'd never done. Then I sat on the floor in front of the TV and clicked on Oprah—my friend and sister, an angel sent to Earth to help save me.

At bedtime, I swayed with Elsa in my arms, singing songs until she fell asleep. Considering the possibility that my flat vocals may have *bored* her to sleep, I smiled and placed her in the crib with her pink bear, tucking them in with a soft blanket.

I watched Elsa's sweet face and form for a long time, wondering how I would protect her. She sighed in her sleep and splayed her arms and legs out like a starfish; the relaxed sleep of one who feels secure.

How long would that last?

I retreated to my spot on the sofa and gazed out the window at a gray sky settling into night. Grackles were coming to roost in a tree outside the window.

They looked like large ravens, with long tail feathers almost as long as their body. Their loud, distinct squawking had become a source of comfort and stability in my chaotic life. I'd come to look forward to our time together in the evenings.

I had never forgotten running through the alley with Maria. And I'd always remembered the police officer and Maria's mother yelling in Polish. But that's all I'd remembered, and wasn't sure it was connected.

I thought it very strange, the way memories presented themselves in jolting, disjointed scraps—the dream of Michael, the visions of Jake, the party, running to Maria's basement bedroom—glued together into the story of a *murder*. Which I could no longer deny.

Outside, the Grackles began quieting for the night.

One way or another, I conceded, dark witches must have been connected to that murder. Witches too dangerous to acknowledge back then. Unbelievable, mind-twisting manipulators of me and Maria and Jake. And Karen, even. And perhaps Michael. All of us so young.

The people of darkness governing my childhood planned my life long before I started school, where I viewed the happenings in the classroom and on the playground as on a movie screen. When I involved myself in the film—which I did, having many friends—I was an actress playing a role. I kept waiting for my *real* life to begin, knowing that the life arranged for me was a stage production.

Hidden in my heart, in a place beyond the stage, I sensed my true life was one planned by a Divine Light of the Universe, though it was impossible to believe when the evil witches shut out the Light with a curtain of hate and fear. The subtle whisper of a Higher Power above and beyond all was elusive. It was easier to believe evil was real.

The dark ones never intended me to be the author of my life. Nor Elsa's.

I was merely a chapter in a story perhaps hundreds of years old, and Elsa was the next chapter. I saw no way to change it.

How could someone like me live a regular life?

I was convinced Elsa would be better off without me. Safer. If I were dead, no one could steal her from me. It made perfect sense. I even discussed it with Ray, whom I continued seeing, of course, shoving aside my hurt feelings that counseling me was his *job*, with time limits.

"Elsa would certainly *not* be safe if you died," Ray said. "Neil would have her. Don't you get that?"

No, I didn't.

Nineteen

My parents are in my bedroom. So is Neil, dressed in surgical gear—a paper gown and cap. I can't see Marjorie and Evert, but I hear them talking to someone else is in the room, though I can't see him either. Marjorie says it's "the doctor." I am lying on the bed Evert bought after Elsa was born, the headboard made of oak slats fashioned into a starburst design. They are performing a surgery on me.

The way the light filters through the shade on the bedroom window, I see it is morning. Neil stands to my right gripping my hand, which I struggle to wrench free, while someone pulls worms from, or places worms inside, my vagina. I have no idea where Elsa is.

It just popped into my mind one day. It seemed to be a dream at first.

Mulling it over later, I wasn't sure if it was a dream or a memory. Perhaps Marjorie and Evert subjected me to a brainwashing technique while they were in Austin, using Neil to assist them in their attempt to maintain control over me by keeping me in fear and confusion. Because I certainly was in fear and confusion. A mock surgery to implant worms or remove them from the most intimate part of my body, the channel from which my cherished baby daughter made her way into this realm. What was it supposed to signify? It was crazy. Maybe they used mind-control to turn off my memory of the incident, while implanting it deep inside my unconscious mind as a ridiculous warning of some kind. Maybe I'd filed it in my mind's amnesia drawer, only to remember when it was safe. What I wanted was for it to be a nightmare, nothing more.

My life was in shambolic disarray. From mid-January to the end of February 1989, my existence was a big paranoia fest. Trying to combat the confusion that kept me in turmoil, I questioned everything in terms of real, maybe real, or not real, and made a list of bullet points:

- Chanting outside my window: Not Real
- Dark figures in the corners of my eyes: Not Real
- Strange woman who wasn't a stranger: Maybe Real
- Dream, or memory, of a mock surgery: Maybe Real
- Dream about Michael: Real dream, maybe revealing a memory
- My father's sexual assaults: Real
- Visit from Marjorie & Evert: Real
- Marjorie & Evert hastily selling house I grew up in: Real
- Emma & Ellyn snooping in the attic for evidence: Real
- Hang-up calls: Real
- Jake holding a gun: Real

I hesitated before adding:

- Murder of the girl at that party: Probably Real

At the end of February, Neil's step-sister called. Cynthia. We'd been friends early on in my marriage to Neil. She'd visit us in Round Rock. She liked western wear, so I gave her my western-style ruffled blouses when I'd moved on from that look to another. I liked Cynthia, was happy to hear her voice. We chatted with the niceties of friends who hadn't spoken for a time.

Then she said, "I was thinking of Neil bringing Elsa up here to stay at my house in Abilene."

"Stay at your house?"

"Yeah. Neil told me you're not doing well. I thought you might need a break."

I tried to remain cool and composed. "Thanks, Cynthia, but it wouldn't be a good idea to separate Elsa from me. She'd be unhappy. But it would be great if you'd come down to Austin. I could sure use some help. For a weekend, maybe?"

"I don't think so, Hanna. Why don't you let me take her? Then you can have some time for yourself." Her tone was not one of love and concern, which I would expect from my friend. Instead, it sounded like an accusation, as if I'd done something wrong and Elsa should be away from me.

"I don't need time to myself. I need help, you're right about that. Things *aren't* going well. And I'm not about to let Neil take Elsa to Abilene, or anywhere else, because he's the biggest part of the problem."

"I've talked to him. He wants what's best." *Oh my God, what is she saying?*

"Cynthia, I'd love to tell you what's been going on. Your friendship would be nice right now. But Elsa is *not* going anywhere with Neil."

"Okay then," she sighed.

I said goodbye with a premonition I would never again share a kind word with her. I felt so alone.

Neil came over that night, threatening me with the same old bullshit of committing me to a "mental institution" and vehemently insisting that I allow my sick, twisted parents to see Elsa. Now he included his resolve to take Elsa to Abilene to stay with Cynthia—another fear added to the popping, sputtering embers of the roaring fire raging through my life, incinerating everything I thought was real. I had to accept *all* of the truths rising from the cinders of my disillusionment, piling Cynthia's withdrawal of friendship on top.

No way was Neil taking Elsa *anywhere*.

Entirely spent, I didn't think I'd hold on much longer, trying to protect my precious angel on my own. The bottle of benztropine pills for the side effects of Haldol, prescribed by Dr. Dumass at the psychiatric hospital in Albuquerque, beckoned me to untwist its cap. I knew they'd knock me out, but was unsure if they'd put me to sleep forever. Needing to know, I called a pharmacy to find out if they were deadly.

"I have a friend who is contemplating suicide," I told the pharmacist. "Will benztropine kill her?"

"Yes, if she takes enough of it," he assured me.

"The bottle has about sixty pills in it."

"Please get help for your friend. Those pills are deadly. If you give me her name, I'll try to help her myself."

"That's very kind of you. I'll help my friend. If I can't, I'll call you back. Okay?" His kindness almost made me want to confess and ask him for help.

He tried to keep me on the phone. "Sure. Please do. Please let me help."

I assumed he knew it was me contemplating suicide. I politely said goodbye and hung up.

At midnight, I fell into a fitful sleep of crazy dreams, scenes of chaos jumping around, exhausting me further; an exhaustion beyond this world, which was over for me.

I woke up in the morning to pouring rain striking the windows like an angry swarm of bees on a mission to avenge a disturbed hive. I imagined them breaking through the glass to sting me to death, the perfect setting to solidify my suicide plan. Ray and his wife would fight for custody of Elsa, I decided, though I neglected to tell them.

I put my plan into action three weeks before my thirtieth birthday.

The first step was to ask Mrs. Lopez to keep Elsa overnight.

"Of course!" she said. "She can stay as long as you like."

Everyone loved Elsa. She was easy, adapted to any situation, smiled all the time, and even when ill, she was a delight.

"And don't worry," she added, "I won't let Neil have her."

I had recently started drinking an occasional beer. In the 1980s, the state of Texas permitted open containers in automobiles, so I'd swing into any corner convenience store on my way to Ray's office and grab a can or two from a giant barrel filled with an assortment of beer buried in ice. Checkout clerks plunked my single can purchases into beer-can-sized paper bags.

On the day I chose to die, a single can of beer wasn't going to provide the courage I needed to do it. I'd have to get good and plastered.

I convinced Pamela and Judith to go to a bar, wanting to spend my last night alive with my best friends, surprised they agreed to go with me. They hadn't a clue I was planning to commit suicide, of course.

To go out drinking together was unusual for us, something we'd never done. Aside from my recent beers in a bag, none of us were big drinkers. Although Judith drank an occasional glass of wine with dinner, I'd never seen Pamela drink even one beer or a glass of wine.

They picked me up at my apartment to go dancing at a popular club. As usual, like in the old days when I drank all the time, I was the life of the party, dancing and raising hell. Until I got home.

With the desperation of a madwoman, I staggered into the dark bedroom and grabbed the bottle of benztropine off my dresser, where it'd sat looking at me. I was acutely aware of Elsa's absence. Our apartment felt empty without her energy, as if I'd abandoned her. Which, indeed, I was about to do.

I twisted off the cap and, like a drunk in the throes of a binge, I poured all that would fit into my mouth, at least half the bottle, around thirty pills, and started swallowing. I poured in the second half and tried to swallow those, but my gag reflex kept throwing them back up. I made it to the kitchen with my head tilted skyward to avoid spitting them out and drew another glass of water. I swallowed and re-swallowed several times before the entire bottle of benztropine would stay down.

My apartment was dark. I turned on the little light over the stove.

I felt utterly alone, wallowing in self-pity. Although Pamela and Judith and their families cared for Elsa and me, their support had waned during the months of my constant crises. I didn't blame them. Who would want to deal with my bizarre life? I didn't want to. And now my evening with them was over. My life was over. My concern was all for Elsa, longing for her to have a safe and happy life. *Safe*.

I opened a bottle of anti-anxiety pills, prescribed by Dr. Dweebin, that were perched on the edge of the dining table. In one gulp, I swallowed them, too. Then I yanked open the silverware drawer and rattled around for a steak knife, pulling one out to examine it for sharpness. The blade glinted in the little yellow glow over the stove. I brushed it along the vein of a wrist, testing to see if I could do it.

In the kitchen, I teetered on my feet, sinking to my knees as the drugs took effect. I tried not to vomit, keeping my face turned upward as I crawled to the phone and yanked it off the counter by its cord. I called Ray and asked him to take my daughter, begging him to fight for her as I slipped into unconsciousness, the knife slipping from my hand before I could make a cut.

As if in a cave, I saw nothing but black.

Beautiful violin music floated towards me from somewhere far away, vibrating the blackness as it grew nearer. The most exquisite music I'd ever heard surrounded me like a cocoon, calming and soothing my tormented thoughts. I felt no fear in the darkness enveloping me, only peace. A peace that words would never adequately describe.

Drifting far above and away from my body, I still felt like myself, while the violins drew me farther from my life on planet Earth. In total darkness, I floated with the music, on the music, in the music, becoming one with the strings' vibrations. I didn't see the bright white light many people describe in their near-death experiences. Maybe my eyes were closed and I traveled beyond the light. I don't know. In the vast darkness of what must have been outer space, I instead saw a glowing golden planet taking form below.

The violin music cushioned my descent as I drifted toward it, a feather gently cascading to the golden globe.

Floating in the stream of string music, the power of the gold planet drew me to it. I remembered being there as a child of five, when I nearly died the first time, though I did not know how or why. As I was about to alight on the surface—*thunk*—I was back in my body, in my apartment in Austin.

An awful bitterness stung my nostrils. A paramedic was screaming in my face, strapping me down to a gurney. I struggled against the restraints. I couldn't move or speak, like in a dream when you want to run and scream, but you can't.

By the time we reached the hospital, I was unconscious again. Fleetingly, I opened my eyes to bright lights shining above me. A woman bent over my face with understanding concern while someone shoved something down my throat. I couldn't breathe. She nodded knowingly, patted my arm, and I was out again.

When I fully regained consciousness the next day, I was sprawled on a bed in the emergency room in my underwear, looking down at my chest and bra covered in black stuff that looked like charcoal. A kind nurse said, yes, it was charcoal, used to pump my stomach. She told me how deeply concerned she had been, thinking I must have been in severe anguish to want to die so badly.

"Even after pumping your stomach, we lost you several times during the night," she said, patting my hand.

Sometime later, she returned. "Here," she said, handing me the bedside phone. "Dr. Gunn wants to speak with you."

She smiled, patted my arm, and left.

Dr. Gunn, Ray, said I had to be admitted to a psychiatric hospital, that it wasn't an option, legally, because I had attempted suicide.

"I've made all the arrangements," he said. "I'll be by to see you tomorrow afternoon."

I went home for a few things. Judith agreed to keep Elsa at night and take her to Mrs. Lopez's during the day.

Neil didn't like it, of course. I figured his compensation was me going to a mental institution at last. Strange thing is, he never said a word about it, aside from protesting Elsa staying with Judith, which I ignored.

Ted, Pamela's husband, picked me up at my apartment and drove me to the psychiatrist hospital. On the way, he told me what happened.

"Ray called and woke me up the night of your suicide, asking me to check on you," Ted said. "I went over to your place and when you didn't come to the door, I looked in the window through a bent slat in the blind and saw you lying on the floor."

Ted called 911 and stayed until the police arrived and broke down the door.

"When they turned on the lights, your eyes were open and staring," he said. "It was terrible. You weren't breathing, and you had no pulse. Paramedics had to revive you with smelling salts."

Hence the bitter, burning sensation in my nose. I cringed. What a pathetic story. *I* was pathetic.

"Please, Hanna, *promise* me you will never do this again."

"I'm sorry," is all I said.

"Call *us* when you're feeling bad. We're always here for you. Always!"

As soon as I arrived at the psychiatric hospital, Dr. Dweebin, the assigned psychiatrist, began pumping me with Xanax. "For your depression," he said.

That night, thinking about my near-death experience, I knew I survived for a reason. The Light Beings came to me in a strange dream, urging me to embrace life, that I was needed. But I wanted to go back to the peace I felt with them.

In the morning, Dr. Dweebin told me he'd consulted with Ray about my childhood abuse. He knew a woman, Hillary, with in-depth knowledge about my abuse, even the Ritual Abuse, as he called it, which she too had survived.

"I conduct group therapy in my office once a week, and Hillary helps me," said Dr. Dweebin. "It's a mix of men and women survivors of childhood sexual abuse. Would you like to meet Hillary and join the group?"

"Sure," I said, eager to meet Hillary.

She came to the hospital later that day. Tall, around six feet, her long dark hair, hanging loose on her shoulders, was starting to gray. She shared her story of abuse, holding my attention with intense, large, gray eyes. Hillary grasped Occult Abuse better than anyone I'd talked to thus far, with a no-nonsense, all business, yet gentle manner. She understood my anxiety and turmoil about all the children abused every moment of every day. She, too, was consumed by that fact.

"It's killing me, eating me alive," I said. "I can't go on living in a society that does little or nothing to help children."

"You *can* go on living. Trust me, I understand your longing to help." Hillary paused, looking up at the ceiling as if searching for something up there. She dropped her gaze to my face and said, "I've learned ways to cope, which I'll teach you in Dr. Dweebin's group."

"Thank you so much," I said, clasping her hands, not wanting to let go.

After she left, I pondered all she'd validated. A vague notion took shape, almost like a memory, of something I was supposed to do, my purpose for being alive, forgotten long ago. I would have to heal from the past if I were to find my purpose again, including no more alcohol. I didn't want anything mind-altering, especially not the Xanax prescribed by Dr. Dweebin, which I knew was habit-forming. I took it, though, while I was in the hospital. Man, was I high.

"Dr. Dweebin, I'm still groggy from the drugs I took, and the Xanax is making it worse."

"You're severely depressed. After all, you tried to get attention with your suicide attempt," Dr. Dweebin said, looking down at my chart. "So, you've got our attention. Xanax will help with your depression."

His patronizing attitude cut like a shard of glass. He'd been kind and understanding when I met him. He wouldn't even look at me now.

"I was told I was dead when they found me. When I came to in the hospital, a nurse said I died several times during the night. You believe that was only for attention?"

Dr. Dweebin finally looked up at me.

"I swallowed and re-swallowed an entire bottle of benztropine. I don't see how adding Xanax is going to help right now."

"Enough about the drugs," he said with finality. "You're depressed. End of story. The Xanax will take the edge off, and I'm also prescribing Prozac, which you may have to take every day for the rest of your life."

I took the Prozac and Xanax, and was totally wasted until the day of my discharge, when I dumped the Xanax in the trash.

* * * *

1964. I'm five years old. I'm leaving Earth, floating in blackness. I'm not afraid. I feel free. Pretty violin music is taking me on a journey. Down below, I see a beautiful place with gold rocks, gold dirt, and even gold people.

I arrive. I feel like I belong here.

Warm, tranquil, goodness surrounds me.

The most beautiful music I've ever heard fills everything. It permeates the warmth, the rocks, and the sky. I don't want to leave, so I'm hiding behind a big gold rock, trying not to be seen by these beautiful people of pure gold, only they aren't regular people. They're glowing, golden lights shaped into people. I want to stay with them, but I can tell they won't let me. That's why I'm hiding.

One of them, Agnes, finds me behind the rock. She and the others don't talk with words. They speak with their minds, like Emma and I do when it isn't safe to talk out loud. That's how I know her name. She doesn't have a face, and neither do the others. Like the others, Agnes wears a long robe of glittering gold, but her robe glitters over a lighter colored, golden-white gown, filmy, like a nightgown. High shimmering collars curve over their heads like halos.

Agnes is beautiful, pure, shimmering light. She swirls and vibrates with the soothing violin music, which is a part of her. Peace and love pour out of her and over me. She tells me, in her way, that it is not my time yet and I can't stay. You have a job to do on Earth, her vibrational mind tells me. She grabs my hand, and we travel at light speed through a tunnel of white lights.

Thunk—I'm lying in a box looking up at Emma, my beloved twin. She's sobbing frantically. Our mother peers over her shoulder, a tight-lipped look of anger creasing her face. I blink up at her. She grunts in disgust and walks away.

I've come back from the dead. I don't know how I died or why I'm lying in a box. And I don't understand why my mother is angry at me. . . For being alive?

In modern science, a wormhole is a narrow tube in space that, if stretched, may one day transport a spaceship—a tunnel leading to the outer reaches of space, or possibly another dimension. When I learned this, it reminded me of my two near-death experiences. Perhaps what scientists are discovering is the transport of the soul.

Twenty

My death journey's unearthly sense of peace faded during five days of bright lights and Dr. Dweebin's "professional" advice at the psych hospital. Mercifully, a lingering golden light remained, unquenched, changing me in ways I would not fully comprehend for many years.

I returned to my apartment with a fresh view of life, inspired, ironically, by my desperate desire to end it the week before.

It was *me* Elsa needed. There was no doubt about that.

With a new, acute awareness that she would indeed suffer if I died, I was dismayed to think I considered leaving her for even one moment. From hence forth, my determination was to fill Elsa's life with joy and laughter, to nurture her toward a blissful awe for living.

On our first evening back together, Stevie Wonder was on the radio singing "For Once in My Life." I grabbed Elsa's chubby hands to dance. Throwing her head back, she laughed with open-mouthed hilarity:

> For once, unafraid
> I can go where life leads me
> Somehow, I know I'll be strong

Elated, I scooped her up in an arc and slung her onto my hip. Holding her little hand, I stretched out her arm in a jubilant, spinning dance, singing as loud as I could with Stevie:

> For once, I can say
> This is mine, you can't take it
> As long as I know I have [Elsa]
> I can make it
> For once in my life
> I have someone who needs me

We collapsed on the floor in joy.

My exuberance for life endured for a few more days. I looked at life through Elsa's eyes, reborn into a new world unlike anything I'd known. We giggled, played with toys, and went for long walks in the evenings. It was fabulous.

Fabulous until the dark side of my life revisited, reminding me with what I still needed to contend. It began with a phone call from my sister Lorain.

"I'm going to call mom and dad in Florida and tell them you're dead," Lorain blurted when I answered the phone. She said they were at Bob and Joy's condo, their friends from childhood.

I didn't bother asking how Lorain knew Marjorie and Evert were in Florida. Ellyn must have told her, despite her denial of having any kind of communication with them. My real life, barging its way into the new one I was creating for my daughter, was an intrusion I didn't appreciate. I preferred not to know how Lorain found out Marjorie and Evert were vacationing in Florida.

"Why would you do that, Lorain?" I said, completely flabbergasted.

"To fuck with them," she said with vengeance. I heard the hurt of a child.

I half-heartedly asked her not to do it, curious to see how Marjorie and Evert would respond to the news of my death.

Two hours later, Lorain called back. "They didn't believe me at first, but I convinced them you killed yourself."

"Oh, Lorain, I wish you hadn't done that. Now what?"

"They said they were getting the next flight out."

"*What?*" I panicked. "To where? Austin?"

"I don't know. I was so happy to disrupt *their* lives for a change, I didn't ask."

I felt a rush of satisfaction, yes, but mostly of fear.

"What am I supposed to do if they come here? I *am* alive, you know."

"Oh, who cares? Let them come. Maybe our *father* will have one of those heart attacks our *mother* always said he'd have if we told him the truth about anything." She said it just like that, not dad and mom, but father and mother, putting a formal distance between them and us.

"Yeah, Lorain, but then I'll have to face them."

I listened to her rant and rave, which I didn't deny her. She wanted to fuck with their heads like they'd fucked with ours—confuse them and make them wonder what's real.

I didn't want to have to see their faces when they learned I was alive. Honestly, it would have been equally painful to see relief as it would disappointment.

"Lorain, give me the number where they're at."

"No way."

"I have to tell them I'm alive."

"*I'll* call and tell them you're alive. Then I'll wait a while, call back, and convince them you really are dead. Then call back and say you're not. They'll be all flustered, not knowing what's what, making them putty in our hands."

"To what end, Lorain? Either you or I *have* to tell them I'm alive."

"But we've got them by the balls. Isn't this great?"

"What if they show up here? What am I supposed to do? Invite them in for a party or something?"

Lorain raged some more, then became quiet.

"Lorain?"

"Yeah, I'm here. Sorry. I hadn't thought about what it would be like for you if they went to Austin. I was just happy to hurt them. Make them *suffer*," she added with a ragged edge to her voice.

"I know, Lorain. I understand."

I couldn't be angry with her raw emotion. I shared it. We were treading down the dark, twisted path our parents had laid for us.

Together, Lorain and I were capable of a heinous psychological plot against our parents. I felt pleasure envisioning them out of their minds in anxiety, not knowing the truth, pacing the floor of their vacation condo, writhing in agony.

I'd been living with that agonizing, mind-bending frustration every time the phone rang at 3 a.m. *And* whenever Neil threatened to have me "committed." The agony that had invited me to swallow the pills that temporarily killed me.

"Lorain, we can't do it. It's not right. Either you call them or you give me the number."

She reluctantly turned over Bob and Joy's Florida phone number.

We'd known Bob and Joy our whole lives; Marjorie and Evert's lifelong Swedish friends. I'd always liked them, and wondered about their involvement in the cult. They seemed like such normal people, it was difficult to believe they were evil witches. I had no memory of their involvement, but that didn't mean they weren't. I didn't want to believe they were. I didn't want to believe any of this. Yet, the way Lorain wanted to fuck with our parents' heads, and the fact that she and I knew how, was confirmation of any lingering doubts of an evil cult.

But I refused to play tit for tat with Marjorie and Evert, to turn their sick mind games onto them for revenge. My goal was moving on, keeping Elsa safe.

Fucking with Marjorie and Evert was not the way to freedom. It took every ounce of courage I possessed to pick up my heavy phone. Marjorie's voice was shaky when Bob put her on the line.

"Oh, Hanna, why did you and Lorain do this to us?" Her voice cracked in a way that'd always pulled at my heartstrings.

On the defensive, I disdainfully proclaimed, "I did *nothing* to you. You did it to yourself." Then I added, like a good little tattletale, "Besides, it was Lorain's idea, and I told her not to do it."

Marjorie handed the phone to Evert.

"Is that honestly you, Hanna?" I heard a crack in his voice, shattering my heart.

"Who else would it be?" I snapped. I wouldn't give in to sympathy for them.

"Are you sure you're not pretending to be Hanna?"

His voice quavered. I heard fear. It occurred to me that my father probably cared more about us playing games with his sense of reality than whether or not his daughter was dead. Good, I thought. Now he knew how we had felt throughout our childhoods.

Caught up in the thrill of beating him at his own game, I wanted to laugh and say I was Emma and that I, Hanna, *was* dead. I willed myself with all my might not to feel sorry for him and Marjorie, but I couldn't do it. I refused to be like them. I convinced Evert it was me.

"Listen, your mother and I will come there to get you. We'll move you back to Chicago. You and little Elsa can stay with us." That's the way he put it, not mom, but your mother, putting a formal distance between them and me. "I know a psychiatrist you can see," he said. "So you can stop all this nonsense."

I laughed. "Yeah, right."

"I'm serious. You are a very sick woman. You need help, and I've got a doctor for you." His voice clipped with condescending mockery, believing he'd regained control as the puppet master, attempting to attach his strings.

"Yes, I *do* need help. Thanks to *you*. You're the crazy one if you think I would *ever* see a psychiatrist you chose or *ever* allow you to run my life. I only called to tell you I'm alive because it seemed the right thing to do. That's it."

"We'd still like to come and get you and the baby, and—"

"Don't you *dare* show up here! I'll call the police if you do." I hung up, my hands shaking.

Tucking Elsa into bed that night, I realized there had been no three-ring phone calls that day.

They resumed at 3 a.m.

For several weeks I nervously anticipated the arrival of Marjorie and Evert, relieved beyond words that they stayed away.

With my prescription for Prozac, I resumed daily sessions with Ray, followed by The Oprah Winfrey Show. I started Dr. Dweebin's weekly therapy group on Tuesday nights as well, and let Neil babysit.

Dr. Dweebin sat on the floor with us, his patients, learning from Hillary how to work with us. She was an incredible healer, and the one actually running the group. Hillary gently and lovingly coaxed out the destructive behaviors we'd developed to cope with our abuse, getting to our gut-level feelings of shame. We loved her. She helped me see more deeply into how I used confusion as a defense against the truth, having developed during the twisted head games Marjorie and Donald played with me.

I found out a few years later that Dr. Dweebin only paid Hillary twenty dollars a session.

There were six of us in the group—Starr, Vincent, Norman, Susan, Peter, me—our insurance agencies paying over one hundred dollars each for every session.

I bonded quickly with Vincent and Starr. They became my best friends, aside from Pamela and Judith, who were busy with their families. I think they

235

were relieved to pass on the torch, so to speak, though Pamela still invited us for dinner and invited Vincent now, too. She'd also babysit so he and I could see a movie or go for a walk. On weekends, Vincent took Elsa and me to the lake and out for dinner, sitting with me in the evenings after Elsa went to bed. He was handsome in a clean-cut way, with light brown hair, brown eyes, and the athletic build of a golfer. I was 5'8" and he was maybe an inch or two taller.

Starr was different from anyone I'd ever met. She was a lot younger than I, fifteen years younger. The first time I saw her, she was sitting on the floor in Dr. Dweebin's therapy room, head bent, hiding her face. Her head was shaved, except for one thick green-and-purple strand of hair cascading down the center of her face, lightly curving across her chin. She wore black pants and a black leather jacket with zippers on the sleeves, down each side, and diagonally across her chest. A painted green dragon filled the back of her jacket from neck to waist. When she stood up, she trudged around in black combat boots, which I soon found she wore with everything, including shorts and the occasional skirt.

I had never been in proximity to a child whom one would expect, by her outward appearance, to be a fallen angel.

When Starr lifted her beautiful, unusual eyes to greet a new member of the group, me, I was startled by the wise, lonely soul peering out of crystal eyes the color of ginger, almost orange, with flecks of sand and chocolate. Meeting her gaze, I witnessed the same vast expanse of the universe in her eyes as I had seen the first time I looked into my daughter's. Starr and I connected immediately, understanding what dwelt behind each other's eyes. A connection unbroken by time and space. Her peacock-feather strand of hair falling over her creamy white face wasn't enough to mask her innocence, nor was her armor of leather strong enough to hide her angelic spirit.

I was astounded to learn that Starr, fifteen, had been living on her own for several months, renting an apartment and eating Ramen noodles for breakfast, lunch, and dinner because she could barely support herself. She mowed lawns

236

and ironed clothes for a living, paid in cash because she was too young for a worker's permit. Her mother drove her to and from Dr. Dweebin's therapy group, which appeared to be the extent of her relationship with her parents.

Starr soon began riding over on a moped her father had given her.

She'd arrive in shorts with a mismatched t-shirt, her feet protected in her ever-present combat boots, which she seemed reluctant to remove, even when we went to my apartment complex swimming pool. I always invited her to stay for dinner. She enjoyed feeding Elsa, nineteen months old.

Elsa adored Starr. During dinner one evening, she took the plate of peas Starr was feeding her and smashed them on her head. Starr froze. I giggled, Elsa giggled, and Starr looked at me to make sure it was okay for her to giggle, too.

Years later, Starr told me she appreciated me allowing her to feed my baby, being that her fallen angel persona—leather jacket, shaved head, combat boots—tended to scare people. "You accepted me as I was. And am," she said.

My upcoming thirtieth birthday charged my brain with notions of life or death. The insight I'd gained into life's infinite possibilities slowly faded, replaced by renewed, unabated suicidal ideation.

I sensed my thirtieth birthday triggered my thoughts of death, though I didn't know how or why. I told Vincent everything, including the patterns of three I saw everywhere. Vincent, a former engineering student with a pragmatic mind, said with a smile, "I think you're suffering from over-thinking." Then added, somewhat reluctantly, "But I have to admit, it *is* eerie that your thirtieth birthday is falling on Good Friday," which I hadn't known.

"Oh shit! I didn't know that," I said. "So, my thirtieth birthday, divisible by three, will be on Good Friday! I'm ending the *third* decade of my life, Elsa was born *six* weeks early, and even the day she was born is divisible by three. Come on, Vincent, don't you see?"

"Yeah, but the year Elsa was born is not divisible by three," Vincent interjected. "See what you're doing? You're looking for suspicious meanings everywhere. That's not good for you."

"Oh, so you *don't* believe me. You just pretend you do, so I'll shut up."

Vincent chuckled, flipping his light brown bangs. "That's not true."

"I don't see what's so funny, Vincent." I pulled away and crossed my arms over my chest.

He pulled me over and put his arm around me. "I *believe* you." He looked into my eyes, his chin slightly bent, earnestness swimming in his cocoa eyes. "But let's look at the facts, okay? The phone calls logically *can* occur, right? And logically, maybe they are coming in patterns—"

"Aha! See, you don't believe me."

"I didn't say that," he rushed on. "The phone calls are in patterns of three, okay? But, seriously, think about it. Elsa was born in 1987, in August, the eighth month of the year. Neither of those numbers are divisible by three. So what if the day is? Nobody could possibly have made you give birth to her on *that* day. Think about it, Hanna."

"Well, yeah. I guess I *am* getting a bit squirrelly," I sighed. "Even so, Elsa *was* born six weeks early."

"Oh, geez. Yeah, that's true, I'll admit, and creepy. But Hanna, no one could have arranged her birth on that exact day. Right?"

"I suppose. I'm sorry."

"Don't be sorry. It's understandable. You've been trying to sort through a lot of stuff." He placed my head on his shoulder.

Tears flowed down my face like rain on Marjorie's kitchen window, in the only home I knew as a kid. I thought about the day when Marjorie, the only mother I knew, sat at *my* table looking out *my* window, right here in this apartment. I missed Marjorie's kitchen window. But I kept it to myself. I never told anyone how much I missed her.

Before I could crawl deeper into self-pity, an idea climbed up the ladder of my lost memory vault, shutting out my grief and replacing my sorrow with fear. Had I been programmed to kill myself on my thirtieth birthday? Were the phone calls a trigger to make me do it?

A bizarre recollection insinuated itself upon me. Could it be? The dark, earthen place made of rock, where faint, flickering light illuminated the floor, ceiling, and walls—it was there I learned about the number three, in a weird class I attended, instructions on the ways of The Circle, the coven. I was supposed to be in a trance during my training, but I never fully succumbed, thanks to the games Emma and I had played to stay in touch with reality.

I told Vincent as it came to me, thankful to have someone to tell who wasn't restricted to an hour at a time. Sitting beside me on the couch, his arm around my shoulder, he just listened, nodding his head.

Some practitioners of Satanism and black magic use the number three in their occult practices to signify the Holy Trinity in Christianity—the Father, the Son, and the Holy Ghost. They believe that through the innocence of children they can capture the power of God—the true Source of all Power—harnessing it to conjure spirits of darkness to do their bidding.

TwentyOne

Vincent brought over a flier for a public lecture on Austin-area Satanic ritual crimes, presented by Sergeant Lamar Daniels, an Austin police detective. I stared at it in astonishment.

"Do you wanna go?" Vincent asked.

"Uh, yeah. Of course I do!"

"Okay, I'll pick you up."

Seargeant Daniels was tall and solid; medium-build with a fat-free physique. His dark, military-style haircut was cropped close to his head, his receding hairline barely noticeable. He wore black pants and a beige, western-style shirt, looking more like a Deputy Sherriff or Texas Ranger than a police detective.

His lecture began with a slide show of Satanic activity on the outskirts of Austin, and in the more remote areas of Travis County. Scenes of Satanic graffiti veneered the walls of abandoned buildings and houses, with remnants of bonfires blackening floors. One site depicted a pentagram drawn in the dirt outside an old abandoned house in the woods.

"These particular crime scenes," said Sergeant Daniels, "are rituals that were performed in remote locations to avoid detection. And they are the surface crimes."

He described them as hedonistic rituals orchestrated by adults to lure troubled kids into Satanic cults.

"Mostly teenagers," he said, pointing to a slide of a graffiti-covered wall. "Like the ones who created this lovely artwork."

The audience murmured faint chuckles.

"These groups recruit younger children as well, but we know little about how they do it. Or, rather, we can't seem to gather substantial evidence," he said. "With troubled teens, cult members promise everything they desire if they join the cult, though they do not describe themselves as a 'cult,' In their indoctrination into Satanism, the teenagers will participate in increasingly violent rituals, given free drugs. It's a step-by-step process of elimination to see how far they can push, choosing the young people who will unquestioningly follow along."

Sergeant Daniels bent to retrieve a bottle of water beneath the podium.

"At some sites, we've found gruesome animal sacrifices, which I will not show you. These are the later stage rituals in coercive indoctrination."

My skin prickled. I rushed to the restroom and sat on a toilet, my face in my hands. Vague pictures of butchered animals crept into my mind.

I splashed water on my face, averting my eyes from the mirror. When I returned to my seat, Vincent took my hand.

The remaining lecture described Sergeant Daniels's research on the origins and history of Satanism. His demeanor was calm and straightforward, presenting the information matter-of-factly.

"Basically," he said, "white witchcraft is the innocuous worship of Mother Nature, such as some Wiccan and Neo-Pagan groups. Black witchcraft involves individuals and groups practicing black magic for evil purposes, including those identifying themselves as Satan worshippers. Their crimes, I'm sorry to say, consist of child abuse, animal sacrifice, and even some human sacrifices."

A gasp from the audience.

After the lecture, I introduced myself, briefly outlined my history, and asked if we could talk further. Sergeant Daniels offered me his card and an invitation to meet the following afternoon at his office in the police department.

I arrived promptly at 1 p.m.

I liked Sergeant Daniels straight away. It was easy to trust his warmth and sincere understanding. He said he'd been investigating Satanic cults for several years. He answered my questions intelligently, and with great respect. His knowledge of Satanism—the term he used to encompass all forms of occult crimes—was extensive. Eager for an investigation into my history, I gave him the names of my parents, their friends, and other family members possibly connected to the coven.

"This is a good start for an *un*official investigation," said Sergeant Daniels. "If I find tangible evidence, I'll make it official and contact the FBI, who I've been working with for a few years on national child pornography cases." He took a sip of coffee. "Recently, I've hooked up with FBI agents who are also trying to expose Satanic crimes. Because, unfortunately, child porn is a prime bankroller of Satanic cults." He paused, looking directly into my eyes, and cleared his throat. "I think we can classify your parents' group with Satanic, even though you don't call them Satanists, per se."

He stood to usher me out the door and walked me to my car.

"Don't get your hopes up too high," he said, leaning on my open window. "The chances of obtaining hard evidence linked to prosecutable ritual crimes are rare."

"Okay. I understand. Thank you for even trying, Sergeant Daniels."

"Hey, would you be willing to meet with me again to tell me your whole story?"

242

"Sure," I said. "I'd like that."

I drove off, elated by the chance to talk to someone with his knowledge of the occult, which Ray lacked.

The following week, I told Sergeant Daniels about the party when I was fourteen, that I thought a girl had been murdered, and that maybe her name was Karen. Though I didn't know her last name, where she lived, or if Karen *was* her name, Sergeant Daniels promised to look into it. We agreed to meet every week, so I could tell him everything.

Two weeks later, I got the courage to tell him about bright lights and my father's locked cabinet crammed with blue-gray metal containers of 8 mm films. Sergeant Daniels tenderly asked for descriptions of scars, moles, or any other marks my twin sister and I might have on our bodies. He and his FBI friends were pouring over old 8 mm child pornography films they'd confiscated and would look for us on those films.

He jotted down the identifying descriptions of me and Emma, which I gave him with downcast eyes. I felt terrible sadness and shame, afraid Sergeant Daniels and the FBI would find us in those films, fearful of their low opinions of us if they did.

"All types of organized cults, including street gangs, acquire or make these films to sell to the average-Joe pervert, and to each other," said Sergeant Daniels. "Cults and gangs finance their activities by selling drugs, too, and producing and distributing snuff films—porn films where people are sexually tortured and then murdered."

Horrified, I sat speechless. I hadn't wanted to believe snuff films were real, like I hadn't wanted to believe my life was real.

I didn't tell Neil anything about Sergeant Daniels, certain he'd tell my parents. He was still threatening to commit me to an insane asylum whenever I brought up divorce, failing to mention that I'd already been in one after trying to kill myself. Surprisingly, Neil and my parents never used my suicide attempt against me.

Meanwhile, memories of Thanksgiving 1987 re-surfaced in waves—Emma and Lily's faces in the dark hallway at the back door ebbed and flowed across my mind's movie screen. I'd pull the power cord on the projector before it showed more. My fear that someone from my past would take Elsa intensified as my thirtieth birthday neared, and I believed Neil would let them. Once again, I felt my only way out was death. My former resolve to refuse the self-destructive ideology that had been drilled into my mind—to die rather than *ever* speak out— weakened as those waves of memory crashed on the shore of truth.

Concerned I might swallow more pills, Ray enlisted the help of Sergeant Daniels to locate a safe place for me and Elsa to spend my thirtieth birthday. Sergeant Daniels gave him contact information for a Christian group in San Antonio that provided safe houses for people leaving Satanic cults.

"What's a safe house?" I asked.

"To my understanding, safe houses are where people leaving Satanic cults can live secretly. Hide from the cult."

Curious, I agreed to allow Ray to inquire on my behalf.

When I got to his office, he clapped his hands and declared, "Good news! They'd love to have you spend your birthday with them in San Antonio."

Sergeant Daniels instructed me to go alone, so I left Elsa with Mrs. Lopez on the morning of my birthday, Good Friday. I drove as directed to an office building unoccupied for the weekend, right off I10 near the center of downtown San Antonio. An odd place to meet.

Iris, the director of the Christian organization, met me at the door. She was plump and motherly, dressed a bit on the shabby side in a nondescript beige pants suit.

She ushered me inside the weekend-quiet building to an inner office where two people she had rescued from Satanic cults greeted me. Adam, sitting on a desk with one leg dangling off the side, and Mishel, standing behind him as if trying to hide. Both were around my age.

Adam was average height and extremely thin, with straight black hair flipping up on the tops of his shoulders. What I found most unusual was his lack of eyebrows, only a few stray hairs poking out here and there like a botched electrolysis job. He noticed me staring and pointed at them. "I shaved them off regularly when I was the high priest of a Satanic cult," he said. "They haven't grown back properly."

He didn't explain why he shaved off his eyebrows, and I didn't ask.

Iris asked him to tell me his story.

"As I said, I was a high priest, the leader of a cult that worships Satan. My wife was also in the cult. She disappeared a few months ago, and I don't know what happened to her." His voice cracked. "I lost all memory around that time." He pushed fingers into his eyes to hold back tears. "I think she's dead. And if she is, I'm not sure if I killed her or if other cult members vying for power killed her. Or if they killed her, but want me to think I did it."

I couldn't believe I was hearing someone say they'd experienced the same type of mind-fuck I'd been afraid to face—the confusing torment of not knowing what happened. Adam's story was a validating mirror of my own questioning self-doubt, reminding me of the weeks I had worried I would find Elsa dead in her crib, terrified someone would kill her and make me think I did it.

Adam felt wretchedly responsible for his wife's disappearance and was desperate to find her, alive or dead. Running scared, he went into hiding with the Christian group because, he said, "Satanic cult members are not allowed to leave, upon punishment of death."

Another mirrored validation.

Mishel came around from behind Adam and stood next to him. Despite her jumpiness, she had a sweet, gentle way about her. In appearance, we could have been mistaken for sisters—blonde, blue-eyed, slender. We liked each other right off, even though we were cautious of our shared history. Mishel was deathly afraid of the Satanic cult she'd fled from, only recently rescued by our plump hostess. She didn't want to talk about her personal story, except in general terms. She and Adam explained some of the complexities of Satanic cults, vehemently insisting that I believe in the paranormal aspect of Satanism.

"I became completely blind and deaf right before my wife vanished, and for several weeks afterwards," said Adam. "I can't explain it other than a spell cast upon me by the cult members who wanted to take my place of power." He conceded that a drug may have been used to make him blind and deaf, "but no drug *I* knew of, and I was the high priest!" he said. "I would have used it all the time to fuck with people, if such a drug existed."

I gaped in astonishment, speechless, as if Adam's tormentors had cast a spell of muteness upon me.

Adam and Michel overwhelmed me with their confirmation of what I wasn't sure I wanted confirmed. Their understanding of what I'd endured, from their own experiences, was profound—validating in a way Ray and Sergeant Daniels couldn't, and not even Hillary, Dr. Dweebin's assistant in group therapy.

Iris turned to me for my story. She asked me questions in a way a skeptical interrogator might, an edge of sarcasm in her approach that almost shut me down. I needed their help, so I answered her questions as best I could, addressing Adam and Mishel, as their thoughts and opinions were the ones I cared about.

When we took a break, Mishel asked me to go outside with her for a smoke.

The office building sat back from a vast parking lot, on the corner of two intersecting streets beneath I10. Cars roared by on the highway above, making the crossroads below a darkened cavern of traffic echoes. We sat on a curb in the parking lot, knees lightly touching, quietly smoking our cigarettes.

Rising above the resounding street echoes, I heard what sounded like howling wolves, way off in the distance. I looked at Mishel, and she at me. The

246

howling grew in volume, slowly surrounding us—right in the middle of San Antonio!—as if we were in the wilderness about to be pounced upon and eaten by a gathering pack. We stared at each other in disbelief.

"Do you hear that?"

"Yes," I said.

"Do you think it's possible we're having the same auditory hallucination?"

"No," I said.

"Where would wolves come from in downtown San Antonio? And why?"

I shrugged my shoulders, wondering if one of us, or perhaps the Christian group, was being followed by people wanting to freak us out and let us know they knew where we were. If so, how was it done? Loudspeakers?

Iris opened the door to our frantic banging. She held it open, head cocked, listening, and looked around the parking lot, a grave perplexity creasing the space between her brows.

"Do you hear that, Iris?" I asked.

"The howling wolves," Mishel added.

Our benefactress nodded her head once, hustled us inside, and hurriedly locked the glass door. She stood there for a moment, looking out, her left hand on her hip, her right elbow bent, a finger lightly tapping her lips. Then she turned and hurried us back to the inner office, a protective mother with her pups.

Adam rushed out a rear door to return to his safe house. The rest of us spoke little after that.

Mishel and I eventually fell into a fitful slumber on the hard office floor, our protective overseer watching us throughout the night.

In the morning, I drove home. We did not exchange phone numbers. And I didn't even want to see them again. It was too weird, too spooky.

Iris didn't offer me a safe house, which would have meant "going underground," though I did not fully comprehend the meaning, nor was I ready.

Not yet.

For the next month, April 1989, I stagnated in my apartment, unable to do much of anything but take care of twenty-month-old Elsa after picking her up from Mrs. Lopez's in the evenings.

I spent most days in Ray's office, coming home in the late afternoon to watch The Oprah Winfrey Show.

Oprah's television show encouraged me to keep going. Her frank openness and unashamed honesty were inspiring elixirs keeping me alive. She spoke freely about taboo subjects such as the Ku Klux Klan, obesity, homelessness, rape, and even incest and other sexual assaults against children, including her own sexual abuse in her childhood.

On May 1, 1989, Oprah's topic was Satanic cults, featuring the Satanic ritual murder of University of Texas student, Mark Kilroy, on spring break with friends in Matamoros, Mexico.

Seven chairs lined the stage. From left to right sat Mark Kilroy's friend, the last person to see him alive, and his mother; next to them, a woman whose son committed suicide after involvement in a Satanic cult; Texas Attorney General at that time, Jim Mattox; Lauren Stratford, author of *Satan's Underground*; and on the far right, Tina Grossman, a therapist introduced as a Ritual Abuse expert, with a woman sitting next to her introduced as "Rachel," a Satanic cult survivor from the Chicago area.

What?

I moved to the floor, right in front of the TV.

Rachel described the Satanic cult she was raised in as a twisting of Judaic beliefs. She told the audience the cult had used her as a "breeder" throughout her adolescence, wherein she was impregnated by cult members to produce babies for sacrifices. Rachel had developed Multiple Personality Disorder, MPD, to cope with her shameful reality—her mind fragmented into separate people, each with a distinct persona living individual pieces of Rachel's life.

248

Like paper dolls with stick-on hair and facial features that changed at will, MPD allowed Rachel to switch out parts of her mind to protect her from going insane, each personality possessing their own unique ability to withstand different aspects of the abuse Rachel had suffered.

Though Rachel's trauma-riddled childhood resulted from cult practices distorting her Jewish religion, while mine was at the hands of a tight-knit Scandinavian coven of Aryan black witches, the abuse we suffered and witnessed was similar. Her story fascinated me, especially being from the Chicago area. (youtube.com/watch?v=n7QXz6hDtxI)

The following night, Oprah Winfrey was a guest on The Late Show with David Letterman. Letterman wanted to make jokes about her show the previous day.

Oprah steadfastly defended her guests.

"I don't want to make light of it . . .," said Oprah. "I just think that if it happens to your child or your sister or your aunt, it's very serious, and it's not fair for us to make light of it. And I think that a lot of these children disappearing; that's what's happening to them."

"Well, I'm sorry to have brought it up," Letterman replied. "Maybe it's happening more than I thought."

"It is," said Oprah.

(dailymotion.com/video/x2mog9h)

Oprah spoke with such authority it was impossible not to believe her. *Thank you, Oprah!* I shouted at the TV.

Overjoyed by Oprah's endorsement, I fell into a fitful sleep later that night, after singing Elsa to sleep. Like an opened picture book on page ten, my story spoke to me in muted tones of blues and grays . . .

Emma and Lily at the back door.

Emma begs me to get the baby and go home with her and Lily.

I refuse.

They leave.

I notice the setting's strangeness—dim light over the sink in the kitchen and the three candles positioned around my mother and my baby in the living room.

Sitting on her gold lamé couch, the woman I call my mother bends over the chair upon which my baby lies in her basket from Mexico. My mother has that eerie, all-knowing look in her eyes, reflecting the sparkling candle flames.

I hear the tinkle of a bell, signaling the Changing Time.

. . . The living room lights are on now. My father and Donald are holding me down on the carpet. I freak out. Donald? *Why is* Donald *here? A hateful grimace contorts his face, his fist clenched around a bottle of pills—a familiar scenario that I always forget between events.*

"No! This is not happening. This is not happening," I babble over and over.

"Shut up!" That's my mother. "Evert! Get the car."

My father walks briskly through the living room, grabbing his coat from the closet next to the front door.

Elsa is lying next to me, wrapped in the pink and white checked blanket Judith made for her. I struggle free and bend over her, creating a protective cocoon for my little butterfly.

"This is not happening. Leave us alone!"

"Donald, shut her up! She'll wake up the neighbors."

How many times have I heard that *in this house?*

Donald pries open my mouth and shoves in two or three small pills, rubbing my throat to make me swallow, like I'm a dog. What the fuck?

Almost immediately my limbs turn to liquid.

Try as I may, like all the other times when I was a kid, I cannot hold back the effects of the drug, whatever it is. But I'm not totally out of it. I've learned how to fight the drugs over the years, an expert at pretending it has taken full effect—sometimes pills, sometimes a shot, sometimes smoke. I will myself to calm down so they won't give me more, resigning myself to the fact that, yes, it is *happening again—there will be a ritual.*

My father opens the front door, and the glass storm door shudders. I hear the vacuum sound the front door makes when opened, as if the house were an airtight pressure cooker, the front door the release valve.

My father's big car, a rust-colored Chrysler, is parked as close to the front door as possible, engine running. He steers me to the rear door behind the driver's seat, his seat. Donald sits in the front beside my father, and my mother is in the back with me, snapping orders. I hunch over Elsa, not looking at her because I'll come unglued if I do. I repeat to myself over and over that I must stay calm. I can't let them know I'm resisting. Yet, I do resist. My real *mother, or whoever that woman was, told me they could never truly have me. They use my body, not my spirit.*

But it's impossible to accept any of this for my baby. I want to be far, far away from here with my precious darling, somewhere they'll never find us. Why did I come here? I didn't even want to come. Why didn't I listen to my inner voice telling me to stay away? Why didn't I listen to Emma's pleas for me to go home with her and Lily?

There's nothing I can do about it now. I hope that whatever they've got planned, it's over quick.

Groggy and disoriented, like I always felt after memories crept into my consciousness, I walked outside in the night air. I was okay, though, because I wasn't alone anymore.

At least one other person with similar experiences existed—that woman, Rachel, from the Chicago area.

Rejuvenated by her validation, and Oprah defending her on The Late Show, I decided to go look for Rachel in Chicago.

TwentyTwo

"I think it's an excellent idea to try to find Rachel in Chicago," said Ray. "But how will you find her?"

"I figured I'd call The Oprah Winfrey Show and ask for the name of that therapist sitting next to Rachel on the show. She didn't say it, but I got the impression she's Rachel's therapist."

"Hey!" Ray clapped his hands once and crossed them over his chest. "Why don't you see a lawyer while you're in Chicago? Get the ball rolling on that civil suit against your father." We'd been discussing a civil suit. I'd even talked to my sisters about it.

Sergeant Daniels disagreed. He didn't think going to Chicago was a good idea, not for any reason. In our weekly meeting, he said, "I'm not sure you're psychologically up to it. You've been through a lot, and so have your sisters. Do they support you? Are *they* ready to sue your father? Do you know for a fact that they've stopped communicating with your parents?"

"Yeah, my sisters want to sue that perverted bastard too. Except for Emma. She says she doesn't want his dirty blood money. But I'm sure she'll change her mind when I obtain an attorney. And I'm going to call The Oprah Winfrey Show to start my search for Rachel. I have to find her, Lamar. I have to." By now, he insisted I call him by his first name.

Sergeant Lamar Daniels looked worried. Shaking his head, he said, "I understand how you must feel, but I just don't think it's time. If I can't stop you, please be careful. And take my phone number with you, if you really think it's a good idea."

"I do," I said.

He shook my hand and walked me to my car.

In Ray's office the following afternoon, he said, "First, we need to find out how much your father is worth," wheeling his chair over to the couch with a flourish of excitement.

When Evert retired a few years before, he sold his portion of the business to the junior partner, Justus, pronounced *Yoo stus*.

"Justus!" I shouted. "I'll call Justus. He was always nice to me when I worked for them. I think he still owns the company. I don't know why I didn't think of him before."

"Great!" Ray said with that goofy grin of his. It pained me to notice him glance at the clock. He clapped his hands with enthusiasm and stood. "I'll see you tomorrow," he said. He handed me his check for my COBRA premium and ushered me out with a big smile.

Elsa was waiting at the door when I got to Mrs. Lopez's house. I scooped her up and took her to the park for a long walk.

Holding Elsa's hand, I became acutely aware of the warmth in her chubby fingers. She looked up at me, Earth-blue eyes like shining planets. The sun shone sparkles of gold in her soft blonde curls, which were finally thickening. She'd been practically bald until then. At twenty-one months, Elsa had only recently begun running with confidence, delayed by her premature birth. She pulled her hand from mine and ran across the grass, proud of herself. I caught up to her squatting in the grass, examining a tiny white wildflower. I sat on my knees

254

beside her, in awe of her gentleness with the flower, and noticed they were everywhere.

"Mamma." Elsa gazed up at me, her clear eyes filled with curiosity.

I looked around, seeing the world from her point of view. New. Fresh.

"Elsa, I love you more than anything."

She climbed onto my lap. I wrapped my arms around her, resting my chin on top of her head. We gazed at the world together, out toward the mystery of our future. I would do whatever it took to fill her future with love, opening all the doors to her dreams so she could accomplish everything she wanted. I would never leave her. Never.

My hand involuntarily pressed against her chest, her heart.

"Me, Elsa. I'll do it. *I* will be your protector."

She looked at me quizzically. We giggled.

Slowly, we walked hand in hand back to the car.

I made dinner while Elsa played on the living room floor. After we ate, she hummed in the bathtub piled with toys. I brushed her hair, then rocked her to sleep, singing "Song of the Soul."

In the morning, I called Justus.

Justus emigrated from Sweden to the United States a few years before accepting the partnership in my father's business. He was younger than his business partners, Evert and Henry. He was thin and fit, too, with thick, graying hair swept up and away from his tall forehead. Even his style of clothing differed from his partners, looking very Scandinavian, if that's a look.

I didn't quite know what to make of Justus's Swedish mystique, but I liked it. I considered him a friend, a kind uncle who truly wanted nothing from me but to live my life to its fullest.

When I worked for Justus, Henry, and Evert in the early 1980s, Justus often talked to me. Unlike my father, he asked me questions about my life and what I wanted. He even offered to pay for college after he overheard me and Evert arguing about it.

Nine years later, Justus was happy to disclose information about Evert.

"Your father ripped me off. He owes me tousands of dollars," he said in his Swedish accent, no 'th' sound. He pronounced father as fot-her.

Justus's estimate of my father's worth was at least a million dollars at the time of his retirement in the mid-1980s. "A million is a conservative estimate. Your father has *lots* of assets, including military money for his time served in World War II. I don't know where he's stashed it all, but it's hidden somewhere." Unfortunately, there was no paper trail of Evert's worth, hindering Justus's lawsuit.

"Oh sure," he said, "I could proceed anyway, but what good would it do? On paper, your father looks broke."

Ray was optimistic about *my* lawsuit, nonetheless. "So what if Justus doesn't think he can sue your father?" Ray's smiling face was joyous. "Doesn't mean you can't."

Even though Ray and I also never found evidence of Evert's estate, Ray enthusiastically contacted an Austin personal injury lawyer who aired TV commercials at least ten times a day. He made an appointment on my behalf and accompanied me to the meeting.

The well-known Austin attorney patiently listened to my story, agreed I might have a personal injury case against my father, and referred me to a lawyer he knew in Chicago. I made an appointment for the following week.

I asked Mrs. Lopez to keep Elsa while I was away.

"Of course!" she said, as always. This time she added, "Are you okay? Do you need help with anything else?"

The last time I asked her to keep Elsa overnight I had ended up in the hospital, getting my stomach pumped.

I assured her I was fine and said Neil could pick up Elsa in the evenings.

"Neil? Your husband?"

"Yes."

"Are you sure? You said you were afraid of him and think he's not safe for Elsa."

"Yeah, I know. But I'm switching tactics, hoping if I allow him to spend time alone with her as her caregiver, then maybe he'll bond with her like I have. And finally see the need to protect her from my parents."

Mrs. Lopez's forehead scrunched up in thought, her intense, dark brown eyes shining. She hugged Elsa and said, "Okay, if you say so. I hope it'll work."

I fell asleep that night thinking about Evert. And Justus . . .

Autumn. 1981. That's it! I've had enough of my father. I've been working for him for a year now, and I'm not getting anywhere. I even moved with the company from their building on Clark Street to Arlington Heights, out in the suburbs. I'm thinking of quitting, sick of everything about my father, especially his hiring practices. For example, suppose a man calling about a job opening sounds African-American. My father purposely sets up an interview for like 6:00 in the morning, assuming the caller lives on the south side of Chicago, a long way to drive or take a bus at such an early hour. The fact that my father admits this is unusual for him. He's usually subtler in his racism, which I haven't wanted to admit until now, now that I've witnessed what he does firsthand.

I think my father derives much pleasure in his power as a private business owner to lord over people's lives. I don't know what his policy of discrimination was in Chicago, but he had one because I never saw a Black person hired when I worked for them on Clark Street. I've never seen a Black person come in for an interview; not in Chicago, and not here in Arlington Heights.

I'm disgusted by it. I've considered reporting him, but to who? As a private business owner, he can get away with anything he wants.

I don't want to be a part of it. Plus, I'm bored sitting in the front office typing orders and helping the receptionist. At least my father let me learn the computer system, but continues to flatly refuse promoting me to sales.

What I really want is a degree in anthropology, but I don't know if that'll ever happen, so I want to get more involved in my father's business. Why the hell wouldn't he want me to learn all I can? He won't give me a raise, either, because I refuse to tell him how much money I need to live on, which is totally irrelevant to my job. Shit! He's so controlling.

I must admit that I don't like my father. He doesn't like women, and he doesn't want me to learn his business. Yet, when I talk about college, he says he'll pay for it only if I get a business degree, which makes no sense.

Justus, the youngest business partner, asks me questions about myself. He even called me into his office yesterday to ask what I want to do with my life.

"You mean here? At the company?"

"Sure, here," Justus said.

"Here, I'd like to get into sales, but my father won't let me."

"You want to take over the business someday?" he asked in his sing-song Swedish accent.

"Oh, I don't know about that. Clearly, my father doesn't want women in management. It's very frustrating."

"What about college?" Justus asked, ignoring my comment about women in management.

"I'd love to go to college."

"Then go!"

"I, uh . . . well, uh," I stammered. "My father says I'd have to get a business degree, which doesn't even make sense since he doesn't believe women should manage businesses."

I shook my head, trying not to divulge my pent-up frustration and negative feelings toward my father. I felt I needed to protect him, the way people defend and obey abusive captors, like Patty Hearst, who even robbed banks for her abductors.

"What do you want to study tat he won't pay for?"

"Um, uh, anthropology?" I answered as a question, gritting my teeth in a sheepish smile, embarrassed that I'd let slip my heart's desire, feeling I needed to apologize for it.

"And what's wrong with tat?" Justus's sing-song accent made me smile. He relaxed back in his chair and crossed a foot over a knee, lacing his hands behind his head, smiling.

I gasped, unprepared for encouragement to study anthropology. "I don't know. I guess it's not practical?"

"Nonsense!" Justus leaned forward. "All education is good."

"What do you mean?" I said, mystified.

"Anyting you want to study is good. What's important is to get an education. So, how do you want to use your anthropology degree?"

No one had ever asked me what I wanted, had ever endorsed my passion.

"I'd like to study the world's cultures and go to the places I study. I'm interested mostly in ancient civilizations." I couldn't believe I'd said it. Taken aback by my brazen pronouncement, I quickly added, "My father would never pay for that, no way, no how."

"I'll pay for it." Justus slapped his hand on his desk and sat back in his chair in the aforementioned manner.

I practically choked. "I can't let you pay for me to go to college. What would my father say?"

"It doesn't matter what he says. It's a matter between you and me."

"You have your own children to put through college, don't you?"

"I have plenty of money to send you to college, too."

I was astounded. Why would Justus do something so kind for me?

In high school I asked my guidance counselor, the tennis coach, to help me, but not even he would, and that was his job! He practically accused me of being a communist because I wanted to take Russian. I was just a burnout to him, having earned that reputation when I fainted in the hallway near the dean's office after snorting some potent Angel Dust. From Mr. Tennis Coach's point of view, I was nothing but a burnout commie, regardless of the fact that my high school did offer Russian as a foreign language credit.

For some reason, Justus believes in me. The only man I know who does.

"I offer tis because you are an intelligent girl who needs higher education. To live your dreams." He threw his arms up in the air to solidify that fact. "You have a good work ethic, too, except for taking off a lot of Mondays and Fridays," he added with a disapproving frowny face. I grinned an "Oops-sorry" shrug of my shoulders.

I quickly estimated the cost of a university education and wondered how Justus, a junior partner, could have more money than my father. Money has been one of my father's main topics whenever I try to talk about college. He always says he doesn't want to waste money on anthropology, "a Mickey Mouse degree." I thought maybe he doesn't have enough money to send me to college, even though he paid for my brother's bachelor's and master's degrees. He has the money.

"Justus, I don't know what to say."

"Well, you tink about it."

I left his office in a daze, immediately dismissing the idea of taking him up on his extraordinary offer. I could never embarrass my father that way.

I can't help but feel sorry for my father, closed up inside his narrow-minded, misogynist views. He would be mortified if he knew about Justus's offer, so I'm not telling him.

I feel terrible, like I've done something wrong and have created problems between him and Justus because I want to go to college.

260

I'll keep taking two classes at a time at the community college, paying for them myself. Last semester, I took anthropology and political science. Right now, I'm only taking one computer science class. I long for at a bachelor's degree from a university and wonder if it'll ever happen.

With this whole thing with Justus, plus my father's repugnant, racist hiring practices, I quit.

I packed my car in the morning, kissed Elsa goodbye, and drove 1100 miles to Chicago.

TwentyThree

Early May Illinois was still spring-like, unlike Austin that time of year, already drenched in wet, heavy heat. Overjoyed for the chance to spend time with my sisters and my friend Nina, I visited all of them before searching for Rachel and meeting with the attorney to start the civil suit.

I spent the first night with Emma and Lily at their suburban apartment, a good hour's drive northwest from the heart of Chicago, picking up a deep-dish Chicago style pizza on my way. Emma had been drifting day to day between her job and counseling sessions, barely coping, struggling with the incest and deceit of our childhood that'd been trapping her in the past. Her movements were slow and forced, her voice a flat, depressed monotone. Sweet Lily, nine, was quiet and unassuming. It was easy to forget she was there. She'd already learned how to disappear, and my heart ached for her—and Elsa, and Emma, and me.

Next, I spent a night with Lorain and her daughter, Gina, also nine years old, like Lily. Lorain had been my favorite drinking-buddy sister when I drank. I'd been missing her with an ache. She was on a rampage of bar hopping, acting out the tragedy of her childhood, a bubbling cauldron of churning hurt. My darling and beautiful niece Gina, like a wide-eyed waif from a Charles Dickens novel, watched her mother fall apart. Rick, my beloved brother-in-law, Gina's father and soon to be Lorain's ex-husband, was living in his van, struggling through the throes of their pending divorce and the insanity of our now-exposed family secrets, which derailed him as well. He'd been a member of our family for many years, more of a brother to me than Donald. Rick survived two enlistments as a marine in Vietnam, yet couldn't win the war against his wife's reality. Afraid I'd lose him, I wanted to see him, but he didn't want to see me.

Lorain had been the rebel of our family until she moved out at seventeen and I took over that position. Our parents readily allowed their teenage daughter to drive her dark-green VW Bug to Skokie every day to finish high school. She didn't tell them she was moving in with Rick, said she was renting an apartment with a girl from school, which they accepted.

Lorain met Rick, twenty-seven, a couple of months earlier, at a bar. She was on stage dancing with John Prine's band while they performed. Rick, in the audience, fell in love with her on the spot. He swooped in when the set was over and bought her a drink before anyone else could. Throughout their early relationship, they lived on the third floors of lovely old Chicago apartment buildings, where living room bay windows acted as greenhouses for their flourishing houseplants. It was a pain in the ass to help them move to those trademark third-floor apartments. I dreaded it and tried not to come to the phone when they'd call for help. But I never refused. Rick made me laugh.

After Gina was born, they moved their new family to an apartment in the suburbs, the one where I'd made my decision to leave Chicago. It was the last apartment they shared as a married couple. On the third floor with lots of plants, of course, but no bay windows. Maybe that's what went wrong—they tried to live a suburban life, minus the bay windows to extend a slightly curved view of the world.

Rick moved out in the aftermath of my and Emma's disclosure of incest.

Lorain took Gina and moved into another apartment in the building, with a roommate to share expenses.

And that's where I sat now, fifteen years after they'd met, on a chair in Lorain's living room, watching the wreckage of our family playing out in Lorain's world, mayhem spreading across her life like a cancer.

And that's where I sat now, fifteen years after they'd met, on a chair in Lorain's living room watching the wreckage of our family playing out in Lorain's world, mayhem spreading across her life like a cancer.

She opened a bottle of wine and told me all the outrageous things she'd been doing with men since breaking up with Rick. She asked if I'd stay with Gina so she could go out partying with her roommate. I, of course, agreed.

With Lorain and her roommate out at the bar, it was quiet. Gina fell asleep right away. I tucked her in bed with a kiss, stroking her wavy hair, just like her mother's. I made up a bed for myself on the couch with a sheet and a couple of blankets I found in Lorain's bedroom closet.

Lying there in the quiet, I wondered what kind of life Lorain had envisioned for herself as a teenager. Among her many attributes was a lovely singing voice. With practice, she easily could have had a singing career. She'd sing along with Joni Mitchell, melancholy songs she played on the stereo in the backroom:

> I am on a lonely road and I am traveling
> Looking for the key to set me free
> "All I Want"

I fell asleep thinking about my life when Lorain met Rick . . .

Lorain is seventeen and I'm fifteen. We've been going to the Chicago blues bars with her new boyfriend, Rick, but lots of times it's just the two of us. I still hang out at Kostner Park, like every day, but I prefer the bars right now and take every opportunity to go. We've been following John Prine around. I see lots of other musicians and singers, too, at Biddy Mulligan's on Sheridan Road: Koko Taylor, Luther Allison, and other fantastic local blues. I love to dance. I watch the older Black people and copy their smooth, mellow moves. It feels so good to get lost in the rhythm. I rarely get carded. But bouncers will sometimes ask for my ID, so I've learned how to use a razor blade to cut out the year I was born and insert a date that makes me twenty-one, taping the back of my license to hold the new date in place. We all do this. Then we get our driver's licenses laminated to hide the razor blade cuts. It works most of the time.

When Rick isn't with us, Lorain and I get harassed by guys. She taught me how to put those assholes in their place. At first, we're friendly with them so they'll buy us drinks. When they start wanting to kiss us, we tell them we're not interested. Then, if they won't leave us alone, we get right up in their faces and yell, "Fuck off!" That usually does the trick. One night at Biddy Mulligan's, these two guys we met invited us to smoke some reefer in their car. Well, they decided they weren't going to let us out and got real mean. We did some fancy talking to get out of that car—Lorain, mostly.

Lately, we've been hanging out with John Prine's band at a bar on Sheridan Road, south of Biddy's. I don't actually hang out with John, though. I don't think he likes me, or he thinks I'm too young to be hanging out there. I hang out with his lighting technician, Dicky. He tells me he's on the methadone program and seems nervous about it. "It's to help people get off heroin," Dicky says. I think he likes me, but doesn't try to kiss me or anything, just talks about methadone. He doesn't drink or smoke pot.

Lorain and Rick met at this bar. She was dancing with John Prine and his band while they were playing; not as a professional dancer, just a wild, cute young girl they didn't mind looking at. Rick, twenty-seven, was sitting at the bar, watching. He told me he fell in love with her at first sight. She fell in love with him, too. When I met Rick, I couldn't blame her—he looks a lot like Greg Allman, a tall guy with long dusty-blonde hair, a few shades darker than Greg's.

Rick and I came here one night when Lorain was waitressing at her new job at the seafood restaurant. We met an off-duty Chicago cop who turned us on to some primo reefer. I don't much like reefer, but if I'm drinking, it's okay. It felt strange getting high with a cop, and he knew I was fifteen.

Tonight, after the bar closes, Dicky takes me home with him to John Prine's apartment, where he's been staying. It's a beautiful apartment in an old building, with beveled glass in the front door and an enormous bay window in the living room. There are lots of photographs on the walls, one of John Prine with Paul McCartney. I don't know why John would know Paul McCartney—*to me, he's just got a great, fun local band. But Dicky says John's getting to be well known, famous even. Oh, maybe that's why he's kinda snooty and won't talk to me.*

Dicky and I listen to music and he tells me, yet again, that he's on the methadone program when I ask if he wants to get high. We try to kiss, but it's not working out. He's cute, with long black hair and a full beard, but he's boring—he doesn't even smoke pot!

My overnight stopover at Lorain's left me feeling glum.

Lorain and her roommate walked in while I was packing up to leave in the morning.

I poured a bowl of cereal for Gina and sat with her until it was time for me to go. She walked me to the door, clutching my hand. Hugging her tightly, I said, "I love you, little darling."

Gina clung to me, then let go and sat on the couch, drawing up her knees and hugging them to her chest. She watched Lorain stagger around, talking loudly about a guy she'd met at the bar.

I kissed Lorain on the cheek and said goodbye. I hoped she would find her key to freedom one day.

I drove away feeling devastated about Lorain and Gina. And Rick, too. I thought their marriage would last forever.

Next, I went to the city to spend the day with Nina. Emma and I met her when we were nine and she was the new kid in sixth grade. She looked so different from us, with pitch black hair and beautiful eyes the darkest brown I'd ever seen. Her skin turned so dark in the sun I wondered if she had African ancestors, but never asked. Nina was Jewish, and I enjoyed Passover at her house when we were kids. She liked coming to our house, too, and became nearly a member of our family. She loved Christmas and helped Marjorie decorate the tree.

It was lunchtime when I arrived at Nina's 1920s-era apartment in a fantastic Chicago neighborhood of old Greystone walk-ups. She'd jogged down to the deli around the corner for corned beef on rye, which we ate in her enormous kitchen, her toddler, David, a month older than Elsa, strapped in his high chair. I couldn't get good corned beef in Austin, Texas, so I greedily wolfed down two sandwiches. We reminisced about Nina, age nine or ten, standing on her living room couch used as her stage to dramatically lip-syncing songs made famous by Barbara Streisand.

Her favorite was "Don't Rain on My Parade":

Don't tell me not to fly, I've simply got to
If someone takes a spill, it's me and not you
Who told you you're allowed
To rain on my parade?

She'd fly off the couch in a flourish of waving arms.

In her huge, square kitchen twenty years later, Nina threw her head back and belted out the refrain at the kitchen table. We laughed our asses off, picturing Nina with her hairbrush microphone. David looked on with a startled, about-to-cry pout, tears rimming his wide eyes. I grabbed him and rocked him on my lap like a baby, missing Elsa, wishing I'd brought her with me. David squirmed away and stood in front of me, staring, big tears sliding down his cheeks. I wiped them off and tried to hug him. He brushed me off with an indignant shove, making Nina and I laugh harder.

Nina put David down for his afternoon nap and we moved into the beautiful living room of original woodwork and twelve-foot ceilings.

I told Nina everything. She'd heard some of it from Emma, and listened to me with rapt attention. She'd been experiencing her own feelings about what had been exposed, having spent *years* with our family.

"I came to Chicago to find Rachel, the woman I saw interviewed on The Oprah Winfrey Show. I wanna call the show to get the name of the therapist who was sitting next to Rachel, figuring she might be a good start."

Nina handed me her four-inch-thick Chicago white pages, the only phone book she had. I called the number listed in the business section for The Oprah Winfrey Show. Without hesitation, the woman who answered gave me the name of the therapist. Tina Grossman.

There wasn't a business number listed for Tina Grossman in the white pages, but there was a home phone number. I assumed it had to be a different Tina Grossman, doubting a therapist would list a home number. Nonetheless, I dialed the number and she answered on the first ring.

"Is this the Tina Grossman interviewed on The Oprah Winfrey Show?"

"Yes, I am she."

"I'm so happy I reached you. Rachel said she was from the Chicago area, so I thought I'd take a chance and try to find her. I got the impression you were her therapist and got your number in the Chicago white pages."

"And you are?" she asked.

"I'm a survivor of incest and witchcraft. I grew up in Skokie."

Tina inhaled sharply.

"I *am* Rachel's therapist," she said. "And Rachel is *also* from Skokie. I can't believe this. It's astonishing. What's your name?"

I told her my name, and she told me Rachel's real name.

"I know her!" I exclaimed. "We went to junior high school together."

"That's incredible. This is wonderful. Hold on, let me get you her number."

Tina excitedly rattled off Rachel's phone number. I had to ask her to slow down and repeat it several times. Though it seemed highly inappropriate and unethical for Tina to give me her client's real name, plus her phone number, I didn't care.

Rachel answered on the third ring. I recognized her voice at once, the same distinctive voice from junior high school, surprised I hadn't recognized it on The Oprah Winfrey Show. Neither of us *ever* imagined we would find someone we actually knew who shared our bizarre histories from the dark corners of the occult. Rachel gave me directions to her downtown Chicago apartment. I drove as fast as I could.

The doorman buzzed me in after calling Rachel. I ran to the elevator.

"Oh, my gosh! Hanna, it's really you!"

"I can't believe it. How can this be?"

We clung to each other, weeping.

"How/ Emma?" Rachel wanted to know right away.

"Suffering. Like us."

We talked for hours. Rachel had been in therapy for several years and was working on her master's degree in art therapy. As a civil rights activist for survivors of sexual assault, Rachel became involved with Voices in Action, Inc., an acronym for Victims of Incest Can Emerge Survivors, an organization providing information and resources to adult survivors of sexual abuse. They published a monthly newsletter for members. Rachel's affiliation with Voices in Action had introduced her to experts in Ritual Abuse and cult crimes.

269

One such expert in the field, Detective Jerry Simandl, was a Chicago gang-crimes cop touting himself as the leading international expert on Ritual Abuse. Rachel had shared her history with Detective Simandl and provided his phone number to RA survivors who contacted Voices in Action. Simandl validated victims and pursued investigations for those who wanted it. Rachel gave me his contact information that day, and I became a member of Voices in Action, Inc.

I preferred the term Occult Abuse to encompass abuse perpetrated by all types of occultists and cults. Having learned the common term, Ritual Abuse, RA, I began using Occult Abuse and RA interchangeably.

Connecting with Rachel and her resources re-directed the route of my journey from that day forward. I felt hope, genuine hope.

I spent the rest of my trip with Ellyn and my nephew Eric. Being around my big sister was like old times—lots of laughter. She painted on her "I'm fine!" façade each morning with her makeup, dashing off to her downtown secretarial job. I tried to ignore my suspicion that she might still talk to Marjorie and Evert, as my only hope for a family lay in believing my sisters had rid themselves of them. My appointment with the personal injury attorney was a few days off, so I hung out with Eric while Ellyn was at work.

Eric played high school football. He was a busy guy, so when I say we hung out, it was only when I begged him.

Eric was huge. And exceptionally handsome. The perfect combination of his pretty Swedish mother and gorgeous Guatemalan father. Eric had his father's deep brown Latin eyes, unlike the blue eyes of his mother's family. Marjorie used to gush over Eric's stunningly handsome father back when he and Ellyn were dating, but Evert never quite took to him and opposed their mixed-race marriage, which lasted less than two years.

Ellyn and Eric lived in an enormous apartment on the third floor of a 1930s building in Skokie, scarcely three blocks from the house of horrors in which we all grew up. Yes, all of us—Ellyn and Eric lived with Marjorie and Evert on and off throughout Eric's childhood, and when they lived elsewhere, Eric spent most weekends with Marjorie and Evert, and sometimes even during the week.

On a day Eric was too busy for me, I searched for the place I'd met Karen, the girl from the party when I was fourteen. I thought it was north, so I headed that way on Edens Expressway. As if my car knew where to go, I kept getting off the highway to turn back south. Frustrated, I gave up on the third turnaround and stopped at Lockwood Castle, a popular lunch and ice cream spot south of Skokie.

I hadn't planned on contacting Michael, but if he could point me to the place I sought, then perhaps my dream signified an actual event connected to Jake and the gun, and that girl, Karen. I decided to call him, but the number I had was no longer in service.

At dinner that night, I mentioned my disappointment to Ellyn. To my great surprise, she gave me Michael's new phone number. They'd kept in touch after I left Chicago in 1984. It was now 1989, five years later.

"How come you never told me you talk to Michael?"

"Oh, he's just my pot supplier," she said offhandedly. "He likes to talk about you while we pass joints."

I put aside my puzzlement and called Michael the next day, Saturday. He invited me to his house, which he'd bought the year before, and which Ellyn also knew about and hadn't mentioned.

We sat on a worn-out couch in the back of Michael's house, his main living space. His handsome face made my heart flutter. Rejecting the beer he offered, I said, "This might sound strange, but I'm trying to find a place I think you took me to after we met. There was a girl there my age. Fourteen."

Michael looked up at the ceiling, his pointer finger on his chin. "Hmmm, I can't recall any specific place or girl that stands out in my mind. What did she look like?"

"She had long light-brown hair and very pale skin."

"Oh, that narrows it down." Michael smiled that sexy half-smile of his.

I pried my eyes loose from his magnetic lips.

"Her name may have been Karen."

"I don't know, Hanna."

"I have a vague idea of where we may have met her."

"Where?"

"Somewhere with a lot of trees. And a hill overlooking a big grassy meadow, with maybe a small river or a stream?"

"That sounds like the forest preserve Andy hung out at." Andy was the only friend of Michael's I liked.

"Did you ever take me there?"

"Probably. I can take you there now."

Michael drove south to the exit for Lockwood Castle, where I'd stopped the day before when I'd been so confident the area I sought was in the opposite direction. Michael passed the restaurant and turned into the entrance of a forest preserve. From the parking lot, I saw it was the place I had envisioned.

Standing at the summit of the hill, I barely breathed, gazing across the meadow below to trees lining the banks of a creek. Michael, sober that day, stood quietly beside me, his arm touching mine.

Filled with emotion, I told him about my dream when I was pregnant, that I thought it was a memory, and that I'd met Karen with him, at this forest preserve.

"I saw her again at a party in the city," I said. "Something happened to her, and even though you weren't there, you might know something, but you've forgotten."

"*Forgotten?*" Michael snickered. "That sounds kinda nutty, Han."

"I know it does. But it seems like someone instructed us to forget, and we did. That's how afraid we were."

Michael said nothing. Never even asked me to explain.

He leaned into me in his gentle way, and we stood side by side, gazing down at the meadow. Turning slightly, he glanced into my eyes, then back to the meadow. He lengthened the connection of his arm against mine, from shoulder to wrist, invitingly. I adored him when he was sober. We stood that way for a long time, lost in memories.

On Sunday, he came to Ellyn's apartment, sober. I hadn't realized how much I missed the authentic Michael, the beautiful, sober Michael with a kind heart. He brought his girlfriend, which didn't bother me. I wanted him to be happy.

Later that night, Ellyn proclaimed her enthusiasm for the civil suit against our father and took Monday morning off to join me at the attorney's office.

Arnold Preston greeted us at the door, offered us coffee, and ushered us into his office, motioning us to adjacent chairs in front of his desk.

Ray had given him the basic low-down on our case, so Arnold began by asking about our family. I told him about the incest and other family secrets, such as alcoholism. Out of the corner of my eye, I saw Ellyn roll her eyes, almost imperceptibly shaking her head back and forth, negating everything I said.

Arnold glanced back and forth between us.

I pretended I didn't see Ellyn's eye rolls and continued with an account of our parents' occult activity, prompting a more vigorous head-shaking from Ellyn, which was impossible not to notice.

Nevertheless, I stashed her sabotage of our lawsuit in my mind's denial drawer, in the file marked "Ellyn," along with the implication of her treason—to benefit Evert and Marjorie. I *had* to deny her betrayal. I didn't want to give her up. Besides, my childhood conditioning to refute reality ran deep, though I was not yet aware of it.

I left Arnold's office in a daze. Dissociated.

My wish to believe in Ellyn took a lot of psychic energy. All that shuffling of files in my mind's denial drawer drained me. Continuing to ignore my inner voice, keeper of the truth, I resumed telling Ellyn whatever information she cheerily asked for, revealing everything I'd remembered. I even told her about the party, leaving out the part about the murder.

It may sound bizarre that I'd tell Ellyn *anything*, especially about the party. I wasn't aware, yet, that my parents' coven trained me to tell on myself to keep tabs on me: what I knew, where I was, who I was with, what I was doing. Though the survivor deep inside tried to keep quiet, I couldn't escape the programming.

I drove home to Austin. Arnold Preston never returned my calls.

* * * *

My new friend, Dianna, took me to Kostner Park last week. Looks like we'll be hanging out there now. There's a guy there she likes, nicknamed Eagle because of the intense look in his Mediterranean-blue eyes, like an eagle.

Yesterday, I was standing on the sidewalk around the corner from White Hen Pantry, across the street from Kostner Park. I watched a car approach, a really cool white Pontiac GTO convertible with the top down. Everything turned into slow motion as it crawled to the curb, with this absolutely, positively, no question about it, most gorgeous guy behind the wheel. His long brown hair was blowing around his head in the breeze like a silent movie scene slowed to a crawl to memorialize an important event. When the GTO stopped, right in front of me, I saw his muttonchop sideburns and square chin. He's gorgeous! *And* soooo *cool!*

Marvin was standing next to me when the man of my dreams, the love of my life, my soul mate, drove up. "Marvin, who is that?"

"Him?" He pointed sideways. "That's Sieben."

"Please, please, can I meet him?" I begged.

"Okay," Marvin said and walked me over to the car.

Weak in my knees, I approached the GTO, a chariot from heaven.

The interior seats were red vinyl, and I heard Led Zeppelin's "Misty Mountain Hop" blaring from the 8-track player:

Sitting in the park just the other day, baby
Whad'ya, what do you think I saw?

As long as I live, I will never forget when Sieben looked up at me and smiled. Then, in slow motion, he said, "Hiiiii," and my heart, also beating at a snail's pace, literally stopped for a second. His smooth voice weakened my knees.

"I'm Miiiikkee," he drawled, and I almost fainted. Tongue-tied, I couldn't speak, but in my mind, I screamed, I LOVE YOU!

Michael J. Sieben is his name. I'm thinking about getting a tattoo.

The next day I was sitting on a picnic table bullshitting when I watched, in disbelief, Mike's GTO flow to a stop at the curb. Marvin was in the passenger seat, smiling, white teeth flashing, motioning me to come over to the car. Marvin is my new bestest friend in the whole wide world.

Mike politely invited me to get in.

Marvin grinned and climbed from the front seat to the back. I was now sitting close enough to Mike to reach out and actually touch the object of my deepest desire. He looked at me with a half-smile and said, "Hello." I may have literally passed out for a second. Struck mute, my thoughts twisted into a tight knot, my mouth so dry I couldn't even swallow, much less speak.

Everyone calls him Sieben or Mike. But if I ever get the nerve to speak to him, I will call him Michael because his formal name suits him. Michael. An ethereal spirit, like the leader of the angels for whom his mother named him.

Michael picks me up at my house every day now. We spend all day and night together. He tells me he has a girlfriend who's on a trip to Colorado to celebrate high school graduation. She'll be back soon. I just graduated junior high school.

Dianna is working as a nanny this summer for a family living across the street from Oakton Park. Michael and I hang out there during the day, making out and listening to The Moody Blues album, Days of Future Passed. *We also cruise up and down the highway, hang out at Kostner Park at night, and wherever we are, do* a lot *of kissing. I love spending time with Michael.*

The two weeks are up today.

Michael and I just pulled up and parked at White Hen Pantry and his girlfriend, Robin, gets out of her car and walks into the store, her super-long black hair swaying, a white halter top accentuating her summer tan. She sees us, but says nothing.

I'm crushed. There's no way I can compete with her.

That happened yesterday. Right now, I'm sitting on the couch looking out the picture window, grieving.

To my surprise, Michael drives up in his GTO and parks across the street, dead center in front of the window. He's not coming to the door, just sits in his car for a long time, in a light rain. I stare out the window at him, crying tears of heart-wrenching despair.

I didn't know love could hurt so bad.

And guess where my parents are forcing me to go on a family vacation tomorrow? Colorado!

TwentyFour

Elsa ran to me with outstretched arms when I walked in the door, a Mother's Day gift clutched in her left hand.

"Elsa!" I scooped her up to hug her, swinging her back and forth.

I sat in my rocking chair to open her gift, a small heart-shaped frame with a picture of her smiling face (I still have it). She draped herself over my knees, hugging them.

"Thank you, little darling," I cooed, petting her golden curls. I pulled her onto my lap to give her a squeeze.

I thanked Neil, too, as he obviously framed the photo. In fact, the three of us drove to the top of Mount Bonnell to watch the sunset.

Neil had his moments. He was hilarious, with a contagious laugh. He told all kinds of zany stories, silly tales with a southern or Texas theme. I liked that side of him. I still wanted us to parent Elsa together. Friends. Since he'd taken care of Elsa while I was in Chicago, I hoped his time with her had somehow proven how much I needed him to help me protect her from my parents.

Vincent deemed it highly inappropriate for me to spend any time at all with Neil, considering the situation.

When he found out I'd taken Elsa to Mount Bonnell with Neil, he told me to get a divorce or forget about him.

"Vincent," I pleaded, "I'm not *with* Neil and I'm not going to be. He's my daughter's father, and I'm trying to have a friendship with him, so we can both be her parents."

"What about him refusing to give you a divorce, threatening to have you committed, and worst of all, talking to your fucked-up parents?"

"I'm hoping he'll stop, that he'll realize we're not getting back together and agree to a divorce and be friends with me. For Elsa's sake."

"You can want that to happen all day long and into next week, but wishing won't make it happen. Face facts. He's crazy."

I liked Vincent's country phrases, such as *all day long and into next week*. Trying not to smile, I said, "Vincent, please understand."

"Nothing to understand. Meanwhile, I come hang out with you and Elsa, and yeah, I'd like to be more than a friend, but you're married."

"I'm married only on paper."

"No. I don't see it that way." He stormed out the door, threw himself into his car, and drove off. Slowly. Very slowly.

I wanted to go after him, even walked out behind him after he shut the door in my face. But I didn't know what to say. I hadn't considered a romantic relationship with Vincent. I didn't think I'd be good for him, with all my complicated problems.

With Neil, I kept hoping if I gave it a little more time, everything would be all right; maybe he'd change. Accepting that he probably would not change was heartbreaking, which he soon proved.

The following weekend, Neil was on his best behavior, having dropped his campaign on behalf of Marjorie and Evert for a few days. He persuaded me to go to a park in the hill country west of town. It took an hour to get there.

"Neil, how did you find this place way out here?"

"Just out exploring one day. Thought Elsa would like it."

We turned left onto a gravel roadway leading to a large campground, not a park. In the center was a large fire ring with the charred remains of bonfires. Nailed on many trees were narrow wooden planks with peculiar names burned onto them, such as Gowdie, Blight, Nurse, and Wilde. They looked as if they'd been there for years. I got a creepy sense of doom and dissociated into panic.

I told Neil I wanted to leave at once. He said I was ridiculous and headed off on a trail by a creek that led into a wooded area, Elsa's tiny hand in his.

A few days later, Neil supposedly came over to see Elsa, but hardly said hello to her. Instead, he loomed over me, renewing his fight for Marjorie and Evert's *right* to see Elsa.

"What the hell, Neil. I'm begging you to listen to me. We *must* protect our daughter from them." I had so hoped he would change his mind after spending time with Elsa. "I'm not repeating this again."

Neil stared at me with his unblinking coldness that sent ice through my veins. "Well, Hanna, I could commit you to an insane asylum. Do you want that?"

That was it. I was done fighting. Exhausted, utterly depleted, I said nothing more.

That night, after he was long gone, with Elsa asleep in her crib, the quiet of the living room gave voice to the slides snapping across my mind's projector screen, which slowly evolved into a moving picture show . . .

Three candles in the living room. The woman I call my mother bends over my baby.

The tinkle of a bell signals the Changing Time.

Donald forces me to swallow a pill, his face so ugly in violent rage.

My father pushes me into the back seat of his car, behind the driver's seat.

We arrive at a building with marble steps leading to an ornately carved, massive wooden door.

Evert heaves the door open, and we step inside onto a marble floor with marble pillars evenly spaced across the entryway.

Another ornate wooden door leads into a large room, like a banquet hall, only there are no tables set for a fancy meal. Instead, I see people in black robes.

Like the parting of the Red Sea, an aisle opens in the middle of the throng. I'm pushed toward it from behind, aware that I am the only person without a hood. I notice Elsa is wrapped in a black cloth now. Who changed her frilly pink and white blanket to black?

A woman is waiting at the front of the room.

Shuddering, I stood and walked outside, willing the pictures away. Standing in the warm night air, listening to far-off traffic, I finally faced the fact that Neil would not become my ally. I wondered what his motive had been for taking Elsa and me to that strange campground with the fire circle and wooden name planks.

I had to do something, but what? I was physically, emotionally, psychically, and spiritually drained. In my next meeting with Sergeant Daniels, he told me I had no legal clout without evidence of my parents' occult crimes, aside from my verbal testimony, which wasn't enough. If any of my sisters had been willing to corroborate my story, there may have been legal help, but I could do nothing alone. And my parents had money. He also said he'd found an old FBI flier from 1973, of a missing girl that fit my description of the murdered girl, Karen.

"Hanna, I, um . . ." Sergeant Daniels cleared his throat. "I think you should drop it."

"What? Why?"

"Because when I attempted to retrieve the FBI file, it was gone."

"Gone?"

"Yep. It wasn't there. And, Hanna, that's not normal. Missing person cases are never closed and that file should have been there. This is serious."

I had so hoped it was my imagination—the party, the rape, the girl, the blood. And now this. More validation of what I didn't want to be true.

"Because you don't know if Karen *is* her name, this could be coincidental, but . . . forget about it, Hanna, and go on with your life with your little daughter." He looked into my eyes. "I'm so sorry, Hanna. For everything." His eyes had a ring of tears he wouldn't let fall. "You do not deserve *any* of this."

I stood up in a daze. He patted my shoulder and walked me out.

If it was true, I wanted to find that murdered girl for her family.

And protect my own little joy, creating a happily-ever-after for her. For all children. Was that too much to ask?

At home, I sat at the table with the phone in my hand, seeking counsel from Rachel, expressing my grief and outrage.

We'd been talking on the phone every day since I'd found her on The Oprah Winfrey Show. Rachel understood the driving force behind my determination to protect my child, and shared my resolve to end childhood abuse for every child.

"I'm concerned about you and Elsa," Rachel said. "Especially now, with this new information about the missing FBI file on a girl who may have been murdered."

"I don't know what to do, Rachel."

"I know of an organization, MARC. Mother's Against Ritual Crimes. I've hesitated mentioning it until now, because I didn't think you were ready to hear about it."

"What do you mean?"

"MARC is an underground network providing safe houses and identities for moms and kids like you guys, who aren't able to get legal protection."

I'd been hearing about Faye Yager on the news.

Faye was a mom refusing to divulge where she'd hidden her daughter. She was the so-called leader of the new "underground railroad" helping other mothers like herself, with no legal protection, hide their kids from abusers. Usually fathers.

I wasn't going to get legal help either, according to Sergeant Lamar Daniels in Austin, Detective Jerry Simandl in Chicago, and Dale Griffis, PhD in Ohio, a self-proclaimed cult expert working with MARC. Rachel had introduced Dr. Griffis to me via telephone a few days before. He was the person recommending MARC.

"I hate to think I need to do something so drastic, Rachel. I'd prefer believing the underground had only been necessary during slavery times."

"Underground networks have always been around," said Rachel. "These days, they help people escape from abuse."

"Which, when you think about it," I said, "is what enslaved African people were fleeing."

"Yeah. Unfortunately, we still live in a world that doesn't protect vulnerable people. Laws are created by, for, and enforced by men. In the U.S., that means white men."

"That's true, for sure. And it's not fair. Why should I have to consider going 'underground' to keep my daughter safe?" And then it hit me. "Wouldn't we be leaving *everything* behind?"

"Yes, you would. And you wouldn't be able to tell anyone where you are, either. You and Elsa would disappear."

Disappearing sounded nice.

With everything that'd happened since my birthday in San Antonio, I now understood the need for safe houses. Dropping more of the denial I'd been holding onto in my yearning for an everyday kind of life, it was time to consider going underground.

Dr. Griffis told me that many people worked together to help mothers vanish with their children; including police officers, therapists, doctors, abuse survivors, and various others dedicated to transporting moms and kids to the underground.

It sounded like a place of innocent purity, a life-saving network of people wanted to embrace me and my daughter in arms of compassionate understanding.

Even if for just a little while, how wonderful it would be to revitalize my self-esteem and courage among folks strong enough to accept me.

Time to examine the Facts, with a capital "F":

Flashbacks were relentless interrogators coercing me to turn my life over to them, which I had been doing for months.

Ray had been pulling away since my suicide attempt. He didn't know what to do, and wouldn't admit it. Not to me, anyway. The effect of counseling me to remember, remember, remember was keeping me in a constant state of turmoil.

My relationship with my sisters had also deteriorated. I couldn't give them up, not even Ellyn, despite the lies she told every time she opened her mouth.

I obsessively clung to the 3 a.m. hang-up calls, lying awake waiting for them. I needed those calls. They gave me a sense of truth, forced me to face the sinister place from which I'd come, and was not yet free.

Neil's weekly hundred-dollar bill had dwindled to fifty bucks or so, sometimes nothing, and my unemployment was about to run out. Ellyn wanted to buy my car, and I needed the money, so she flew to Austin, gave me two thousand dollars, and drove off with it.

Neil. . . . He was an addict. Thus, his reduction in child support. As with all addicts, drugs and alcohol came first. Period. And my parents easily manipulated him with the cash payments he used to buy the drugs and alcohol. His allegiance was to my father's money, not to me and our baby. At least he thought enough of us to not want me carless, so he gave me the old Buick LeSabre parked at his ramshackle house, the car we'd bought for me to get to and from work when we moved to Round Rock.

Proof of Neil's involvement with my parents came to light when that fuck-head admitted Marjorie had been writing him letters. He said Marjorie and Evert had enlisted his help to commit me to a psychiatric institution, where they planned to twist my PTSD symptoms into a story of insanity.

Neil. My husband, and father of my child, was going along with it.

We were standing in my kitchen when he produced Marjorie's most recent letter, outlining their plan to come to Austin to help Neil commit me to the state hospital. I leaned against the stove for support, staring at the letter, aching from and longing for the familiar handwriting of the only mother I'd known.

I looked at Neil's cold, flat, toad-green, lagoon eyes. Further begging was useless. I had genuflected before him more than once as to a God, groveling, my sorry and despair spilling over the edges of my childhood story. He placidly leaned against the counter, watching me with unblinking eyes, and said, "Our daughter belongs with both of her parents, living in the same home."

"And if I don't agree with that, Neil?"

He shrugged his shoulders. "Well."

There was nothing left to say.

Neil was a monster who had crawled out of a murky lagoon. His absurd, active participation in my parents' plan to gain access to Elsa by getting rid of me made Elsa and me easy fodder.

I didn't sleep that night. The phone rang every hour, three rings. Finally, I ripped it from the wall.

Though I longed to keep my comfortable blanket of denial wrapped tight around me, it had worn thin. All that was left was an old threadbare idea of what I'd wished my life had been. The truth was so very disappointing—I was a mamma bear with no rights to scare off predators.

On the bright side were my warrior sisters, Pamela and Judith, pushing me to keep fighting. As was Dr. Faget.

Sergeant Lamar Daniels, too. He wasn't afraid of my history, and helped me stay focused on Elsa. He shared my passion for freeing all the children being kidnapped and abused *every moment of every day*. His validation boosted my determination to keep my promise to the angels who'd visited me when I was six years old, my promise to be the voice for children.

Lying awake that night, chain-smoking cigarettes, another fearful memory surfaced . . .

Michael's girlfriend, Robin, came home from Colorado two days ago. And here I am with my parents and sisters on our way for a family vacation in COLORADO! Heart-sick, I'm slumped in the back seat, smashed up against the car door by Lorain, sitting between me and Emma. I'm not talking to anybody.

Colorado Springs is beautiful! This morning, we drove up Pike's Peak, on a one-lane road with cars coming and going in both directions. It was terrifying! I thought my mother would have a heart attack; she kept stomping on an imaginary brake pedal on the passenger side floor. At the top of Pike's Peak was a patch of snow, in the middle of summer! I didn't think it could possibly be real. It wasn't even cold outside.

This evening, at the motel high in the Rocky Mountains, the sunset view of the valley below is spectacular! I've never been to such a beautiful place. I've determined that I'm a mountain girl.

Every opportunity I get, I slip off with rolling papers to roll a grass-green joint that isn't very strong but does the trick. It's homegrown pot an ex-boyfriend gave me earlier in the summer. Even though I know Lorain would love to smoke this reefer with me, I'm not sharing. It's my only escape from a family vacation.

Well, a family vacation on the surface. Something isn't right, but I can't put my finger on it. It's a familiar feeling, but . . . I don't know.

My mother wakes us up in the motel room during the night and hustles us into the car. My father drives us in pitch darkness—no lights, no moon—on a winding mountain road.

That feeling of something not right fills my stomach with nervous butterflies.

From my back seat position in the middle between Lorain and Emma, all I see out the windshield are trees whizzing by in the headlights, tall evergreen trees. We turn left onto a bumpy dirt road. Up ahead, I see the light of a massive bonfire. I panic, feeling like a small child.

. . . I wake up in the car leaning against Lorain, daylight hurting my eyes. Where are we? I bolt upright to look out the car windows. Nothing but trees. I hear low voices, my parents speaking to someone. They get back in the car without looking at us, and we drive away.

I can't remember what happened last night. I think I don't want to remember. Maybe I was dreaming.

We're on the road again, vacationing as if nothing happened.

We are *sightseeing and visiting stupid tourist traps. Except for Yellowstone National Park, not stupid at all. Old Faithful geyser shoots up out of the ground and way up into the sky at precise, predictable intervals. It is so cool!*

Once daylight established itself, I picked up the phone from the floor where I'd thrown it, plugged it back into the wall, and called Rachel.

"All right," I said. "I'm ready."

The director of MARC called an hour later. Denise ran the organization from her home in New York. Assuring me I was not alone, she told me that they, the underground network, had helped many mothers who needed to protect their kids. And even a few fathers. She asked if I would be willing to tell no one, not one single person, our destination.

"I guess so."

"No guessing so, Hanna. You must be certain."

"I think I am."

"There will be no trace of you or your daughter, so it's crucial you understand how important it is that you are truly ready to disappear."

286

To vanish would be a splendid relief. I would walk off with Elsa into the sunset, on through the night, and into the sunrise of a new life.

"Okay, I'm ready, Denise. I can't wait to be free."

"Are you absolutely positive? Because it's not only your safety we must consider, it is for everyone else we help, too."

"Yes, I'm positively ready to leave. Really, I am," I said.

"Okay, then. If you all agree it will be a good match, you'll be living with two women, Tovah and Jane."

Tovah called later that day. Within an hour, we agreed.

"For security," she said, "you'll find out where you're going when you pick up your plane tickets at the airport."

I explained my relationships with Ray and Sergeant Daniels, asking if I could tell them.

"You can tell Ray where you are *after* you get here. And *only* Ray," said Tovah. "And go buy as much of whatever you'll need as possible, enough to last a while."

"I don't have money for that. I'm sorry. I'm totally broke."

"You're going to cease to exist, so it's okay to write bad checks."

"But that would be stealing."

Tovah assured me it would be okay, in this instance, because I was a desperate mother on the run to protect my child.

Every other time I'd run away, I'd run broke. When I ran away at twelve with Adrienne and Alex, I only had five dollars and no shoes. When I boarded the plane at O'Hare airport at age twenty-five, I had only twenty dollars and bad checks for my plane ticket and car rental.

Now, five years after running away from Chicago, I was running away from Austin, writing bad checks once more to pay for my escape. It felt good to place whatever I wanted in the shopping cart without penny-pinching, even though my checks would definitely bounce this time; my father would not be bailing me out again.

Ray acted surprised that I contacted MARC without discussing it with him first. His eyes turned into big circles, and he flinched as if I'd struck him. Gaining composure, he said, "Well, you know, I don't think it's a bad idea. I was going to suggest it myself."

"I just don't see what else I can do, Ray. Do you?"

"No, I'm sorry, I don't."

"I still don't understand all this shit! Like the woman in my apartment, if she was really there. And the phone calls. And those fucking letters Marjorie writes to Neil."

"Why are you surprised? You gave your parents your phone number and address, and they were in your apartment. You *are* aware that they've used brainwashing techniques to control you. So why would you doubt anything at this point?"

Ray was right about the brainwashing. But he didn't understand the depth of the embedded messages of what they wanted me to do, who they wanted me to be, and how to make me believe I would never be free.

It was a miracle I left them.

When I told Ray that Tovah instructed me to write bad checks for diapers, he sighed, "Well, ya gotta do what ya gotta do," glanced at the clock, clapped his hands, and said with a smile, "Looks like you've made your decision."

He stood up, hands on hips, his eyes darting to the clock.

Had Ray always watched the time during our therapy sessions?

I stood and crossed the short distance to the door. It seemed like a mile.

"Goodbye, Ray."

He opened his arms for a hug, as usual. I walked out without it, not usual.

Where once I'd known comfort in Ray's arms, wanting to stay there forever, I now felt emptiness.

Ray sent another of his clients over to my apartment to pick out whatever she wanted, including my silverware and the beautiful afghan Grandma Elsa crocheted for me when she was ninety-two years old. The woman promised she would hold on to my afghan and everything else she took and return it if I ever came back to Austin or contacted her. But I never saw any of it, or her, again.

I gave Ray my apartment key a few days before Elsa and I left. He'd offered to make the arrangements for my furniture, and everything his client hadn't taken, to be sold at a consignment shop. He said he would send me the money.

Pamela and Ted invited me and Elsa for dinner one evening, not knowing it would be the last time they'd see us. I brought over a box of stuff I thought I might want back someday, to leave in their garage. I said I needed to store it there because I was moving soon and wanted to lessen the load. Ted looked at me curiously, but said nothing.

We went to Judith and Denny's for pizza and a movie on our regular Saturday night get-together.

And we spent time with Starr and Vincent on Sunday.

I told each of them how much they meant to me, feeling guilty for leaving without saying goodbye.

Then I packed all the clothes I could fit into my Grandma Elsa's blue suitcase, and in June 1989, Sergeant Lamar Daniels drove me and Elsa to the airport, despite Tovah's instructions to have Ray drive us or take a cab. I felt safer with Sergeant Daniels, a police detective who wasn't afraid of anything.

Lamar insisted he park his unmarked car and take us to our departing gate.

At the ticket counter, he glanced over my shoulder at the tickets. I smiled. He smiled. We hugged.

He walked silently by our side to the gate. When Elsa wanted to walk, I held her hand, slinging her up on my hip when she grew tired.

Lamar nodded a farewell at the gate, looking into my eyes. At the entrance to the tunnel leading to the plane, I handed our tickets to the flight attendant and turned to look past the scurrying passengers boarding behind us. Lamar, Sergent Daniels, stood like a soldier at ease: legs apart in a triangle, hands crossed behind his back. He nodded his head as if to say, "go on now," and I sensed him standing there until the plane left the runway.

> My child
> I love her so completely
> I would do anything for her
> Jump into a raging river to rescue her
> Throw a big party with lots of friends
> So that she may never be lonely
> Take her tiny hand and run
> To the opposite end of the earth
> To protect her from monsters
>
> --Ann Willow

The end of Summer. I'm in the woods and don't know how I got here.

A path leads out of the tiny grove I'm standing in, lit by low flickering candles spiked in the ground, lighting the way for a robed figure slowly walking toward me.

I see a building where the path begins, glowing orange, reflecting the firelight of a bonfire. The floating figure approaches me, bends down to kneel before me, and lifts her face with icy blue eyes and bright-red, fresh-blood-colored lips. She's a smiling rescuer, a woman I know well. She says she is my mother. You're not my mommy, are you? *And I slip into darkness.*

A few hours, days, weeks pass, and I see the lady I think might be my real *mommy, the one who could rescue me if only she would—the woman who whispers words of love and tells me I must be quiet, very quiet, and I cannot cry when she leaves. My twin sister, Emma, is with me for this encounter with a mother's love, strong and deep.*

"A love you will only have to think of to know," the lady tells us. "God is real. The love of God is Divine, and angels are watching over you." She hugs us, promising us that angels watch over our sister Lorain, too. "I must leave now," she says.

We cling to her, begging her to take us with her. She tells us we cannot cry and that we must pretend we know nothing about her or the love of God.

"God is, and always will be with you," whispers the kind lady. "When you are older, you will be safe. One day, you will tell this story. You will yell it from a mountaintop."

Dear Reader,

My story continues in my next memoir, *Seeking New Identities*, available in 2026. Read the first chapter pages at the back of this book.

At the beginning of *Remembering Changes Everything*, I stated that my memoirs are based on my true story, which means dates and details may not be exact, and I combined some events and dialogue for readability. I've written this book from memory and the numerous journals I kept during the events you have just read. This story is from my perspective, as I lived it. Certain memories are imprinted in vivid detail in my mind, while others are obscured by time, drugs and alcohol, or intentional processes of brainwashing conducted by my abusers.

It's a funny thing about memory. Certain memories are etched in steel— every minute detail—while others are obscure ghosts. Yet, even in a steel-tight memory . . . is that exactly how it happened, what was said? Maybe yes, maybe no. Regardless, what I've found is that the crux of a memory is true, though the way I may remember a ritual, for example, represents the way in which the event affected me; meaning it did happen, but two people may have varied recollections based upon how they were affected. For instance, they remember the basic details: there was an altar, there was a person on the altar, there were hooded people chanting. They remember how they felt during the ritual, which may not be the same, casting a slant on the details—perhaps one will remember the anguish a participant tried to hide; the other may remember the pale face of a child staring without blinking.

Thus, other people involved in the events I have described may have varying perspectives on what happened. They are welcome to write and publish their accounts, and have the right to do so.

I think of all the missing children and know my life will have meaning only when I do my part to expose the kidnappers, rapists, and traffickers exploiting their innocence. I write my story for the ultimate love of my child, for all of you with abused and missing children, and for those of you who were abused and may also be missing.

In descriptions of Satanic/Occult Abuse, I want to make it perfectly clear that I do not stand in judgment of anyone's spiritual or religious beliefs, nor ethnicity or political affiliation. My concern is in exposing those people who use their authority and belief system to use and abuse vulnerable populations of society, regardless of what those beliefs are, or where or how they came to be. I hope that by doing so, I may help empower their victims.

Some names and locations were changed.

Ann Willow

ACKNOWLEDGEMENTS

Thank you to everyone who helped make the telling of this story possible.

First and foremost, I would not have written this book without Starr Gregg, my adopted sister who believes in me more than anyone. Her persistent pushing has been the axle of dependability upon which I have relied.

I would not have published this book without Tracy Stewart, founder of Freshly Press, Paris (FreshlyPress.com). Tracy bestowed confidence in my writing and belief that I am doing the right thing in bringing my memoirs to light.

My editor, Kjirsten Territ, was also instrumental in turning this story into a published book. As were the invaluable editing recommendations from William Greenleaf and Vicki Holmsten.

Thanks to the providers of feedback, useful information, undying support, and places to write: Glyn Garcia, Joseph Garcia, Gary Gregg, Linda Riddle, Robin Kennedy, Joe Becker, Greg Armstrong, Les Williston, Cheryl Whitetail, William Bernhardt, Jim & Susan Vigil, Randy Smith, Erny Zah, Mary Caroline Rogers, Olga Avalos-Tesillo, Ron Kohn, Michael Farber & Cindy Shelton, Carmen Martinez, Wesley Justice, Dezbah Benally & Mel Sharp, Karen Ellsbury & Patrick Hazen, Gotham Writers, Chicago Writers Association, Southwest Writers, people of the Choctaw Nation, and all the coffee shops, diners, and libraries I frequent across the U.S. And for those no longer with us: Diane Tidmore, Emma De La O, Joe Dillion, and Sister Delores "Dorie" Kincaid.

Thank you, George, for helping me see I was never one of them.

Thank you, Oprah, for your courage in openly addressing controversial ills of society, while championing the inspiring unsung heroes and angels who would otherwise not have a voice.

And thanks to my daughter, Elsa, for giving me her blessing.

REFERENCES

Castaneda, Carlos. *Journey to Ixtlan: The Lessons of Don Juan*. New York, NY: Touchstone, 1973.

May 1, 1989 Oprah Winfrey Show:
Cristian, A. [ArthurLoveForLife]. (2011, October 12). *Vicki Devil Worship—1st May 1989 Oprah Winfrey Show Interview with a Jewish Woman* [Video]. YouTube. www.youtube.com/watch?v=n7QXz6hDtxI or bit.ly/3Tn6jz0

May 2, 1989 Late Night with David Letterman:
Fagan, S. (2015). *Oprah on Letterman 5/2/89 Feud* [Video]. Dailymotion. www.dailymotion.com/video/x2mog9h

The Holy Bible: King James Version. *Psalm 23*. Public domain.

Le Carre, J. (1979). *Smiley's People*. United Kingdom: Hodder & Stoughton.

Masson, J. M. (1984). *The Assault on the Truth: Freud's Suppression of the Seduction Theory*. New York, NY: Farrar, Straus and Giroux.

Seltzer, D. (1976). *The Omen*. New York, NY: Signet.

Video for the entire May 1, 1989 Oprah Winfrey show:
Whitman, R. [GeneralJDRipper]. (2022, December 27). *Satanic murders full episode - Oprah Winfrey Show (1989)* [Video]. BitChute. www.bitchute.com/video/nydgPgyYSd1N/

Every effort was made to obtain permission to use lyrics from the following songs, which I have used sparingly. My deepest gratitude to these writers, composers, and performers. United States record labels, except where otherwise noted:

"All I Want" by Joni Mitchell. Recorded by Joni Mitchell. *Blue*. Reprise Records, 1971.

"American Tune" by Paul Simon. Recorded by Paul Simon. *There Goes Rhymin' Simon*. Columbia, Warner Bros. Records, 1973.

"Don't Rain on My Parade" by Bob Merrill & Jule Styne. Recorded by Barbara Streisand. *Funny Girl*. Capital, 1964.

"Downtown" by Tony Hatch. Recorded by Petula Clark. *Downtown*. Pye Records (UK), Warner Bros. Records (US), Disques Vogue Records (Canada), 1965.

"Flying Cowboys" by Sal Bernardi, Rickie Lee Jones, Pascal Nabet-Meyer. Recorded by Rickie Lee Jones. *Flying Cowboys*. Geffen Records, 1989.

"For Once in My Life" by Ron Miller and Orlando Murden. Recorded by Stevie Wonder. *For Once in My Life*. Tamla/Motown, 1968.

"Helan Går" Swedish drinking song of uncertain origins. Early mention in 1843 operetta.

"The Horses" by Rickie Lee Jones and Walter Becker. Recorded by Rickie Lee Jones. *Flying Cowboys*. Geffen Records, 1989.

"Karn Evil 9: 1st Impression, Part 2" by Keith Emerson and Greg Lake. Recorded by Emerson, Lake & Palmer. *Brain Salad Surgery*. Manticore Records (UK), 1973.

"The Lee Shore" by David Crosby. Recorded by Crosby, Stills, Nash & Young. *4 Way Street*. Atlantic Records, 1971.

"Michelle" by Paul McCartney. Recorded by the Beatles. *Rubber Soul*. Parlophone (UK), Capital (US), 1965.

"Misty Mountain Hop" by Robert Plant, Jimmy Page, John Paul Jones. Recorded by Led Zeppelin. *Untitled Led Zeppelin IV*. Atlantic Records, 1971.

"Song of the Soul" by Cris Williamson. Recorded by Cris Williamson. *The Changer and the Changed*. Olivia Records, 1975.

"Twist & Shout" by Phil Medley and Bert Russell. Recorded by the Beatles. *Please Please Me*. Parlophone (UK), 1963.

"War Pigs" by Tony Iommi, Geezer Butler, Bill Ward, Ozzy Osbourne. Recorded by Black Sabbath. *Paranoid*. Vertigo Records (UK), Warner Brothers (US), 1970.

RECOVERY RESOURCES

Books

Bass, Ellen and Laura Davis. (2008). *The Courage to Heal: A Guide for Women Survivors of Sexual Abuse.* 20th Anniversary Edition. New York, NY: HarperCollins.

Beresford MD, Thomas P. (2012). *Psychological Adaptive Mechanisms: Ego Defense Recognition in Practice and Research.* New York, NY: Oxford University Press, Inc.

Davis, Laura. (1991). *Allies in Healing: When the Person You Love was Sexually Abused as a Child.* New York, NY: HarperCollins.

Frankl, Victor E. (1963). *Man's Search for Meaning.* Boston, MA: Beacon Press.

Jung, Carl G. (1933). *Modern Man in Search of a Soul.* New York, NY: Harcourt, Brace and Company.

Masson, Jeffrey Moussaieff (1984). *The Assault on the Truth: Freud's Suppression of the Seduction Theory.* New York, NY: Farrar, Straus and Giroux.

Oksana, Chrystine. (2001). *Safe Passage to Healing: A Guide for Survivors of Ritual Abuse.* Lincoln, NE: iUniverse.com, Inc.

Peck, M. Scott. (2006). *People of the Lie: The Hope for Healing Human Evil.* London, GB: Cornerstone.

Ross MD, Colin A. (2006). *The C.I.A. Doctors: Human Rights Violations by American Psychiatrists.* Richardson, TX: Manitou Communications.

Ross MD, Colin A. (2008). *The Great Psychiatry Scam: One Shrink's Personal Journey.* Richardson, TX: Manitou Communications.

Ryder, Daniel. (1992). *Breaking the Circle of Satanic Ritual Abuse: Recognizing and Recovering from the Hidden Trauma.* Minneapolis, MN: Hazelden Information and Educational Services.

Sakheim, David K. and Susan E. Devine, Editors. (1992). *Out of Darkness: Exploring Satanism & Ritual Abuse.* New York, NY: Lexington Books, an imprint of Macmillan, Inc.

Smith, Michelle and Lawrence Pazder, MD. (1980). *Michelle Remembers.* New York, NY: Pocket Books.

Spencer, Judith. (2000). *Suffer the Child.* Lincoln, NE: iUniverse.com, Inc.

Stratford, Lauren. (1991). *Satan's Underground.* Gretna, LA: Pelican Publishing Company, Inc.

Streiker, Lowell. (1984). *Mind Bending.* New York, NY: Doubleday.

Thomas LCSW, Shannon. (2016). *Healing from Hidden Abuse: A Journey Through the Stages of Recovery from Psychological Abuse.* MAST Publishing House.

Alcoholics Anonymous
www.aa.org
New York, NY
USA
(212) 870-3400

Adult Children of Alcoholics & Dysfunctional Families
www.adultchildren.org
Lakewood, CA
USA
(310) 534-1815

SUGGESTED LISTENING

Every effort was made to obtain permission to use lyrics from these songs that ran through my mind as I wrote *Remembering Changes Everything*. Regrettably, I received no replies to my requests. Nevertheless, I would like to salute the writers, composers, and performers who provided the words and music to accompany me through the rough times, as well as the not so rough. United States record labels, except where otherwise noted:

"A Child in These Hills" by Jackson Browne. Recorded by Jackson Browne. *Jackson Browne*. Asylum Records, 1972.

"Angel" by Jimi Hendrix. Recorded by Jimi Hendrix. *The Cry of Love*. Polydor/Track Records (UK), Barclay (France), RTB (Yugoslavia), Reprise (US), 1971.

"Carpet Crawlers" by Peter Gabriel, Tony Banks, Mike Rutherford. Recorded by Genesis. *The Lamb Lies Down on Broadway*. Charisma Records (UK), Atco Records (US), 1974.

"Close to the Edge" by Jon Anderson and Steve Howe. Recorded by Yes. *Close to the Edge*. Atlantic, 1972.

"Closer to Fine" by Emily Saliers. Recorded by Indigo Girls. *Indigo Girls*. Epic Records, 1989.

"Crossroads" by Tracy Chapman. Recorded by Tracy Chapman. *Crossroads*. Elektra, 1989.

"Dawn: Dawn is a Feeling" by Mike Pinder. Recorded by The Moody Blues. *Days of Future Passed*. Deram Records (UK), 1967.

"Doctor, My Eyes" by Jackson Browne. Recorded by Jackson Browne. *Jackson Browne*. Asylum Records, 1972.

"Dream On" by Steven Tyler. Recorded by Aerosmith. *Aerosmith*. Columbia Records, 1972.

"Ebony and Ivory" by Paul McCartney. Recorded by Paul McCartney and Stevie Wonder. *Tug of War*. Parlophone/EMI (UK), Columbia (US), 1982.

"Empty" by Ray LaMontagne. Recorded by Ray LaMontagne. *Till the Sun Turns Black*. RCA Records (US), 14th Floor Records (UK), 2006.

"Five to One" by Jim Morrison, Ray Manzarek, Robby Krieger, John Densmore. Recorded by The Doors. *Waiting for the Sun*. Elektra Records, 1968.

"Freedom Rider" by Steve Winwood and Jim Capaldi. Recorded by Traffic. *John Barleycorn Must Die*. Island Records (UK), United Artists Records (US), Polydor (Canada), 1970.

"Hidden Treasure" by Steve Winwood and Jim Capaldi. Recorded by Traffic. *The Low Spark of High Heeled Boys*. Island Records (Worldwide), Polydor Records (Canada), 1971.

"I-Feel-Like-I'm-Fixin'-to-Die" by Country Joe McDonald. Recorded by Country Joe and The Fish. *I-Feel-Like-I'm-Fixin'-to-Die*. Vanguard Records, 1967.

"If You Could Read My Mind" by Gordon Lightfoot. Recorded by Gordon Lightfoot. *Sit Down Young Stranger*. Reprise, 1970.

"Imagine" by John Lennon. Recorded by John Lennon. *Imagine*. Apple Records (UK), 1971.

"The Last Time I saw Richard" by Joni Mitchell. Recorded by Joni Mitchell. *Blue*. Reprise Records, 1971.

"The Low Spark of High Heeled Boys" by Steve Winwood and Jim Capaldi. Recorded by Traffic. *The Low Spark of High Heeled Boys*. Island Records (Worldwide), Polydor Records (Canada), 1971.

"Mr. Blue Skies" by Jeff Lynne. Recorded by Electric Light Orchestra. *Out of the Blue*. Jet Records (UK), United Artists (US), CBS (Int'l), 1977.

"Mother's Little Helper" by Mick Jagger and Keith Richards. Recorded by The Rolling Stones. *Aftermath*. Decca Records (UK), London Records (US), 1966.

"Quicksand" by David Bowie. Recorded by David Bowie. *Hunky Dory*. RCA Records, 1971.

"Running Hard" by Michael Dunford and Betty Thatcher. Recorded by Renaissance. *Turn of the* Cards. BTM (UK & Europe), Sire Records (US & Canada), 1974.

"Satellites" by Rickie Lee Jones. Recorded by Rickie Lee Jones. *Flying Cowboys*. Geffen Records, 1989.

"Show Me" by Chrissie Hynde. Recorded by The Pretenders. *Learning to Crawl*. Sire Records, 1984.

"Stairway to Heaven" by Jimmy Page and Robert Plant. Recorded by Led Zeppelin. *Untitled Led Zeppelin IV*. Atlantic Records, 1971.

"Sympathy for The Devil" by Mick Jagger and Keith Richards. Recorded by The Rolling Stones. *Beggers Banquet*. Decca Records (UK), London Records (US), 1968.

"That's the Way I've Always Heard it Should Be" by Carly Simon and Jacob Brackman. Recorded by Carly Simon. *Carly Simon*. Elektra Records, 1971.

"The Way It Is" by Bruce Hornsby. Recorded by Bruce Hornsby and the Range. *The Way It Is*. RCA Records, 1986.

"Thick as a Brick" by Gerald Bostock (Ian Anderson). Recorded by Jethro Tull. *Thick as a Brick*. Reprise (US, Japan, Oceania), Chrysalis (Europe), 1972.

"Thumbelina" by Chrissie Hynde. Recorded by The Pretenders. *Learning to Crawl*. Sire Records, 1984.

"Trip to the Fair" by Michael Dunford, Betty Thatcher, John Tout. Recorded by Renaissance, *Scheherazade and Other Stories*. BTM Records (UK), Sire Records (North America), RCA Records (Europe and Japan), 1975.

"Two Little Sisters" (from Marvin's Room soundtrack, 1997) by Carly Simon. Recorded by Carly Simon and Meryl Streep. Carly Simon, *Anthology*. Rhino Records, 2002.

"What's Going On" by Marvin Gaye, Al Cleaveland, Renaldo "Obie" Benson. Recorded by Marvin Gaye. *What's Going On*. Tamla Records, 1971.

"When the Levee Breaks" by Kansas Joe McCoy and Memphis Minnie. Recorded by Led Zeppelin. *Untitled Led Zeppelin IV*. Atlantic Records, 1971.

COMING SOON

Seeking New Identities

Book II

Ann Willow

Summer 1989

And if the situation
Should keep us separated
You know the world won't fall apart
And you will free the beautiful bird
That's caught inside your heart
Can't you hear her?
Oh, she cries so loud
Casts her wild note
Over water and cloud
That's the way it's gonna be
Little Darlin'
We'll go riding on the horses
Way up in the sky, Little Darlin'
And if you fall, I'll pick you up

--Rickie Lee Jones, "The Horses"

One

Seattle was a city of trees. Enormous evergreens. I arrived with Elsa, soon to be two years old, on a gray day in early June 1989, welcomed by coolness unknown to the sweltering summers of Austin, Texas, from whence we'd fled. Seattle was a city of water, too, with fingers of waterways stretching into the continent as if grabbing a handful.

Seattle. Our underground destination. Tovah and Jane's house in the University District, brought there by my husband's refusal to help me protect our daughter, his insistence that my parents, Marjorie and Evert, should have access to her. Marjorie and Evert. . . . I had ceased calling them my mother and father months ago, after I remembered the incest and bizarre black magic rituals to which they'd subjected me.

MARC, Mother's Against Ritual Crimes, an underground network promising new identities for me and Elsa, had made the arrangements for our escape. I was introduced to them by "Rachel," a guest I saw on the Oprah Winfrey Show the previous May, after tracking her down in Chicago. Tovah and Jane, MARC cohorts, had offered their home as a "safe house" in which to hide.

1

Despite my self-preoccupation with my past and present dilemmas, it was evident from the get-go that something wasn't quite right with them. One thing I found strange, and which confused me, was who exactly was in charge. It seemed that Tovah controlled everything with her loud demands, but maybe it was Jane, quietly playing the director from behind the scenes. Either way, my inner radar switched on, alerting me to pay attention. And I wondered how the hell those two ended up together.

Tovah was a bulldozer. John Deere indestructible. Large in stature and weight, pushing six feet tall and well over two hundred pounds, she was imposing in both appearance and personality. She wore her thin, dull, charcoal hair up in a sort of twisted ponytail at all times. Even first thing in the morning, there she'd be, stomping into the kitchen, hair pinned up so that it was impossible to tell its precise length. She was around my age, thirty, maybe a bit older. As sweet as pie as long as things were fitting exactly to her plan. Anything got in her way, anyone opposed her—well, she'd roll right over it, them. She was a furious tornado, apt to spin out of control at any moment. I could see, just behind her eyes, that I'd better do as told, lest the thunder of her torrential rage crash down upon me.

At first, I thought Tovah's rage was about all the unprotected and abused children in the world, including herself. After a day or two, flinching from her harsh tone and wondering about her relationship with Jane, it became clear that Tovah's always-present anger was attributable to more than outrage over neglected children. I, however, didn't stay long enough to find out.

Jane was a marshmallow. Jet-Puffed spongy. I'll call her Jane because I cannot remember her name, nor does it matter, really, being that she and Tovah changed their names regularly. She was pushing sixty, much older than Tovah, with a soft, pear-shaped, middle-aged roundness to her. Jane was also much shorter than Tovah, maybe 5'5" or so, although her heavy-burden stoop made it difficult to know for certain. An aging woman, Jane's thinning, boy-cut mousy hair had probably been a shiny chestnut at one time. In contrast to Tovah's dense olive skin, Jane's was a finely creased, creamy white with pink cheeks. Her eyes were oceans of sadness, deep blue-green, lined with a downward wrinkling of mourning, as if sorrowful memories floated on the surface about to spill over. I felt I'd drown in her grief the first time I looked into her eyes.

Jane said she was an incest survivor, too. She seemed docile and meek, speaking softly at all times, with the demeanor of a woman wracked with guilt, a downhearted face of shame and low self-esteem. It didn't take too many days, however, to question her seeming innocence. She claimed she'd rescued Tovah from a Satanic cult when Tovah was eleven years old. I just didn't buy it. She was way too vague about how this "rescue" took place. Her evasiveness bothered me. Yeah, I believed Tovah had been abused, and yeah, probably by Satanists, but questioned Jane's role: Rescuer? Or kidnapper of a vulnerable child?

Me? I was right between them in height, 5'8", and very thin at thirty years old, having lost a lot of weight remembering my real life—I called it my stress diet. I tied my thick, long blonde hair into a twisted ponytail when wet to keep it from frizzing, loose when it dried. As for my personality, you already know I was a fucked-up mess; albeit, trying the best I could to be a good mommy.

In addition to Tovah and Jane, and now me and Elsa, two gigantic dogs inhabited their house, easily over one hundred pounds each. They were an unusual breed, giant orbs of fur with variegated colors ranging from tan to black.

"They're Caucasian Shepherds," Jane said proudly on the day we arrived. She said the breed originated in the Caucasus Mountains of Russia, and they'd been used as guard dogs for centuries.

Tovah added, "In more recent history, they've been used to guard prisoners in the Soviet Gulag, and later to patrol the Berlin Wall."

As she said this, her black eyes bored into me with jolting intensity.

Elsa wasn't a bit afraid of those dogs, even though they were rambunctious and knocked her down a few times. She just laughed and pulled herself up by their fur, which they didn't seem to mind. Way too large to wander around the small house, the dogs lived in enormous cages while inside, spending a good portion of the day outside in the backyard.

Tovah and Jane lived in an eclectic neighborhood filled with coffee shops, cafés, used bookstores, and University of Washington students from countries around the globe. It was a hip neighborhood, if slightly run-down. Shabby chic. I liked the intellectual mood of the area. Yet, each time we drove away from their congested neighborhood, the trees diverted my attention from all else, reminding me of the northern Illinois and Wisconsin woods of my childhood, locations of black magic rituals. The Seattle evergreens, mimicking the tall trees that forested my youth, triggered memories of those rituals, mocking me, it seemed, as they dragged me back to the roots of my life as a child. And Seattle waters, too, filling every nook and cranny dipping into land surface—lakes, ponds, rivers, and creeks *everywhere*—flooded my mind with mysterious, wavy memories of northern Wisconsin, the Chain of Lakes area where my sisters and I spent summer vacations with our parents and their "vacation club" friends that met once a month during the year to plan those summer trips.

Not all Wisconsin memories were mysterious. I was a kid, with kid ways, always exploring. My twin sister, Emma, and I dug up the muddy banks at the shallow edge of the water for crawdads, and took rowboats out into the channel that ran along the edge of the resort, rowing up to piers where we freed minnows from fishermen's buckets tied to docks. We fed chipmunks and watched in the early evening for deer arriving at salt blocks, breathing in the cool evening air with a scent of pine, like Christmas in summer. At dusk, us kids piled into one of our parents' cars for a teenager to drive us to the dump to watch bears lumbering around like rolling black boulders, their flab rippling across their bodies.

Those pleasant memories of my summers in the north woods of Wisconsin brought great sorrow, wishing my bright days with Emma and evenings with the older kids hadn't been tainted by nighttime rituals in the woods. . . . Fifteen years later, one of those kids committed suicide; hung himself from a rafter in the garage of the house he'd been raised in.

I had to tell Tovah and Jane I was dissociated and frightened, constantly looking over my shoulder. After all, until the final moment we left Austin, I'd been in daily therapy sessions with Ray Gunn, PhD, encouraged to remember, remember, remember every detail of childhood abuse I'd suffered and witnessed. The endless dredging up of memories had kept me in a nearly perpetual state of Post Traumatic Stress flashbacks. I was a mess when I came to Tovah and Jane. A desperate, confused, scared, freaked-out mess. Arriving in Seattle for what was to be my underground escape with my little daughter, faced with forests and waterways triggering memories of my childhood, I could not turn off the flashbacks, nor had any of the therapists I'd sought for help taught me how.

I wanted to ask if the underground network—Mothers Against Ritual Crimes, MARC—had other places to choose from. Like maybe a desert, mountains, or a sunny beach? But I was far too lost in my anguished past to think I deserved to ask for somewhere else to start a new life. I didn't wish to be a burden, which I felt from the moment I met Tovah and Jane.

And their relationship baffled me. Were they adopted mother and daughter? They had separate bedrooms. Or were they lovers? They usually slept together in Tovah's room, though they seemed to want to keep it a secret. They argued like an old married couple and went to weekly couples' counseling, which I was required to attend and to sit, my daughter on my knee, in the waiting room because they would not leave us alone for a second.

Whatever the nature of their relationship, it certainly was not a mother-daughter sort of thing, which one would expect, being as Tovah had lived with Jane since age eleven, when she still needed a mother, and Jane would have been in her late twenties then, maybe early thirties. If they were now lovers, which seemed the case, Jane had incestuously violated the mother-child relationship, had she not? No better than the place from which she had taken Tovah.

Maybe this was the source of Tovah's turbulent anger, and Jane's floating sorrow.

The first time Tovah and I talked about what was going to happen now—I thought of us already as *prisoners* of the underground network, though it was hard to pinpoint why, other than wondering how those guard dogs would be used—was the morning after our arrival, finishing a breakfast of cereal, bacon, and iced tea.

Tovah put the dogs outside and directed me to her small bedroom off the kitchen of their rented house. Elsa got up to follow, but Jane put her hand atop Elsa's, asking soothingly, "Wouldn't you like me to read you a story?" Elsa didn't look happy, so I took her hand and said, "That's all right, she'll come with me."

Tovah and Jane shot looks at each other and Jane released Elsa's hand as if removing it from a hot stove.

I placed Elsa on the floor with a couple of books Jane reluctantly handed me, and sat down in front of Tovah, who faced me from behind her computer screen that took up most of her desktop. Her room felt damp and chilly, with a somber mood matching the perpetual gray Seattle sky. An old woolen blanket hung in the single window, partially draped down to expose outside light. Tovah's gigantic, Gothic-style bed crowded the wall beside it.

"Yeah, we bought that bed when we were in the Netherlands. Amsterdam," she said when I commented on its immensity. "I fell in love with it and had to have it."

"It's remarkable." I said, impressed by the massive, medieval darkness of it. The headboard's intricately carved wood, in an unusual pattern of swirling vines, looked very old.

"I saw it in an antique shop in a building that was probably over 200 years old." Tovah laughed, sort of like you'd expect from Boris Karloff, the evil character actor in movies of the 30s and 40s. "It's just one of the many things we bought in Amsterdam, and all over the Netherlands."

She explained that their Netherlands spending spree was only one such spree they'd indulged in over the years, acquiring new identities after each extravagant binge.

"How in the world did you get that monster of a bed back to the States?"

"We had it shipped."

"That must have cost a fortune."

"Well, yeah, it did. We used a credit card." Tovah hadn't diverted her eyes from the computer screen, scrolling. "We knew we'd change our names again when we got back to America, so we figured, why not get everything we want?"

Since Tovah and Jane had to wait until the bed arrived before changing their identities, they continued stacking up credit card bills which they shredded and tossed away, along with the names on those cards, after the shipping company wrestled the bed into the house they were renting.

Tovah explained, "It's fairly easy to change identities because we, MARC, have access to unused and obsolete social security numbers."

"Obsolete?"

"Yeah. Obsolete, like when people die."

"Oh." I paused, surprised and curious. "Really?"

"Yeeesss." Tovah drew out the word like speaking to a half-wit.

"Oh," I said again, sheepish.

"Jane and I, from time to time, rack up a lot of bills. Then we change our names and move." Her voice trailed off for a moment while she read something on her computer screen, her eyebrows scrunched in concentration. "We've lived in a lot of places," she said, chuckling Boris Karloff-style. "You'll get to do that now, like when I told you to buy stuff for the baby before you left Austin."

I sat rigid, not knowing if I should say something.

Tovah continued staring intently at her computer screen. Then she added, rather condescendingly, "It's a good thing we *have* these social security numbers, huh? Cuz you're sure gonna need one whenever you want a new identity."

The sarcasm in her tone startled me, and the implication behind it. I hadn't realized I could change our identities as often as I pleased. I thought this was a one-shot deal, for the sole purpose of our safety. It didn't seem right, changing identities to avoid paying bills, and that's not why I'd brought Elsa there. Would Elsa and I forever be associated with this underground network, expected to change our identities regularly, via them?

"Yeah, I guess so, Tovah." That was the best comeback I could come up with. I'd just met the woman, felt I had to go along.

Next, I was required to hand over my identification. Tovah held out her hand for the items, wriggling her chubby fingers impatiently while I rummaged around in my purse for my driver's license and empty checkbook, the only identification I had. When I asked why the rush to hand it over—my identity—Tovah's eyes darkened and her face pinched as she replied, "In case you change your mind."

Alarms went off deep in my mind. *What? I don't have that option?*

Adrenaline pumped through my body, heart aflutter, eyes wide. It hadn't occurred to me that accepting their help to protect my daughter would require me to relinquish our identities to them and then be monitored . . . forever?

In fear, I didn't ask what the consequence would be if I were to change my mind and want out. I didn't want to face the possibility that I had made the biggest mistake of my life. The control they'd wield wasn't what I had expected, Tovah's anger not what I'd sensed over the phone when we discussed my emergency to leave Austin with my child. I thought we'd board the plane, instead of the proverbial train, en route to the safety of "the underground," a place of nourishing compassion with understanding people who would provide my longed-for new identities. Then off I'd ride with Elsa into the sunrise of a new life. Free.

Listening to Tovah from behind her computer screen listing social security numbers that would forevermore tie us to her, I did not see freedom in our future.

From that moment onward, gazing at the backside of a computer containing my unexpected and unwanted fate, my time in Seattle became hazy. Like UFOs in films of sightings, events flitted all over the place, the camera shaking and never coming into focus, leaving one to doubt the authenticity and wonder, *Is this real?*

Why I don't remember is a mystery. I can only speculate that the ensuing drama triggered Traumatic Amnesia. Or possibly Tovah and Jane drugged me, beginning with that first breakfast.

I ask you to bear with me as I relate what I *do* remember, events of which I recall with the clarity of the miraculous way the camera comes into focus for UFO witness interviews. . . .

East is Lake Michigan. That's how I learned my directions.
West is everything on the other side of Eden's Expressway,
over the bridge to Adrienne and Alex's house.
South is downtown Chicago.
North is Wisconsin.

Ann Willow is an award-winning author and playwright loving life in the American Southwest, inspired by its mystical landscapes, unique history, and diverse quirky folk. *Remembering Changes Everything* is her debut memoir, a psychological thriller of survival, redemption, and love. Ann's next book, *Seeking New Identities,* continues her story. Look for it in 2026.